# BROKEN CHURCHES, BROKEN NATION

# BROKEN CHURCHES, BROKEN NATION

Denominational Schisms
and the Coming
of the American Civil War

BY
C. C. GOEN

MERCER

ISBN 0-86554-187-6

All books published by Mercer University Press
are produced on acid-free paper
that exceeds the minimum standards set by the
National Historical Records and Publications Commission.

♾

*Library of Congress Cataloging in Publication Data*
Goen, C. C.
  Broken churches, broken nation.

  Includes bibliographies and index.
  1. United States—Church history—19th century.
2. Christian sects—United States—History—19th
century. 3. Evangelicalism—United States—History—
19th century. 4. United States—History—Civil War,
1861–1865—Religious aspects. 5. United States—
History—Civil War, 1861–1865—Causes. I. Title.
BR525.G56    1985    277.3'081    85-7131
ISBN 0-86554-187-6

# CONTENTS

# TABLES

*To the Memory of*
Sydney E. Ahlstrom
*Teacher, Counselor, Friend*

" . . . *how little is to be expected from any other* Union, *if the union of Christians fail.*"

—correspondent for *The Charleston Mercury,*
reporting on the formation
of the Southern Baptist Convention, 9 May 1845

# ACKNOWLEDGMENTS

It is a pleasure to acknowledge the assistance of those who helped me organize my inchoate ideas about the divided denominations and the antecedents of the American Civil War. In the ten years of research and contemplation that preceded my decision finally to let go of a work I still consider unfinished, librarians and archivists at many institutions have been unfailingly helpful. I am especially indebted to the gracious people at the Wesley Theological Seminary Library, the American Baptist Historical Society, and the Presbyterian Historical Society.

During her years as a seminary student, Rebecca Abts Wright served me so proficiently as research assistant, typist, and critic that I almost regretted to see her graduate and go on to other duties that she doubtlessly found much more fulfilling.

Early expositions and progressive refinements of the central thesis of this book not only were inflicted on several generations of my students but were presented to the Homewood Seminar in American Religious History at The Johns Hopkins University, the 1979 annual session of the American Society of Church History, and a conference on "Religion in the American South" at Florida State University. Discussants at these meetings included John B. Boles, Timothy L. Smith, Robert T. Handy, William A. Clebsch, Donald G. Mathews, and Samuel S. Hill. I remain grateful for their comments—some confirmatory, some corrective, some provoking, and all helpful. Additionally, Handy went far beyond the expectations of professional collegiality to read a near-final version of the entire manuscript and offer many wise suggestions for improvement. J. Philip Wogaman, professor of Christian Social Ethics at Wesley Theological Seminary and a treasured colleague, helped me refine the argument of the last chapter. Betty Ruth Goen, my wife and always my most persistent encourager, read with the critical eye of an elementary-school reading specialist; her comments gave a good indication of the likely reaction of the proverbial "general reader" that every author aspires to interest.

The dedication witnesses to a debt difficult for tongue to tell or life repay. Professor Ahlstrom's comments on the early conception of this work inspired me to continue its pursuit. I deeply regret that he did not live to see its completion.

Portions of chapter 4 served as my presidential address to the American Society of Church History in December 1982 and were printed as "Broken Churches, Broken Nation: Regional Religion and North-South Alienation in Antebellum America," *Church History*, 52 (March 1983): 21-35. I thank the journal's editors for permission to use that material here.

*C. C. Goen*
*Wesley Theological Seminary*

# THE PROBLEM
# AND THE HYPOTHESIS

Politicians, secular and religious journals, pamphleteers, men in all classes of society, freely lay the blame of this Rebellion, in great measure, or wholly, at the door of the Church; charging the ministry, more especially, with having caused it. This is a very prevalent sentiment, if we may judge from what has been said and written. There is undoubtedly justice or injustice in the charge, according to the direction given to it. It is then essential that the matter be probed, so that if the Church or its ministers are improperly impugned, they may have justice done them; and that the really guilty may be held responsible.[1]

Those words were written in 1864 by Robert Livingston Stanton, professor of practical theology in the Theological Seminary of the (Old School) Presbyterian Church at Danville, Kentucky. The question he addressed at the height of the Civil War was one that many thoughtful Americans had been pondering for more than a quarter of a century. Although systems of slavery had ex-

---

[1]Robert Livingston Stanton, *The Church and the Rebellion: A Consideration of the Rebellion Against the Government of the United States; and the Agency of the Church, North and South, in Relation Thereto* (New York, 1864) vi. Stanton (1810-1885) was educated at Princeton. He had served pastorates in New Orleans and Chillicothe, Ohio, before coming to the Danville seminary in 1862.

isted for centuries with little challenge, it was inevitable that sensitive observers should be troubled by the paradox of human bondage in a professedly free society—even a Christian republic, as many claimed. Early protests came from individuals and groups whose libertarian ideas rested as much on the doctrine of Christian freedom as on the Enlightenment philosophy of natural rights. But American churches were growing institutions; and for the most part they equivocated on the question of slavery, stumbling uncertainly between stern pronouncements and ambiguous enforcement. When they proved themselves unable or unwilling to deal intramurally with slavery in terms of their own moral discipline, and some sundered over the issue, fears grew that the visible fracturing of religious institutions presaged the rupture of the nation.

An early prognostication came from William Lloyd Garrison in a Fourth of July address at Providence, Rhode Island, in 1837. Commenting on the schism between Old School and New School Presbyterians which had occurred the preceding May, Garrison prophesied:

> Our doom as a nation is sealed . . . the day of our probation has ended, and we are not saved . . . *the downfall of the republic seems inevitable.* . . . The corruptions of the CHURCH, so-called . . . are obviously more deep and incurable than those of the STATE; and therefore the CHURCH, in spite of every precaution and safeguard, is first to be dashed in pieces. . . . Look at the recent turbulent and despotic transactions in the Presbyterian General Assembly at Philadelphia: that mighty denomination is severed in twain at a blow. *The political dismemberment of our Union is ultimately to follow.*[2]

Whatever allowances one may wish to make for Garrison's characteristically extremist rhetoric, his words still seem uncannily prescient, rendering a solemn judgment, as it were, before the event. When telegraphs clattered the news of Lincoln's election across the land in November 1860, *The Presbyterian Herald* warned solemnly:

---

[2]*The Liberator*, 28 July 1837, in *Documents of Upheaval: Selections from William Lloyd Garrison's* The Liberator, *1831-1865*, ed. Truman Nelson (New York, 1966) 123.

> The very worst omen of the times is the fact that the religious men of the country stand apart to so great an extent in this hour of trial. Most of the Churches have split on the very rock upon which the State is foundering. In fact their divisions have prepared the way and laid the political foundations for the political divisions which now exist.[3]

As national disruption came closer to realization, many speakers and writers took for granted the connection between ecclesiastical and political breakdown. And many were ready to fix a significant portion of blame upon the churches.

Certainly, as one sensitive historian has cautioned, "the sight of any people drifting toward civil war calls for much more than the distribution of blame."[4] But the relationships of religious ideas and institutions to social and political realities are both extensive and profound, and there seems to be a closer link between the denominational schisms and the coming of the war than has been commonly recognized. This investigation, therefore, proposes to focus on one aspect of those relationships in antebellum America—not so much the churches' massive support for the war itself, which has been amply documented by such scholars as James W. Silver, Chester F. Dunham, and James H. Moorhead,[5] but the way in which the division of the churches and their subsequent behavior reinforced a growing sectionalism that led eventually to political rupture and armed conflict.

The runaway growth of sectionalism and the cumulating alienation of the sections in the 1850s remain major problems of American historiography, and completely satisfactory explanations

---

[3]*The Presbyterian Herald* (Louisville), 30:21 (November 1860): 2, quoted in Chester F. Dunham, *The Attitude of the Northern Clergy Toward the South, 1860-1865* (Toledo, 1942) 127.

[4]Avery O. Craven, *An Historian and the Civil War* (Chicago, 1964) 232. Craven has been called "the scholar who has wrestled most persistently with the problem of why the American nation broke apart a century ago" (Don E. Fehrenbacher, "Disunion and Reunion," in *The Reconstruction of American History*, ed. John Higham [New York, 1962] 117).

[5]James W. Silver, *Confederate Morale and Church Propaganda* (New York, 1967); Dunham, *The Attitude of the Northern Clergy Toward the South;* James H. Moorhead, *American Apocalypse: Yankee Protestants and the Civil War, 1860-1869* (New Haven, 1978).

continue to elude scholars.[6] The present essay will suggest that one significant factor in the disuniting of the United States, largely unexplored in the massive outpouring of publications about the Civil War and its antecedents, was the division of America's popular churches into sectional factions several years before the political break. The divided churches painfully exposed the deep moral chasm between North and South, furthering the alienation between sections and contributing to the eventual disruption of the Union.

This is not another search for the "causes" of the Civil War, although the study may shed some light on the reasons for that national trauma.[7] The question to be pursued in these pages is not whether the conflict should be regarded as repressible or irrepressible, needless or inevitable, the work of an evil or a blundering generation, the result of excessive democracy or conspiratorial politics, the inexorable operation of grand elemental forces or the random working of accidental factors. Lee Benson rightly dismissed such considerations as trivial, questions that often divert the investigator away from the search for plausible historical explanation. A better question, he suggested, might be: "What conditions made it likely that a group would form who wanted to create a new nation in the Old South and who were prepared, if necessary, to use revolutionary violence to achieve their goal?"[8] One should also ask what conditions led to the formation in the North of a group that deter-

------

[6]Cf. David M. Potter, *The Impending Crisis, 1848-1861* (New York, 1976) 30.

[7]After more than a century of inquiry into the causes of the war, there is no conclusive result that can pass for a consensus and the problem remains a major issue in the historiography of the United States. See Howard K. Beale, "What Historians Have Said About the Causes of the Civil War," in *Theory and Practice in Historical Study* (New York, 1946); Kenneth M. Stampp, *The Causes of the Civil War* (Englewood Cliffs, 1959); Thomas J. Pressly, *Americans Interpret Their Civil War,* 2d ed. (New York, 1962); William Dray, "Some Causal Accounts of the American Civil War," *Daedalus,* 91 (1962): 578-98; and Eric Foner, "The Causes of the American Civil War: Recent Interpretations and New Directions," *Civil War History,* 20 (1974): 197-214. The number of books dealing with the American Civil War has been estimated at more than 100,000, and works treating even its historiography are multiplying.

[8]Lee Benson, *Toward the Scientific Study of History* (Philadelphia, 1972) 316. Cf. also Benson's "Causation and the American Civil War," *History and Theory,* 1 (1961): 163-75.

mined to maintain a Union in which slavery would be confined until it could be eradicated and then reached the point where, if necessary, they were willing to use military force to achieve their goal.[9]

Perhaps the really crucial question can be narrowed further, for in the 1850s the substantive issue—in contrast to wildly exaggerated fears about it—had nothing to do with the spread of slavery into the few remaining territories of the United States, none of which were economically attractive to the slave system in any case. David Donald observed that "no responsible political body in the North in 1860 proposed to do anything at all about slavery where it actually existed and no numerous group of Southerners thought their peculiar institution could be extended into the free states." He then asked, "Do we not have to inquire why public opinion, North and South, grew so sensitive over what appears to be an abstract and unimportant point?"[10] The immediate answer is that the South's almost pathological fear of antislavery resulted from its attachment not so much to a system of labor as to a structure of race domination and social control, while the North masked its racial objections to an expanding black presence behind a self-righteous call for "free soil." That is what turned the dispute over slavery in the territories into the gravest question of the day.

It is becoming increasingly clear that questions dealing with group perceptions and popular sensitivities, especially in nineteenth-century America, cannot be answered fully without taking into account the role of the churches—particularly the large evangelical denominations with national constituencies—as significant influences on public opinion and popular feeling. Historians have examined at length the conditions that led to violent conflict between North and South, but most of their studies have been un-

---

[9]Phillip S. Paludan, "The American Civil War Considered as a Crisis in Law and Order," *American Historical Review,* 77 (1972): 1013-33, argued that the main question of the *war* (not secession) was why Northerners rushed to fight for the preservation of the Union. He proposed that an answer lay in their attachment to the law and the orderly processes of democratic government, which they felt secession had disrupted.

[10]David Donald, "An Excess of Democracy: The American Civil War and the Social Process," *The Centennial Review of Arts and Science,* 5 (1961): 24-25.

dertaken mainly in geopolitical terms. Since a final definitive statement on the whole nexus of historical events that led to the Civil War seems to remain beyond the reach of present-day scholarship, it may further the discussion to suggest a factor that so far has escaped close analysis.

The present investigation originated in the suspicion that the behavior of the popular denominations—their own inner conflicts and eventual rupture—formed a set of determinants with a significant impact in their own right. Although there is always the danger of the *post hoc ergo propter hoc* fallacy and of mistaking simple contemporaneity for correlation or even causation, it seems plausible to hypothesize that when Presbyterian, Methodist, and Baptist churches divided along North-South lines, they severed an important bond of national union; that the forebodings of their leaders and of contemporary observers regarding the probability of disastrous political consequences were well founded; and that the denominational schisms, as irreversible steps along the nation's tortuous course to violence, were both portent and catalyst of the imminent national tragedy.

Such a hypothesis is not entirely novel. Nearly all the standard textbooks in American religious history make brief reference to the idea, though they rarely argue the case or document it with hard evidence. Several examples may give some measure of its currency. William W. Sweet found "good arguments to support the claim that the split in the churches was not only the first break between the sections, but the chief cause of the final break."[11] Clifton E. Olmstead fixed responsibility for secession largely on the Southern churches, while Winthrop S. Hudson called the division of the churches "prophetic of the political division that was to follow." H. Shelton Smith added that "ecclesiastical division not only foreshadowed political disunion, but actually prepared the moral ground for it." Robert T. Handy observed that the church schisms over slavery

---

[11]William Warren Sweet, *The Story of Religion in America*, rev. ed. (New York, 1950) 312. Sweet had affirmed earlier that "the snapping of the ecclesiastical cords binding the North and South had considerable influence in making the final break between the sections" (*The Methodist Episcopal Church and the Civil War* [Cincinnati, 1912] 43).

shattered evangelical hopes for fashioning America into a great Christian commonwealth, and then commented:

> The religious ties that had been shaped during the Great Awakenings and that had helped to bring a nation together, ties that had been strengthened in the Second Awakenings to the point that the Kingdom seemed close, were now rudely broken. The separations not only foreshadowed the political division but prepared the arguments by which each section would claim its cause as God's cause.

Even the bibliographer of American religion could not refrain from remarking *en passant* that "the schism in the Methodist Church was important because of the church's national character, and hastened the trend toward political schism." Sydney E. Ahlstrom, in his magisterial *Religious History of the American People,* underscored "the full dimension of the churches' involvement in the era's sectionalism" and concluded that the division of "churches in the socially dominant Protestant mainstream, with large constituencies in both regions, anticipated the national rift." More than other church historians, Ahlstrom returned several times to "the churches' large role in dividing the nation."[12]

Most denominational historians have treated the point gingerly, if at all. There are a few one-liners like Wade Crawford Barclay's confession that the division of the Methodist Episcopal Church not only foreshadowed but also contributed to "the greater national division and sanguinary fratricidal strife yet to come." Similarly, Benjamin F. Riley acknowledged that Southern Baptists,

---

[12]Clifton E. Olmstead, *History of Religion in the United States* (Englewood Cliffs, 1960) 388; Winthrop S. Hudson, *Religion in America,* 3d ed. (New York, 1981) 204; Perry Miller, "From the Covenant to the Revival," in *The Shaping of American Religion,* ed. James W. Smith and A. Leland Jamison (Princeton, 1961) 367; H. Shelton Smith et al., eds., *American Christianity: An Historical Interpretation with Representative Documents,* 2 vols. (New York, 1960–1963) 2:178; Robert T. Handy, *A History of the Christian Churches in the United States and Canada* (New York, 1970) 194; Nelson R. Burr, *A Critical Bibliography of Religion in America* (Princeton, 1961) 691; Sydney E. Ahlstrom, *A Religious History of the America People* (New Haven, 1972) 659, 665, 673.

by withdrawing from their national organizations, "sowed the seeds that brought forth the harvest of national dissolution in 1860-61."[13]

"Secular" historians have not been entirely oblivious to the influence of the churches on sectionalism, secession, and war. Monroe L. Billington, in his study of the South, commented that "the split of three major Protestant churches in America was an ominous sign of what the entire nation was to face in 1861." Avery O. Craven, who regarded the years from 1844 (the date of the Methodist schism) to 1860 as "something of a watershed in the history of the democratic process in the United States," observed that the division of the churches over the question of slavery marked the moment when the slavery controversy "had passed out of the realm of abstract discussion and had begun to influence the every-day affairs of men and institutions. When churches divided, how long could political parties withstand the disrupting force?" Allan Nevins, who furnished what is still the most comprehensive account of America in mid-passage, noted in his massive study of "the ordeal of the Union" that by 1857 Northerners and Southerners had almost become separate peoples and the divided churches had contributed significantly to the estrangement.[14]

According to David Potter's fine work, *The Impending Crisis*, the Wilmot Proviso of 1846 "raised the curtain on the sectional drama." Although Potter did not catch the opening act of a few years earlier when the churches began to divide, he did find massive evidence for the fact that "the idea of secession as a possible recourse first won widespread acceptance in the South during the last half of the fifth decade."[15] The timing is too close to the denominational schisms to be coincidental. This essay will elaborate on how the Southern Presbyterians, Methodists, and Baptists, in separating

---

[13]Wade Crawford Barclay, *Early American Methodism, 1769-1844*, 2 vols. (New York, 1950) 2:110; Benjamin F. Riley, *History of the Baptists of Alabama* (Birmingham, 1895) 153. Cf. also Nolan B. Harmon, "The Origin of the Methodist Episcopal Church, South," in *The History of American Methodism*, ed. Emory S. Bucke, 3 vols. (Nashville, 1964) 2:98.

[14]Monroe L. Billington, *The American South: A Brief History* (New York, 1974) 55; Avery O. Craven, *Civil War in the Making, 1815-1860* (Baton Rouge, 1959) 69-70, and *The Coming of the Civil War* (New York, 1942) 201; Allan Nevins, *Ordeal of the Union*, 2 vols. (New York, 1947) 2:553.

[15]Potter, *The Impending Crisis*, 18, 122.

from their national organizations, gave powerful impetus to the secessionist idea.

Carl N. Degler studied "the other South"—Southerners who opposed both slavery and secession. Although he ignored the influence of the churches and the role of religion in shaping Southern society and the course of Southern history, he unwittingly suggested an important clue: "Most Southerners were never torn by the wrong of slavery, but every Southerner had to confront at the time of secession the conflict of loyalties to region and to nation."[16] One need only add the obvious: churches that had been national, but were now regional, clearly helped to define loyalty in both sections. As evidence adduced in the following chapters will show, the division of national denominations into sectional bodies both provided a persuasive example for reluctant secessionists and inspired the zeal that turned sectional interests into a holy crusade.

More narrowly focused studies of the Old South are sprinkled with comments on the social and political consequences of the denominational schisms. One of the conclusions of Charles S. Sydnor's detailed study of Southern sectionalism suggests ramifications far beyond the ecclesiastical context. Observing that "the churches were among the great cohesive forces in America, serving along with the Whig and Democratic parties, business organizations and other institutions to reinforce the Federal government in the maintenance of the American Union," Sydnor noted that the snapping of any one of these bonds under the stress of sectional tension inevitably increased the strain upon the others. "The churches were the first to break; and when they did, tension upon other national organizations was brought nearer to the danger point."

Clement Eaton likewise remarked that "ever since 1844 when the Methodist church had broken asunder over the slavery question, the mystic bonds of sentiment holding the Union together had begun to snap." Henry Thomas Shanks described how the division of the churches reinforced sectional animosities in Virginia, which as a border state had affiliates of both Northern and Southern wings of the divided churches. Especially did the alienation between the

---

[16]Carl N. Degler, *The Other South: Southern Dissenters in the Nineteenth Century* (New York, 1974) 4.

two branches of Methodism carry over into the political contests and influence the people's decisions on political alignment when secession became an accomplished fact. In its areas of influence, Shanks noted, Southern Methodism spread sectional sympathy through "religious literature designed for the purpose," while in the western part of Virginia, where Northern Methodism was strong, "the sentiment in 1861 for the Union was overwhelming." Other scholars agreed that the separated churches played an important role in dividing the nation, but none pursued the point in any detail.[17]

A few special studies have dealt more directly with the issue. John Nelson Norwood, in *The Schism in the Methodist Episcopal Church*, included an appendix on "Political Implications of Schism," describing the interest taken in the Methodist split by John C. Calhoun, Henry Clay, and various political commentators. James W. Silver asserted in the opening chapter of his *Confederate Morale and Church Propaganda* that "secession in the church was a natural prelude to secession in the state." He concluded his last chapter by declaring that Southern clergymen, as no other group, "were responsible for a state of mind which made secession possible, and as no other group they sustained the people in their long, costly, and futile War for Southern Independence." Silver's book marshals so much evidence for the Southern churches' uncompromising support of the Lost Cause that one wonders whether secession and the resort to arms could have existed at all without them.

Chester F. Dunham, in *The Attitude of the Northern Clergy Toward the South, 1860-1865*, documented a similar role for church support of Northern sectionalism and the Union cause. A more sophisticated study of "Yankee Protestantism" by James H. Moorhead, while devoting minimal attention to the antecedents of the conflict, shows convincingly that the war evoked "universal clerical support." In religious rhetoric the Union cause became a holy crusade,

---

[17]Charles S. Sydnor, *The Development of Southern Sectionalism, 1819-1848* (Baton Rouge, 1948) 299-300; Clement Eaton, *The Mind of the Old South*, rev. ed. (Baton Rouge, 1967) 284; Henry Thomas Shanks, *The Secession Movement in Virginia, 1847-1861* (Richmond, 1934) 82. Cf. also Percy Lee Rainwater, *Mississippi: Storm Center of Secession, 1856-1865* (Baton Rouge, 1938) 173.

the climactic apocalypse which would unveil "the glory of the coming of the Lord."[18]

Donald G. Mathews noted some years ago that the dissolution of the national identity of the popular churches institutionalized the moral disjunction of the United States. In a later essay on religion in the antebellum South, he observed that the divisions of the churches had greater significance than any philosophical debate because "if religious people who valued forgiveness, reconciliation, and love could not resolve their differences, what hope for compromise was there for politicians—most of whom were lawyers—whose philosophy of social action was based on an adversary view of issues?"[19]

The moral disjunction was rendered more intractable because the break in the churches, as in the nation, was over the enslavement of black people. If there has been a single constant in the American experience, it has been that where a racial factor is present, the values of "forgiveness, reconciliation, and love" have been largely impotent—even in church—to resolve conflict and stave off strife. Thus the best treatment of the controversy that sundered the popular denominations remains the one that focuses quite explicitly on the racial factor, namely H. Shelton Smith's *In His Image, but . . .: Racism in Southern Religion, 1780-1910*.[20] Smith demonstrated beyond reasonable contradiction that the slavery dispute was the fundamental issue in ecclesiastical rupture, but he did not go on to relate the church schisms to the political breakdown.

Paul C. Nagel traced the development of American concepts of the Union from Experiment to Absolute, showing that in the 1820s only "madmen or vicious demagogues" would think of dismembering the indivisible nation. Before the rise of militant abolition-

---

[18]John Nelson Norwood, *The Schism in the Methodist Episcopal Church, 1844: A Study of Slavery and Ecclesiastical Politics* (New York, 1923) 187-94; Silver, *Confederate Morale and Church Propaganda*, 16, 101; Dunham, *Attitude of the Northern Clergy Toward the South*, 35; Moorhead, *American Apocalypse*, x.

[19]Donald G. Mathews, *Slavery and Methodism: A Chapter in American Morality, 1780-1845* (Princeton, 1965) 290, and *Religion in the Old South* (Chicago, 1977) 159.

[20](Durham, 1972). For an insightful treatment of the earlier period, see Lester B. Scherer, *Slavery and the Churches in Early America, 1619-1819* (Grand Rapids, 1975).

ism and the intransigent Southern defense of slavery, members of all political parties and citizens of all geographical regions regarded the Union as (in the words of Congressman Owen Lovejoy of Illinois) "a holy instrument around which all American hearts cluster and to which they cling with the tenacity of a semi-religious attachment."[21] Between such convictions and the deepening disaffection of the 1850s lie the denominational schisms, marking a sectional division of such import that it seems strange that they have not attracted more historical investigation than they have. Since it is now generally conceded that "simply as an important value-generating institution and source of status and power, religion cannot exist without seriously affecting the nature of political discourse,"[22] it is time to look more closely at the role of the churches in the disruption of the nation and the coming of the Civil War.

To be sure, the causes and course of the nation's greatest trauma have been debated more than any other feature of American history; and as David Potter noted, there is a great deal of irony in the fact that disagreements of interpretation persist even though our historical knowledge is vastly increased.[23] But the very complexity of the factors that influenced the sectional conflict demands that we attempt to analyze each one which may have any significant bearing on the nation's course to war. How then may we assess the churches' influence?

The argument outlined in the following pages is built around four theses that correspond roughly to the first four chapters:

(1) Evangelical Christianity was a major bond of national unity for the United States during the first third of the nineteenth century. "Evangelical" as used here refers to the conviction that the Christian life begins with a personal experience of conversion and issues in a life of strenuous moral endeavor.[24] In antebellum Amer-

---

[21]Paul C. Nagel, *One Nation Indivisible: The Union in American Thought, 1776-1861* (New York, 1964) 9, 283.

[22]Seymour Martin Lipset, "Religion and Politics in the American Past and Present," in *Religion and Social Conflict,* ed. Robert Lee and Martin E. Marty (New York, 1964) 70.

[23]David Potter, *The South and the Sectional Conflict* (Baton Rouge, 1968) 146.

[24]For further explication of this and related terms, see C. C. Goen, "Editor's Introduction," in *The Great Awakening,* vol. 4 of *The Works of Jonathan Edwards* (New Haven, 1972) 1-4.

ica, the techniques of evangelicalism were mainly revivals and the numerous missionary, benevolent, and reforming organizations which they generated. The revivals produced conversions (or at least acceptable surrogates) in great numbers, and the phalanx of voluntary societies offered the converts suitable outlets for their moral zeal.

(2) The chief institutional forms of evangelical Christianity were the large popular denominations (churches of the people, namely, Methodist, Baptist, and Presbyterian), each with nationwide constituencies. The voluntary societies represented another important "institutional form" of evangelicalism; many of these enlisted national memberships and several suffered sectional losses because of the slavery controversy, but they did not break cleanly into ongoing sectional organizations and hence are not the primary objects of this study.

(3) These three denominations were increasingly agitated by the dispute over slavery, found the problem unmanageable in terms of their own intramural procedures, and divided their national organizations into Northern and Southern factions. Occurring more than fifteen years before the Civil War, these divisions marked the first major national cleavage between slaveholding and nonslaveholding sections.

(4) The denominational schisms presaged and to some extent provoked the crisis of the Union in 1861: they broke a primary bond of national unity, encouraged the myth of "peaceable secession," established a precedent of sectional independence, reinforced the growing alienation between North and South by cultivating distorted images of "the other side," and exacerbated the moral outrage that each section felt against the other.

These are not propositions to be "proved" but theses to be examined. No inexorable linkage of causation is claimed between them and the war. With Kenneth Stampp, I would endorse Richard H. Rovere's piece in *The New Yorker* of 28 October 1967:

> I hold a kind of Tolstoyan view of history and believe that it is hardly ever possible to determine the real truth about how we got from here to there. Since I find it extremely difficult to uncover my own motives, I hesitate to deal with those of other people, and I positively despair at the thought of ever being really sure

about what has moved whole nations and whole generations of mankind. No explanation of the causes and origins of any war— of any large happening in history—can ever be for me much more than a plausible one, a reasonable hypothesis.[25]

The search for plausibility, however, need not end in total agnosticism. The evidence to be adduced for the above theses is often more suggestive than demonstrative; but it cumulates through successive chapters, so that the material of the later chapters reinforces the exposition of earlier ones. The reader should remember that historians simply cannot evaluate with precision the influence of a sermon, a tract, or a book (even *Uncle Tom's Cabin*). Often one must be content with witnesses who testify to the impression of a pervasive influence, knowing that quantification of such influence remains beyond the reach of available evidence. This is particularly true of ministers and churches, who, as one scholar remarked, "have a following among the mute millions that written records never can reveal."[26] Pervasive the churches were, and influential too—as chapters 1 and 2 will demonstrate—but there was no opinion poll to measure their sway to the nearest percentage point.

The final chapter, in addition to carrying forward the effort of historical explanation, will essay to suggest some dimensions of a social ethical critique of the developments described in chapters 1 through 4. Such an attempt is tricky business at best, and it should be recognized at the outset that no critique can possibly please every reader. It may be useful, therefore, to offer a description of the perspective from which such a critique will be mounted.

As a white Southerner educated partly in the North and now a longtime resident of the "neutral territory" of Washington, D.C., I have strong feelings about the moral import of the events that I shall attempt to describe and interpret. These subjectivities will become clear enough, though I trust that even on so debatable a subject as the provocations of the Civil War, they will not distort my historical perception overmuch. At the risk of offending some purists who

---

[25]Quoted by Kenneth M. Stampp, "The Southern Road to Appomattox," *Cotton Memorial Papers*, no. 4 (February 1969): 3.

[26]Charles C. Cole, Jr., *The Social Ideas of the Northern Evangelists, 1826-1860* (New York, 1954) 4; cf. also Benson, "Causation and the American Civil War," 173.

still entertain the notion of "unbiased" history, I make no apology for offering moral judgments on historical events, for as John Higham has argued persuasively, moral evaluation—with proper regard for its many pitfalls—is part of the historian's professional task.

> In the simplest sense, the historian commits to moral criticism all the resources of his human condition. He derives from moral criticism an enlarged and disciplined sensitivity to what men ought to have done, what they might have done, and what they achieved. His history becomes an intensive, concrete reflection upon life, freed from academic primness, and offering itself as one of the noblest, if also one of the most difficult and imperfect, of the arts.[27]

The story of the human past is inescapably a tale of moral struggle; and as many historians of quite different perspectives view the evidence, the Civil War erupted in the context of a supremely transcendent moral issue. A society set for the defense of such an evil institution as chattel slavery, as Arthur Schlesinger, Jr., once pointed out, "forces upon every one, both those living at the time and those writing about it later, the necessity for moral judgment; and moral judgment in such cases becomes an indispensable factor in the historical understanding." Honest and fair criticism, Schlesinger added, must be directed toward issues and not toward individual persons caught in a tragic web of circumstances over which none of them had full control.[28] One may spare individuals, perhaps, but what of a class of persons—such as the clergy? Or what of influential institutions—the churches? Chapter 5 will attempt to

---

[27]John Higham, "Beyond Consensus: The Historian as Moral Critic," *American Historical Review*, 67 (1962): 625. Gordon Wright's 1975 presidential address to the American Historical Association likewise urged historians to operate out of a "central core of values by which to judge the past and to relate that past to the present" ("History as a Moral Science," *American Historical Review*, 81 [1976]: 9). More recently John Muresianu reinforced the admonition; see "Toward a New Moral History," *The History Teacher,* 17 (1984): 339-53. Bibliographical notes in both articles guide the reader to several other writings on the point.

[28]Arthur Schlesinger, Jr., "The Causes of the Civil War: A Note on Historical Sentimentalism," *Partisan Review,* 16 (1949): 977. Schlesinger did not consider another question over which some of the protagonists travailed, namely, whether slavery was a greater immorality than a war that left 600,000 Americans dead at their brothers' hands.

explore this point further, because nowhere have I felt more strongly the force of C. V. Wedgwood's warning that to write history without comment "is, inevitably, to underline its worst features: the defeat of the weak by the strong, the degeneration of ideals, the corruption of institutions, the triumph of . . . self-interest."[29]

Critical interpretation is precisely what distinguishes a historian from a narrator or chronicler. Such interpretation inescapably requires moral judgment, and therein lies both the fascination and the risk of the historian's vocation. Since our greatest national trauma erupted in the context of a moral issue of overwhelming magnitude, it demands all the critical discernment we can bring to it, even though the disagreements that persist in Civil War historiography warn us to temper our judgments with discretion. In offering this exposition of the nineteenth-century American *kirchenkampf* as intrinsic to the wider struggle over fundamental American values, I have tried to follow the wisdom of Gaetamo Salvemini: "Impartiality is a dream and honesty a duty. We cannot be impartial, but we can be intellectually honest."[30] Various readers, following their own biases and values, will judge differently about how well I have succeeded. But that too, I trust, will further the ongoing historical enterprise.

---

[29]C. V. Wedgwood, *Truth and Opinion: Historical Essays* (London, 1960) 52.
[30]Quoted in Jacques Barzun and Henry F. Graff, *The Modern Researcher,* 2d ed. (New York, 1970) 181.

CHAPTER ONE

# THE
# EVANGELICAL BOND

John Adams once explained to Hezekiah Niles that, in the
United States, the achievement of unity out of so much diversity
was a modern marvel in nation-making.

> The colonies had grown up under constitutions of govern-
> ment so different, there was so great a variety of religions, they
> were composed of so many different nations, their customs, man-
> ners, and habits had so little resemblance, and their intercourse
> had been so rare, and their knowledge of each other so imperfect,
> that to unite them in the same principles in theory and the same
> system of action was certainly a very difficult enterprise. The
> complete accomplishment of it, in so short a time and by such
> simple means, was perhaps a singular example in the history of
> mankind. Thirteen clocks were made to strike together—a per-
> fection of mechanism which no artist had ever before effected.[1]

Adams had the good fortune to die before the clocks fell into rau-

---

[1]John Adams to Hezekiah Niles, 13 February 1818, in *The American Enlightenment: The Shaping of the American Experiment in a Free Society,* ed. Adrienne Koch
(New York, 1965) 228-29. Niles was founder and editor of the *Weekly Register,* a
popular nationalist periodical.

cous discord. It would take a bloody fratricidal war, now regarded as "the spiritual center of American history," to confirm the truth and validity of *E Pluribus Unum*. But this should not mask the fact that what had existed as autonomous towns and self-interested colonies began very early to knit themselves together in the bonds of a union that would soon be celebrated as a transcendent value. David Potter captured the paradox of the process: "Perhaps the United States is the only nation in history which for seven decades acted politically and culturally as a nation, and grew steadily stronger in its nationhood, before decisively answering the question of whether it was a nation at all."[2]

The British colonies in North America made substantial progress toward an integrated social order through their maturing political institutions, their widening religious fellowships, and their expanding economic pursuits. Social intercourse among eighteenth-century colonials had not been quite so rare as John Adams remembered it. The postal service flourished, an expanding network of roads linked together scattered communities, newspapers and books circulated widely, colleges attracted students from diverse regions and sent them back with better knowledge of their remoter neighbors, the American Philosophical Society provided a forum for interchange among the intelligentsia, and local governments consulted each other freely on matters of mutual concern ranging from commerce to defense.

Adams was even more mistaken about "so great a variety of religions" among Americans of the Revolutionary epoch. Belonging as he did to a regional denomination and being predisposed to favor outward uniformity in religion, he misread the variety of sectarian labels as being diversity in religious faith itself. The majority of religious groups in late eighteenth-century America bore "the stamp of Geneva" in one way or another, and the similarities among

---

[2]David M. Potter, *The Impending Crisis, 1848-1861* (New York, 1976) 479. Marcus Cunliffe wrote in a similar vein that "America became a nation legally before it was one emotionally" (*George Washington: Man and Monument* [London, 1958] 165).

them far outweighed the differences.[3] Adams's own New England Congregationalists had formalized by 1801 a growing rapprochement with Presbyterians in the Plan of Union, and most other Protestant groups shared with them a sense of common identity, purpose, and mission. The "perfection of mechanism" which made Adams's thirteen clocks strike together, in fact, owed a great deal to the pattern of religion brought to the New World by Puritans and pietists, particularly as these groups revived and proliferated through common experiences shared in the evangelical awakenings.

There is an important clue to the nature of emerging American unity in H. Richard Niebuhr's reference to the Great Awakening of the mid-eighteenth century as "our national conversion."[4] He meant, of course, not that the whole population was converting to evangelical Christianity, but that America's religious revivals transcended local and particular allegiances, stimulating and reinforcing a rising national self-consciousness. The Awakening, in short, began the conversion of scattered and diverse colonists into one people with a common sense of nationhood.

The paradigmatic figure of the movement was George Whitefield, the "grand itinerant," who cross-pollinated earlier local buddings of revival. Ignoring boundaries of province, denomination, education, and class, he pressed into every colony from Georgia to Maine, evoking everywhere a massive popular response that was without precedent (as one contemporary put it) "since ye days of ye old Apostles." There is persuasive justification for calling Whitefield "the first American." He was clearly the first popular leader with national recognition, seen and known in all the colonies, whose mere presence was sufficient to guarantee a crowd. His name was a household word throughout the country long before any of the Revolutionary heroes attained such fame. When he died on 30 September 1770, scores of memorial services held across the land

---

[3]Cf. Winthrop S. Hudson, *American Protestantism* (Chicago, 1961) 1-33. More recently, John Higham has pointed out the significance of "a peculiarly American combination: institutional decentralization and ideological conformity"; see "Hanging Together: Divergent Unities in American History," *Journal of American History*, 61 (1974): 11.

[4]H. Richard Niebuhr, *The Kingdom of God in America* (New York, 1937) 126.

bore witness that "his death affected many Americans more deeply than the report of the Boston Massacre."[5] Through his wide-ranging ministry he had become both instrument and symbol of an emerging intercolonial unity.

The Awakening that Whitefield and other evangelists fostered was national in more than a geographical sense. According to John Higham, it "marks the moment in American history when ideology undertook the task of forging a new solidarity among individuals who had lost through immigration and competition any corporate identity."[6] The ideology of the Great Awakening was evangelicalism, which united its subjects in a common bond of nonsectarian piety. The conversion experience produced a "religion of the warm heart" that had no need to insist on subscription to any creed, and it was available to all people regardless of affiliation or status. The Awakening moved easily across existing lines of social and political separation, shattering the parish structure of traditional society and to some extent the class structure also. By pressing its message of the need of every person for God's forgiveness and offering that forgiveness to all, it widened the awareness of common concerns and facilitated the acceptance of common values. In hundreds of churches new and old, converts enjoyed a new opportunity of participation and even a degree of social leveling that spilled over into their other relationships. The Awakening thus brought thousands of Americans in the pre-Revolutionary generation to share as never before in a common world of experience; it spread common interests and loyalties among a people who previously had lived in provincial isolation from one another.

This unitive thrust of the revival is a primary datum for understanding the national identity that took shape in the Revolutionary era. When Patrick Henry declared in 1775 that "the distinctions between Virginians, Pennsylvanians, New Yorkers, and New Englanders are no more," and Tom Paine added, "Our great title is AMERICANS," they were articulating a New World nationalism that

---

[5]Alan Heimert, *Religion and the American Mind from the Great Awakening to the Revolution* (Cambridge MA, 1966) 142.

[6]Higham, "Hanging Together," 12.

the Great Awakening had set in motion a generation earlier.[7] As Robert T. Handy explained, "many of the bonds of national feeling that later helped to give a sense of unity to [the American] people were first forged in the warmth of religious renewal."[8] To be sure, the process of converting the dispersed colonies into a united nation was long and complex, but the sweeping revival movements of the eighteenth century gave Americans a decisive thrust in that direction. By transcending their intellectual disagreements, provincial isolation, and cultural separateness, the Awakening helped to shape a new national spirit, a *consensus cordum* that became one of the most cherished values of the American people.

Ezra Stiles extended the point in 1761 with his *Discourse on the Christian Union*. As minister to a refined congregation in Newport, Rhode Island, Stiles had little feeling for the revivals; to him the Great Awakening was a time when "multitudes were seriously, soberly and solemnly out of their wits."[9] But even so, his treatise sustained the social impetus of the Awakening by trumpeting a call for continental religious unity that strikingly paralleled the aspiration for political union. Motivated by the urbane rationalism of his own "gentle Puritanism," Stiles's widely circulated pamphlet reinforced two legacies from the Great Awakening: the aspiration for unity engendered by the "heart-felt" experiences of the revival, and the quest for liberty on the part of the multitude of new converts who wanted to express their own convictions in their own way.

Carl Bridenbaugh, a close student of eighteenth-century America, perceived that the Revolution "resulted quite as much from a *religious* as from a political change in the minds and hearts of the people"—a change that pushed the colonists in the direction of both unity and freedom.[10] And the popular unity, which was indispensable to the success of the movement for freedom, rested as

---

[7]Robert Douthet Meade, *Patrick Henry, Patriot in the Making* (Philadelphia, 1957) 325; William M. van der Weyde, ed., *Life and Works of Thomas Paine*, 3 vols. (New Rochelle NY, 1925) 3:245.

[8]Robert T. Handy, *A History of the Christian Churches in the United States and Canada* (New York, 1977) 113.

[9]Ezra Stiles, *Discourse on the Christian Union* (Boston, 1761) 50.

[10]Carl Bridenbaugh, *Mitre and Sceptre: Transatlantic Faiths, Ideas, Personalities, and Politics, 1689-1775* (New York, 1962) 20.

much on newly awakened religious aspirations as on formal arguments from political theory. The experiential faith preached by the awakeners was inherently better fitted to prepare people for participation in wider community than were distinctly ideological appeals. As Jonathan Edwards saw so clearly, people are moved to action not only by the "stuff" in their heads but by the "affections" of their hearts.[11]

Buoyed by their success in a revolution that has been likened to a religious revival,[12] the newly self-conscious Americans were prepared to assume the task of constructing a Christian republic. What the evangelicals sought, as they announced so often, was to realize their dream of a Christian republic whose mission was to redeem the world by the power of a godly example. Common themes in the rhetoric of the early National Period were the biblical origins of the American republic and the continuity of the Judaeo-Christian tradition in the emergence of the new nation. The United States of America was "God's New Israel," whom the Almighty had delivered from the hand of the British "Pharaoh" and planted victoriously in a land of promise and plenty. The degenerate Christianity of the Old World had corrupted government and oppressed the saints, but in these latter days God had brought forth a reformation that gave birth to a truly Christian republic for the healing of the nations.

Americans saw a striking providence in the belief that the New World remained hidden until a purified church was ready to be transplanted to its uncorrupted paradise. They thought of their country as the New Canaan—in some cases even the new Eden—and of themselves as the new Adam. These ideas became the staple of hundreds of sermons and addresses, as articulate evangelicals

[11]Jon Butler has entered a strong demurrer against extravagant claims for the Awakening's national unitive force in "Enthusiasm Described and Decried: The Great Awakening as Interpretative Fiction," *Journal of American History*, 69 (1982): 305-25; but while his revisionist essay is both cautionary and provocative, its denials seem far too sweeping.

[12]William G. McLoughlin, "The American Revolution as a Religious Revival: The Millennium in One Country," *New England Quarterly*, 40 (1967): 99-110; Perry Miller, "From the Covenant to the Revival," in *The Shaping of American Religion*, ed. James W. Smith and A. Leland Jamison (Princeton, 1961) 350, 353; Heimert, *Religion and the American Mind*, 21.

both reflected and reinforced common convictions regarding the unique identity, mission, and destiny of America. The union that took shape under such influences was thus one of hearts as of minds, of intuition as of law, of convictions about providential purpose as of confidence in human agency. When President John Tyler hailed the United States in 1843 as a "Union of purpose—[a] union of feeling,"[13] he revealed the extent to which the evangelical dynamic had formed American self-understanding.

Once again, a primary engine of nationalism and union would be evangelical Protestantism, and its most effective technique would be revivalism. Probably no scholar has celebrated the revival as a mechanism of cultural cohesion more than Perry Miller. In his final work crowning a brilliant career of provocative and seminal writings, he reaffirmed the evangelical basis of American thought and character. Unceasingly impressed by "the terrific universality of the Revival," Miller maintained that its steady burning, "sometimes smoldering, now blazing into flame, never quite extinguished (even in Boston) until the Civil War had been fought, was a central mode of this culture's search for national identity." Even on the untamed frontier, he asserted, "the pathetic thousands who camped and writhed at Cane Ridge . . . were not preaching nationalism, they were enacting it." But the Second Awakening was far more than a frontier phenomenon; if anything, it was even more pervasive than the first. Miller concluded that massive revivals during the first four decades of national experience gave "a special tone to the epoch; through them the youthful society sought for solidarity, for a discovery of its meaning." From this perspective, the Civil War becomes all "the more poignant, for it was fought, not by Puritans against Cavaliers, nor by republicans against royalists, but among the rank and file, all children of the Revival."[14]

This second wave of revivals, beginning about 1795 and peaking around 1830, carried forward a social process set in motion by

---

[13]Speech at the dedication of the Bunker Hill Monument, 17 June 1843, in *Niles' National Register*, 1 July 1843, 282.

[14]Perry Miller, *The Life of the Mind in America: From the Revolution to the Civil War* (New York, 1965) 6, 7, 11, 14, 47. On the last point, Handy concurs: "that fratricidal strife was in many important respects a war between evangelicals" (*History of the Christian Churches*, 265).

the first: it further set aside old standards of social participation based on ancestry, learning, and wealth, and introduced new ones based on common experiences that affirmed each person's worth and strengthened communal bonds. Donald G. Mathews's study of religion in the antebellum South, where evangelicalism was rapidly achieving cultural dominance, notes that "the community created by personal experience, baptism, and discipline was a reproach to the old order and a promise of a new one."[15] Not even the heady political theories of the Enlightenment reached so many people and transformed their outlook. For the great mass of ordinary Americans, it was evangelical Christianity that helped to define their experiment in freedom and that shaped their visions of national destiny. The revivals and the multifaceted activities they generated laid the foundation for a religiously based nationalism that transcended sectional differences, tamed the "barbarism" of the frontier, and heightened Americans' sense of fulfilling a special vocation in the purposes of the Almighty.

The Methodists were not alone in believing that it was their mission under God to "reform the continent and to spread scriptural holiness over these lands."[16] All evangelicals shared the same conviction and dedicated their considerable energies and resources to an all-out effort to Christianize every corner of American life. Their literature described ambitious plans to saturate the nation with revivals, missionary efforts, Sunday schools, Bibles, religious tracts, and church-related colleges. A far-flung network of regional organizations gave the movements a pervasive influence throughout the country.[17] Even if, on the eve of mid-century breakdown, history had not completely fulfilled their hopes, evangelicals could still look back on a record sufficiently successful to persuade themselves that God had prospered their undertakings.

---

[15]Donald G. Mathews, *Religion in the Old South* (Chicago, 1977) 24.

[16]This was the answer regularly given to the perennial question asked in the annual conferences, "What may we reasonably believe to be God's Design in raising up the Preachers called Methodists?"

[17]Cf. George M. Marsden, *The Evangelical Mind and the New School Presbyterian Experience: A Case Study of Thought and Theology in Nineteenth-Century America* (New Haven, 1970) 16; see also Robert T. Handy, *A Christian America: Protestant Hopes and Historical Realities* (New York, 1970) ch. 2.

Revivalism succeeded as an engine of evangelical advance in part because of the sense of newness cherished by Americans in the early nineteenth century. The United States was not only a new nation but a new *kind* of nation, and its citizens were fond of viewing the past as a sinkhole of corruption from which they were now providentially set free. It was easy for them to think that with their experiment in self-government, civilization itself had been born again. The millennial vision that had occupied so many minds since the Great Awakening of the 1740s lacked for its fulfillment only the winning of the unchurched masses. Since in 1800 not more than ten percent of the population belonged to any church, there was a vast harvest of souls to be converted; and in the traditionless society of the new nation, they could be won most effectively by appealing to immediate experience. Thus the most "successful" preachers were those who could re-create the biblical world in the immediacy of personal experience, because this best suited the mood of the hearers.

Revivalism won the allegiance of a people who had lost touch with liturgical forms and elaborate creeds by the simple expedient of forceful preachers who laid aside doctrinal complexities and pressed on their hearers the dramatic alternatives of heaven or hell. Salvation was a matter of individual choice, and sinners were urged to "get religion." That religion might "get" them was rarely considered.[18] The techniques of revivalism thus evolved into an effective strategy for increasing church membership but, as will appear later, they were not very useful for developing moral discipline and a sense of social responsibility.

Evangelicals could rejoice that their ubiquitous revivals and reforming efforts seemed, for a time at least, to bring much of antebellum America to accord general consent (if not full obedience) to the principles of Protestant Christianity. Equally noteworthy is that evangelical attitudes and assumptions were becoming constituent elements of American nationalism.[19] In 1812 Congressman Josiah

---

[18]Cf. Richard Hofstadter, *Anti-Intellectualism in American Life* (New York, 1970) 84-85.

[19]Cf. Sydney E. Ahlstrom, *A Religious History of the American People* (New Haven, 1972) 382.

Quincy, Jr., of Massachusetts asked, "What is it that constitutes the moral tie of our nation?" It was not, he said in reply, "that paper contract called the Constitution," but a "family compact," a "moral sentiment which pervades all, and is precious to all. . . . The strong ties of every people are those which spring from the heart and twine through the affections."[20] Evangelicals not only understood such language; they created it. They also understood its political utility, for when the American Home Missionary Society sprang to life in 1826, its organizers declared their conviction that "a more extended effort for the promotion of 'Home Missions' is equally indispensable to the moral advancement and the political stability of the United States."[21]

No one questioned basing moral advancement and political stability on the promotion of home missions because of the widespread persuasion that the American experiment in self-government was fulfilling some grand design of Providence. One of the most convincing evidences was the Union itself; out of rampant diversity, unity had been secured not by law or through a legally established church but by "the universal application of religious and moral influence."[22] Such convictions, voiced often, both celebrated and furthered unity in their time. They also prepared a way for the argument to circle back upon itself when the Union began to break apart, for then the urgent call would be to "nobly save, or meanly lose, the last, best hope of earth."[23]

The intertwining of evangelical fervor with the praise of freedom and a certainty about the nation's special place in God's purpose continued to be the major thrust of American nationalism. A writer in Lyman Beecher's periodical, *The Spirit of the Pilgrims*, argued in 1831 for "The Necessity of Revivals of Religion to the Per-

---

[20]Quoted in Paul C. Nagel, *One Nation Indivisible: The Union in American Thought, 1776-1861* (New York, 1964) 73.

[21]*Constitution of the American Home Missionary Society* (New York, 1826) 4, quoted in Charles I. Foster, *An Errand of Mercy: The Evangelical United Front, 1790-1837* (Chapel Hill, 1960) 184. The AHMS further affirmed, "We are doing a work of patriotism, no less than that of Christianity."

[22]Lyman Beecher, "The Memory of Our Fathers," sermon preached at Plymouth, Massachusetts, 22 December 1827, in *Nationalism and Religion in America: Concepts of American Identity and Mission*, ed. Winthrop S. Hudson (New York, 1970) 103.

[23]Abraham Lincoln, annual message to Congress, 1 December 1862.

petuity of Our Civil and Religious Institutions," which prompted Perry Miller to remark that "the fascination of the piece is its stark avowal of what had become in the minds of the revivalists the complete identification of the cause of the Revival with that of the Federal Union."[24]

Horace Bushnell, no revivalist yet no stranger to the evangelical temper, elaborated the same theme, expecting the wilderness to "bud and blossom as the rose before us; and we will not cease, till a christian nation throws up its temples of worship on every hill and plain; till knowledge, virtue and religion, blending their dignity and their healthful power, have filled our great country with a . . . happy race of people, and the bands of a complete christian commonwealth are seen to span the continent."[25] In Bushnell's "Christian commonwealth," religion and morality as defined by evangelical Protestants melded easily with the norms and values of American "democracy" as understood in the Age of Jackson.

Modern scholars see in this construct an extension of Christendom itself, operating now on the voluntary principle but nonetheless enjoying many of the benefits of quasi-establishment. Now that civilization in America had separated itself from the corruptions of traditional church establishments, it could become more Christian than ever before. Even though the churches were now separated from the state, the vision of a Christian social order was as strong as ever. Evangelical Protestantism forged an impressive symbiosis with the ideals of democracy and freedom, seeing in the new nation a destiny-determining opportunity to shape an authentically Christian republic. "The true American union" would emerge out of democratic institutions whose chief sustaining power was the evangelical enterprise.[26]

---

[24]Miller, *Life of the Mind in America,* 69.

[25]Horace Bushnell, *Barbarism the First Danger: A Discourse for Home Missions* (New York, 1847) 32.

[26]See Handy, *A Christian America,* 30-31; Reinhold Niebuhr and Alan Heimert, *A Nation So Conceived: Reflections on the History of America from Its Early Visions to Its Present Power* (New York, 1963) 20; James Fulton Maclear, " 'The True American Union' of Church and State: The Reconstruction of the Theocratic Tradition," *Church History,* 28 (1959): 56; Maclear, "The Republic and the Millennium," in *The Religion of the Republic,* ed. Elwyn A. Smith (Philadelphia, 1971) 205; Alice Felt Tyler, *Freedom's Ferment: Phases of American Social History from the Colonial Period to the Outbreak of the Civil War* (New York, 1962) 45.

Foreign visitors to the United States frequently commented on the cohesive role of religion in American life. Although many were at first puzzled by the seeming paradox of proliferating sects within an overarching unity, the more perceptive observers soon saw that the diversity was more circumstantial than essential. Several concluded that religion itself was one of the major bonds of union for the whole country, facilitating the functioning of religious institutions. Karl Anton Postl is an example; he abandoned the monastic life in Prague and came to America in 1823 to spend five years in travel and observation. He found that beyond all constraints of habit, law, or even patriotism, the tie binding Americans "beyond the reach of all contingencies," a tie not "affected by the workings of . . . fancy or by an overruling power, a tie to which, under every circumstance, [they] will shew proper respect and deference" was the Christian religion.[27]

Others wrote even more directly of Christianity's role in reinforcing nationalism in America. When the renowned Lafayette returned to the United States for his fourth visit in 1824, his secretary Auguste Levasseur kept a full record of the party's impressions. Noting the strong symbiosis between "religious ideas" and "patriotic sentiments," Levasseur observed that the Americans' religion

> resembles a sentiment as much as their love of liberty resembles a creed. Among them a political orator never closes a patriotic address without invoking or returning thanks to the Almighty; as a minister, when he ascends the pulpit, always begins by reminding his audience of their duties as citizens, and [of] the happiness they enjoy in living under wise institutions.

The French secretary marveled that "this mixture of political morality and theology extends through all the actions of the Americans," exerting an influence which he found beyond his capacity to express adequately.[28]

---

[27]Charles Sealsfield (pseudonym for Karl Anton Postl), *The United States of North America as They Are in Their Politics, Religion, and Social Relations* (London, 1828) 165-66.

[28]Auguste Levasseur, *Lafayette in America in 1824 and 1825, or, Journal of a Voyage to the United States,* trans. John D. Goodman, 2 vols. (Philadelphia, 1829); excerpt in *The Voluntary Church: American Religious Life (1740-1865) Seen Through the Eyes of European Visitors,* ed. Milton Powell (New York, 1967) 64.

Alexis de Tocqueville, arriving from France in 1831, immediately became aware of the pervasiveness of religion in American life. "The religious atmosphere of the country," he reported, "was the first thing that struck me." An entry in his private journal that does not appear in his famous *Democracy in America* describes a Fourth of July celebration in Albany, New York. There was first an impressive parade, then the formal program.

> The Declaration of Independence was read in the Methodist church by a magistrate who in America performs functions analogous to those of a *Procureur du Roi*. Into this reading he put much warmth and dignity. . . .
>
> This reading had been preceded by a religious prayer made by a Protestant minister. I recall this fact because it is characteristic of this country, where they never do anything without [the] assistance of religion.[29]

As other foreign visitors invariably did, Tocqueville wondered at the "innumerable multitude of sects," but he soon discovered that beneath their outward diversity in cultic forms they all "belong to the great unity of Christendom, and Christian morality is everywhere the same." This was all the more significant because, in Tocqueville's judgment, no democratic society could function without common moral standards to which all citizens subscribed. Just as the diverse religious groups were united by their common moral sentiments, the standards they upheld and the restraints they imposed were a unitive force for the entire nation.

What surprised Tocqueville most was that the separation of the churches from state support—always the most difficult point for foreign visitors to understand—had not removed them from the political mainstream; *au contraire*, it had greatly augmented their influence. Religion "never intervenes directly in the government of American society," he noted, but it "should be considered as the first of their political institutions" because it "singularly facilitates

---

[29]George Wilson Pierson, *Tocqueville and Beaumont in America* (New York, 1938) 181. Near the end of his massive study of Tocqueville's private papers, Pierson noted that "the value of American religion—both because of its emphasis on morality and because of the republican characteristics inherent in Protestantism—had been mentioned again and again" (722).

their use thereof." This came home to him in such encounters as
his interview with Joel Roberts Poinsett, a South Carolinian who had
just returned from a five-year term as the first United States am-
bassador to Mexico.

> Q. What is your opinion of the influence of religion in politics?
> A. I think that the religious situation in America is one of the things
>     that helps us most to bear our republican institutions.

Tocqueville concluded that the Americans regard religion as "necessary to the maintenance of republican institutions," and this conviction is not peculiar to "one class or party among the citizens," but
is held by "the whole nation" and "all ranks" of society.[30]

Francis J. Grund, an Austrian journalist, spent ten years in
America before publishing *The Americans in Their Moral, Social, and
Political Relations* in 1837. According to a modern scholar, this work
is "grounded on much longer and more intimate experience of
America than most [other] European travelers had." After wide
observation, Grund reported that he had found "no village in the
United States without its church, no denomination of Christians in
any city without its house of prayer, no congregation in any of the
new settlements without the spiritual consolation of a pastor." Such
pervasiveness convinced him, as it had Tocqueville, that Christianity was a dynamic force for social cohesion in the United States, affecting not only private behavior but the conduct of public affairs.
"The religious habits of the Americans form not only the basis of
their private and public morals, but have become so thoroughly interwoven with their whole course of legislation, that it would be impossible to change them, without affecting the whole course of their
government." Carefully pacing his rhetoric, Grund continued:

> Religion has been the basis of the most important American set-
> tlements; religion kept their little community together—religion
> assisted them in their revolutionary struggle; it was religion to
> which they appealed in defending their rights, and it was religion,

---

[30]Alexis de Tocqueville, *Democracy in America* (1835), ed. J. P. Mayer, trans.
George Lawrence (New York, 1969) 288-95. See also Norman A. Graebner,
"Christianity and Democracy: Tocqueville's Views of Religion in America," *Jour-
nal of Religion*, 56 (1976): 263-73.

in fine, which taught them to prize their liberties. . . . It is to religion they have recourse whenever they wish to impress the popular feeling with anything relative to their country; and it is religion which assists them in all their national undertakings. . . . Whatever is calculated to diminish its influence and practice, has a tendency to weaken the government, and is, consequently, opposed to the peace and welfare of the United States. It would have a direct tendency to lessen the respect for the law, to bring disorder into their public deliberations, and to retard the administration of justice.

It is a fair conclusion that Grund found the churches to be "the most powerfully cohesive factors in American civilization."[31]

Many other foreigners who visited antebellum America shared the same perception. The English *littérateuse* Harriet Martineau noted in 1837 that "the democracy of America is planted down deep into the Christian religion."[32] The Reverend James Dixon, sent to represent British Methodism at the General Conference of 1848, deplored the recent division of American Methodists but nevertheless decided that Christianity was "the conservative power of American society," influencing "the entire social and political state." The Bible was "the governing light, the decisive authority, the court of final appeal," and religion itself was the substratum of the earth, "on which all the soils whence the vegetable products spring repose in security."[33] Even John Robert Godley, a bilious Tory, marveled that Americans freely subscribed to the support of churches and ministers "as they did to a fire engine," and this because "they regarded it as useful in promoting law, order, and public welfare."[34]

Such observers made it plain that they saw religion fulfilling in American life the ordering function that aristocratic institutions and inherited privilege served in the older societies of Europe. They

---

[31]Powell, *The Voluntary Church*, 74; Francis J. Grund, *The Americans, in Their Moral, Social, and Political Relations* (Boston, 1837) 163-65. Cf. also Russell B. Nye, *Society and Culture in America, 1830-1860* (New York, 1974) 5.

[32]Harriet Martineau, *Society in America*, 2 vols. (New York, 1837) 2:315. Mrs. Martineau was shocked, however, at the timidity of the American clergy in opposing slavery.

[33]James Dixon, *Methodism in America* (London, 1849), excerpt in Powell, *The Voluntary Church*, 172, 176, 179.

[34]John Robert Godley, *Letters from America*, 2 vols. (London, 1844) 2:124.

concluded that religion in America, though removed from political entanglements by the legal separation of church and state, had become a "unitive, stable force undergirding all social life."[35]

Modern studies of nationalism furnish additional clues for assessing the strength of the religious bond in America during the National Period. Hans Kohn identified the cultural conditions that must prevail before a people can develop a sense of nationhood: common descent (or at least ethnic affinity), common language, common customs and traditions, and common religion.[36] These features (and more) were captured neatly in a patriotic ode sung at a Fourth of July celebration in Charleston, South Carolina, in 1831:

> *By our altars, pure and free,*
> *By our law's deep rooted tree,*
> *By the past's dread memory,*
>
> > *By our WASHINGTON:*
>
> *By our common parent tongue,*
> *By our hopes, bright, buoyant, young,*
> *By the tie of country strong—*
> > *We will still be ONE.*[37]

One sees immediately how each dimension of nationalism—religion (at the head of the list), law, tradition (personified by George Washington), language, and aspiration—converges on the idea of national unity. The ode also adds two important dimensions omitted by Kohn: common hopes and common territory. But before this cluster of affinities can produce a true nationalism, something else is required, something that David Potter called "the dualism of objective and subjective factors, or, one might say, of cultural realities and states of mind." Factors shared in common, however objec-

---

[35]Jerald C. Brauer, "Images of Religion in America," *Church History*, 30 (1961): 7.

[36]Hans Kohn, *The Idea of Nationalism: A Study of Its Origin and Development* (New York, 1944) 14. A brief but incisive essay by Boyd C. Shafer, *Nationalism: Its Nature and Interpreters* (Washington, D.C., 1976) 10-11, proposes an expanded list of ten common elements of nationalism. Shafer, however, regards religion more as "social institution" than as cultural component, which seems unduly to circumscribe its role.

[37]*Niles' Weekly Register*, 16 July 1831, 346.

tively real, will not by themselves produce cohesion "unless those who share them also share a self-consciousness of what they have in common, unless they attach distinctive value to what is shared, and unless they feel identified with one another in the sharing."[38] That is to say, nationalism must be defined ultimately as a personal appropriation, the sustaining *faith* of a people in their common destiny—in short, their "hopes, bright, buoyant, young."

It was precisely at this point that Protestant evangelicalism, with its millennial visions and its immense energies in seeking to establish the kingdom of God on earth, mightily reinforced American nationalism. In the time and place being considered here, one may take for granted the presence of all the cultural realities enumerated by Kohn—even ethnic affinity, for in 1840 the foreign-born among the population of the United States accounted for about one in seventeen, in 1850 about one in ten. America's ethnic homogeneity was probably never greater than at the time the nation was about to break apart over slavery. The crucial factor, the one that linked "cultural realities" to "states of mind" and provided the brightest hopes, was clearly evangelical Christianity. The "common religion" of antebellum America was largely a product of common experiences in the evangelical revivals; and whatever their sectarian label, if any, most Americans shared a feeling of common identity and looked hopefully toward a common destiny with an awareness nurtured by evangelical Christianity.

The religious component of nationalism in America has been the subject of a few special studies. These began in 1924 with the pioneering work of Edward Frank Humphrey. Asserting that "religion was one of the more potent factors in the making of the United States of America," Humphrey argued that "religious forces play[ed] an important role in the formation of a national spirit." Although he limited his focus to the Revolutionary and Constitution-making periods, Humphrey found that for that time, "the pulpit was the most powerful single force in America for the creation and control of public opinion."

Winthrop S. Hudson pushed these ideas back to sixteenth-century English convictions about an "elect nation" and forward to

---

[38]Potter, *The Impending Crisis*, 450.

American justifications of continentalism and imperialism on the ground of "Manifest Destiny." Dorothy Dohen, in a perceptive study of religious nationalism, especially as it pertained to Roman Catholicism in the United States, found that the American sense of mission resulted from "the convergence of political with religious ideas of destiny," so that "it seemed impossible to conceive of one without the other." Religion, she wrote in a Tocquevillian vein, was at the core of American values. It provided "agreement about ultimate national values, as well as about the ultimate meaning of the nation." These writers all document a convergence of religious conviction, political ideology, and concepts of national destiny and mission forming a consensus of values that had been present from the beginning of the nation.[39]

As the largest religious community in the United States, evangelical Protestants had no doubts about that consensus. Romantic nationalism was the mood of the period, and they had helped create it. Long before George Bancroft celebrated it in his grandiose volumes, evangelicals were enacting it in their congregations, revival meetings, and missionary/benevolent/reforming societies. For them the true union, like the kingdom of God, came not with observation but with participation.

One thrust of the campaign to shape a united Christian America was education, for evangelicals were convinced that free citizens of a godly nation must be able both to read the Bible and to participate intelligently in the political process. They therefore invested heavily in the founding of schools at all levels, and they successfully placed their stamp on American education all the way from Sunday and elementary schools to collegiate institutions. Ruth M. Elson's examination of nineteenth-century American schoolbooks showed that young Americans were taught very early to cast their nationalism in the mold of evangelical Protestantism. The schools

---

[39]Edward Frank Humphrey, *Nationalism and Religion in America, 1774-1789* (New York, 1924) 1-4; Hudson, *Nationalism and Religion in America* (see especially the introduction and the appendix); Dorothy Dohen, *Nationalism and American Catholicism* (New York, 1967) 181. A standard work that stresses at many points the symbiosis between evangelical Protestantism and the American temper is Ralph Henry Gabriel, *The Course of American Democratic Thought*, 2d ed. (New York, 1956); see especially chs. 1-3.

were firmly controlled by the Protestant "establishment," and their textbooks identified personal virtue and civic progress with Christianity. "Religion is the only basis of society," they taught; "Christianity is the prevailing religion of the leading nations of the world." Geography textbooks relied on the strength of Christianity in each country to assess the degree of civilization reached there. Although the common schools were "public" and not churchly institutions, they were still an integral part of what evangelical Protestants considered a Christian republic. They nurtured the growth of a Protestant consensus regarding the identity, mission, and destiny of the nation.[40]

The same was true for the development of American legal theory—another illustration that in antebellum society a general consent to the principles of Protestant Christianity was taken for granted. One of the few scholars to explore the influence of religion on the assumptions and practices of law in America was Perry Miller, who cited an instance in which Justice (later Chancellor) James Kent heard an appeal from a man convicted of drunkenly blaspheming the Christian God. From the bench of the New York Supreme Court in 1811, Judge Kent declared that 'the people of this State, in common with the people of this country, profess the general doctrines of Christianity," and that any action against the Christian faith would "weaken the security of social ties." The appellant lost his case. Tocqueville reported that in 1831 a judge in Chester County, New York, rejected a witness who did not believe in the existence of God because "he knew of no case in a Christian country, where a witness had been permitted to testify without such a belief." Instances of this sort occurred with such regularity that newspapers and the general public accepted them without surprise or protest.[41]

---

[40]Ruth Miller Elson, *Guardians of Tradition: American Schoolbooks of the Nineteenth Century* (Lincoln NE, 1964) 46; cf. also Timothy L. Smith, "Protestant Schooling and American Nationality, 1800-1850," *Journal of American History,* 53 (1966-1967): 695. The term *establishment,* of course, does not refer to any arrangement sanctioned in law but to the cultural dominance of the evangelical coalition. Robert T. Handy referred to the later loss of this dominance in a perceptive phrase, "the second disestablishment" (*A Christian America,* 184-225).

[41]Miller, *Life of the Mind in America,* 66; Tocqueville, *Democracy in America,* 293.

Newspapers and periodicals were another important means of drawing Americans together. By extending the world of common experience born in the revivals, they fanned the fires of religious nationalism and contributed to a widespread sense of belonging. The secular press gave extensive coverage to religious affairs; reports of the national voluntary societies and proceedings of annual denominational meetings especially received prominent display in major newspapers. But such papers by no means preempted the market for a growing religious press. The hunger for revival news was the initiating impulse for religious journalism in America: the first such newspaper was *The Christian History,* begun by Thomas Prince of Boston in 1743 specifically to disseminate accounts of the Great Awakening in both America and Great Britain.

As the post-Revolutionary nation took shape, the religious press became a highly significant news medium for antebellum Americans, reporting many happenings outside the churches—presidential messages, congressional debates, international events, and even the latest quotations from commodity markets—often accompanied by editorial comment. A Philadelphia Presbyterian editor's assessment probably would not violate modern standards of truth in advertising:

> In many cases, the religious newspaper is the only channel of communication with the world at large. Not a few families rely upon it entirely for their secular as well as their religious information. . . . It is not simply taken up, hastily run over, and then thrown aside for waste paper, it is returned to again and again, until every article, even the advertisements, has been pored over; it passes into the hands of every member of the family, undergoing in each case, perhaps, a similar process. It is referred to in the conversations of friends and neighbors; its opinions and statements are quoted; in fact, it comes at last to be regarded as a sort of living companion, and as an old and reliable friend. With some, too, it takes the place of books, where books would seldom or never reach them.[42]

The *Christian Times,* a Baptist paper published in Chicago, often

---

[42]*The Presbyterian,* 24 (1854): 174, quoted in Chester F. Dunham, *The Attitude of the Northern Clergy Toward the South, 1860-1865* (Toledo, 1942) 8.

dealt with public affairs and announced on its masthead that it would be "bold to say any truth." The religious press, in short, reported hard news of the nation and the world, and, as Ralph A. Keller has shown, church papers "provide the best running account of religious response to the troubles of the nation."[43]

The number of religious newspapers grew so rapidly that by the time of the Civil War there were upwards of three hundred. Some of the larger ones quickly achieved nationwide circulation and by deliberate design counteracted the provincialism of the regional publications. Although a Georgia Baptist earned the distinction of starting the first religious periodical in the South (Henry Holcombe's *Georgia Analytical Repository*, 1802-1803), Baptists in the South remained largely dependent on the North for their religious publications during the first third of the nineteenth century.

In 1830, for example, the Furman Theological Institution in South Carolina was receiving such denominational papers as the *Baptist Tract Magazine* (Philadelphia), *The Baptist Preacher* (Boston), *The Christian Watchman* (Boston), and *The Columbian Star* (Philadelphia). Southern Methodists founded the *Wesleyan Journal* in Charleston under the capable editorship of William Capers in 1825; and although the paper was well received, after two years it was merged with the *Christian Advocate* of New York expressly to avoid "the danger of collision" between Northern and Southern views.[44] The *Christian Advocate and Journal*, as the combined publication was called, was for several years the world's largest newspaper. In 1828 it reported a weekly circulation of 28,000 copies, far surpassing even that of the London *Times*, which reached only 10,000 in 1835. The New York-based *Advocate* retained a strong influence in the South for at least a decade, but then resurgent Southern interests created the *Southern Christian Advocate*, again under William Capers in Charleston.

---

[43]Ralph A. Keller, "Methodist Newspapers and the Fugitive Slave Law: A New Perspective for the Slavery Crisis in the North," *Church History*, 43 (1974): 319. See also Wesley Norton, *Religious Newspapers in the Old Northwest to 1861: A History, Bibliography, and Record of Opinion* (Athens OH, 1977) ix.

[44]Henry S. Stroupe, *The Religious Press in the Southern Atlantic States, 1802-1865: An Annotated Bibliography with Historical Introduction and Notes* (Durham, 1956) 9.

The *Western Christian Advocate* began in Cincinnati in 1834 and within six years achieved a circulation of 15,000. Complete circulation figures are not available until 1850, when the federal census began to report such data; by that time the 38 largest religious newspapers of the nation were distributing some 245,000 copies every week. By contrast, only a hundred of the nation's 2,024 secular weeklies could boast of a circulation of 5,000 or more; yet every one of the five official papers of the Methodist Episcopal Church far exceeded that figure.

In addition to the established periodicals, there were literally millions of little tracts printed by numerous evangelical societies and distributed by an army of colporteurs, all reinforcing the common moral standards that evangelical pietists thought essential to the character of a Christian republic. The American Tract Society and the American Sunday School Union poured forth a flood of hortatory literature, and religious newspapers carried the same admonitions. Church publications exerted in antebellum America a religious influence second only to that of the pulpit and the revivals; and since they frequently treated the large themes of America's mission and destiny, they have to be counted among the early unitive forces of the nation.

But religious literature could also be turned to the purpose of division. A study of Southern religious publications revealed that during the 1830s regional periodicals and tracts multiplied; there was "a wide use of the word *Southern* in titles" along with "more frequent insertions of articles in defense of slavery."[45] As the dispute over slavery increased in stridency, religious publications became the partisan organs of their respective sections and contributed significantly to sectional self-consciousness and growing alienation.

The presence of such ambiguities has led some modern scholars to perceive the evidence for national unity in antebellum America as mixed. Gordon S. Wood wrote that after the Revolution "the most pronounced social effect of the Revival was not harmony or stability but the sudden appearance of new men everywhere in politics and business." This upset traditionalists like Governor Samuel

---

[45]Ibid., 11.

Johnston of North Carolina, who feared that power would fall "into the Hands of those whose ability or situation in Life does not intitle [*sic*] them to it." But Wood also noted elsewhere that "all those committed to revolution and republicanism in 1776 necessarily shared an essentially similar vision of the corporate commonwealth—a vision of varying distinctness fed by both millennial Christianity and pagan classicism."[46] A dramatic change in social stratification was not necessarily threatening to the overall unity, since the "new men" were largely devoted to the Union; but it is true that social differences that could tear the Union apart were present from the beginning.

Similarly, Joseph L. Davis argued that antebellum rifts began with the factional struggles of the Confederation, wherein Southern republicans contended with Northern federalists.[47] Underlying all such cleavages was always the intractable issue of slavery. Thomas Jefferson had hinted at this in a letter to George Washington on 23 May 1792, observing that "the mass which opposed the original coalescence [the federal union] lay chiefly in the Southern quarter," and that sectional jealousies continued to plague the Congress.[48] James Madison put it more plainly when he told the Constitutional Convention that "the real difference of interests lay, not between the large and small but between the N. and Southn. States. The institution of slavery and its consequences formed the line of discrimination."[49] As the constitutional compromise shows, national union was purchased at the cost of letting Southerners maintain their "peculiar institution" according to their sectional interests—an omen of future instability.

Such lack of cohesion has been described in various ways. Frank L. Owsley found an "egocentric sectionalism" present from the early years of national experience. Rowland Berthoff characterized the

---

[46]Gordon S. Wood, *The Creation of the American Republic, 1776-1787* (Chapel Hill, 1967) 476-77, 60.

[47]Joseph L. Davis, *Sectionalism in America, 1774-1787* (Madison WI, 1977).

[48]In Koch, *The American Enlightenment*, 333-35.

[49]Records of the Federal Convention, 2:9-10, quoted in Winthrop D. Jordan, *White over Black: American Attitudes Toward the Negro, 1550-1812* (Chapel Hill, 1968) 324. Cf. also James Brewer Stewart, *Holy Warriors: The Abolitionists and American Slavery* (New York, 1976) 26-27.

period after 1815 as a time of "unsettled people," when individualism and uncontrolled economic speculation "eroded older elements of a stable social order." Fred Somkin eyed the "unquiet
eagle" of American free enterprise, jumpy because exploitive greed
was displacing communal values. George M. Frederickson found
much anti-institutional bias among Northern intellectuals, many of
whom could be content with no more "community" than one docile
listener, as in the case of Emerson's "churches of two, churches of
one." Stephen P. Carleton documented a "self-contained southern
religious community" that throughout the nineteenth century
reinforced a steady movement toward a closed society in the "integral South."[50]

To the extent that such works reveal objective realities, they
document a mood that appreciably diminished the nation's resources for dealing effectively with the onrushing controversy over
slavery that would eventually sunder both the evangelical churches
and the Union which they helped to hold together. But as Clinton
Rossiter pointed out, many of these studies rest on elite sources that
lead them to exaggerate the orderliness of eighteenth-century
American society and to misread as anarchical what was simply a
proliferation of voluntary popular organizations.[51] Major L. Wilson also examined several of the above arguments, noted the par-
tial truths they contain, and aligned himself decisively with the
conclusions of Perry Miller, William G. McLoughlin, and Ernest L.
Tuveson: "no influence [was] more seminal than the pervasive categories of the revival experience"; it was the "spirit of revivalism
itself [that] became the 'established' means for sustaining unity and

---

[50]Frank L. Owsley, "The Fundamental Cause of the Civil War: Egocentric
Sectionalism," *Journal of Southern History*, 7 (1941): 3-18; Rowland Berthoff, *An
Unsettled People: Social Order and Disorder in American History* (New York, 1971) 175-
232; Fred Somkin, *Unquiet Eagle: Memory and Desire in the Idea of American Freedom,
1815-1860* (Ithaca, 1967) 11-50; George M. Frederickson, *The Inner Civil War:
Northern Intellectuals and the Crisis of the Union* (New York, 1965) 7-35; Stephen Paul
Carleton, "Southern Church Leadership in the Emergence of Sectionalism and
Schism, 1800-1850" (Ph.D. dissertation, University of Chicago, 1975) 188-92.

[51]Clinton Rossiter, *The American Quest, 1790-1860* (New York, 1971) 170. Cf.
also Phillip S. Paludan, "The American Civil War Considered as a Crisis in Law
and Order," *American Historical Review*, 77 (1972): 1028-30.

order."[52] The overriding fact is that whatever divisive forces were surging beneath the surface of antebellum life, the major elements of nationhood were shared by both North and South even in the time of their growing estrangement; and these elements were sustained largely by evangelical Christianity. Both sections shared a common evangelical heritage, and that heritage was one of the strongest bonds between them until it succumbed to the controversy over slavery. Even in the heat of sectional conflict and of the war itself, both North and South drew on that heritage to justify their respective causes.

Americans were bound together in many ways by their fundamental belief that the nation was the product of God's benevolent purpose. Their religion fused with their patriotism in a way that permitted them to think of the Union as Providence incarnate and to find the meaning of America in the kingdom of God. Because of the particular form of religion that spread most widely throughout the United States—Puritanism transformed into evangelicalism and adapted to the methods of revivalism and reformism—Americans found it easy to think of themselves as a peculiar people with a special mission. By identifying the kingdom of God with the American republic, evangelicals forged the strongest bonds uniting the American people during the National Period. There was, it would seem, an almost familial sense of oneness, and even their tensions and quarrels were those of kinfolk rather than of strangers. For one brief moment—before the rise of the Cotton Kingdom, before the abolitionist crusade, before the sectional conflict and the terrible war that ensued—it appeared that there was a viable answer to the question of how an individualistic, revolution-born republic could achieve a genuine sense of community. In 1815 an unidentified orator in Charleston, South Carolina, could declare with no hint of contradiction that Americans "have known each other only as brethren."[53]

---

[52]Major L. Wilson, *Space, Time, and Freedom: The Quest for Nationality and the Irrepressible Conflict, 1815-1861* (Westport CT, 1974) 9-11.

[53]"Permanency of the American Union," *Niles' Weekly Register*, 7 June 1817, 229.

The Civil War was to fracture that bond and demonstrate that the United States could become "one nation indivisible" only through force of arms. Before that fiery trial, Union ideology thrived in synergy with evangelical Christianity. Even though evangelical unity itself would soon fall victim to the conflict over slavery, its myriad organizations and activities formed an integral part of those "mystic chords of memory" by which Abraham Lincoln hoped to heal the broken nation. As late as 1861, a Unionist editor could reaffirm what had been the common conviction of most white Americans, North and South, when he wrote that "the success of our Revolution and the establishment of this Government—of this *union of the states*—-was God's work."[54] But by that time, the work had been undone—by God's own people.

-----

[54]*Morning Courier and New York Enquirer*, 8 January 1861, in *Northern Editorials on Secession*, ed. Howard C. Perkins (New York, 1942) 936.

CHAPTER TWO

# CHURCHES
# OF THE PEOPLE

At the close of the Revolution the American churches faced
three major tasks: securing full religious liberty, completing their
indigenous organization, and evangelizing a nation in which more
than nine-tenths of the population were outside formal church
membership. The first, accomplished quickly and effectively with
the help of enlightened political leaders such as Thomas Jefferson
and James Madison, made possible the second, which in turn facilitated the third. Given the burst of energy that characterized all
the free institutions of the new nation, it is not surprising that the
churches participated fully in the epidemic of organizing that followed the winning of independence. By harnessing the revival's
energies to a free society's principle of voluntary association, the
rapidly growing evangelicals effectively made revivalism serve a
communal purpose. Converts were gathered into churches,
churches were grouped into denominations, and networks of religious organizations spread over the country as parapolitical structures operating alongside the formal legal apparatus of nationhood.
The large popular denominations were living analogues of the nation itself.

Although the churches might seem at first glance to have fragmented themselves by multiplying their separate organizations, there was a solid foundation of common beliefs and cultic practices that belied the diversity and competitiveness on the surface. The evangelical bodies that are the focus of this study quickly rose to cultural dominance mainly because they were all organizing the same basic impulse, sharing common convictions about purpose and destiny, and participating in the common task of creating a Christian republic. This made for greater unity among them than what was implied in the mutual recognitions of the denominations. The churches saw themselves as enjoying a unique relation to God and bearing a special mission for the nation they were trying to shape, a view that comfortably ignored their disparate origins, histories, and confessions. Convictions about their common purpose and destiny "dominated countless Independence Day sermons, inspired the great interdenominational societies, and informed the principal American church historians from Benjamin Trumbull to Leonard Woolsey Bacon."[1]

The national bonding force of the denominations depended in part on their peculiar nature. By definition, to denominate simply means to name, and *denomination* as applied to religious organization in the United States refers by intention and usage to a family theory of the church. Sectarian differences were less important than assurance of the authenticity of God's action in and through each member of the family, for it was the whole family that maintained the common world of experience. At its best, denominationalism produced a working harmony that overcame creedal divergences and, according to a Methodist itinerant on the antebellum frontier, was even a harbinger of the millennium.

> I frequently met with missionaries of other denominations, all of whom were of Calvinist creeds, but who showed a catholic Christian spirit. The question of disputed doctrines was never raised. The heathen to whom we ministered never knew from us the differences between denominations. A missionary to them was the messenger of God; and so far as I could learn the Calvinists never

---

[1]James Fulton Maclear, "The Republic and the Millennium," in *The Religion of the Republic,* ed. Elwyn A. Smith (Philadelphia, 1971) 194-95.

taught their disciples the peculiar doctrines of their creed. Christ, as a savior, to whom all might come and be saved, and repentance and faith as the conditions of salvation, were the burden of all our preaching, exhortations, hymns, and conversation. I could not but think that the missionary spirit, the measures to sustain it, and those measures the means instituted of God, were to bring in the millennium.[2]

It is easy to see how such cooperation among formally separated organizations could draw together a commonalty of experience and aspiration that nurtured a wide consensus and helped to give the nation itself a sense of common meaning and purpose.

Denominational particularity was never totally submerged, of course. Baptists promoted Baptism, Methodists spread Methodism, and Presbyterians Presbyterianism; but all recognized a unity of the church universal that transcended the apparent disunity of denominations by agreeing on the essential fundaments of the Christian faith, especially those of evangelical Protestantism. The revivals had given them a shared experience of heartfelt religion, while their standing as equals in the new condition of full religious liberty took the sharp edges off their traditional rivalries and facilitated mutual acceptance and cooperation. A celebrator of the Union in 1817 noted that "when tolerance is merged in an equal, indefeasible right of conscience and of freedom, the presbyterian, the catholic, the episcopal, the quaker, knows his fellow-citizen only as a fellow-Christian."[3]

What furnished the bedrock foundation of unity for all groups was widespread confidence that the American experience originated in providential design and was destined to consummate the divine plan. By taking as their common mission the fulfilling of God's purpose for the nation, the American churches resisted narrow tribalism and kept themselves within the larger context of the whole nation.[4]

---

[2]Alfred Brunson, *A Western Pioneer*, 2 vols. (New York, 1879) 2:136.

[3]"Permanency of the American Union," *Niles' Weekly Register,* 7 June 1817.

[4]Cf. Russell E. Richey, ed., *Denominationalism* (Nashville, 1977) 161-62, 168.

Denominationalism, as Philip Schaff noted almost a century ago, is "an American term of recent origin."[5] As a mode of organizing religious life in a religiously neutral state, denominationalism flourished as a unique product of the American experience. Unlike the established state churches of traditional Christendom, the denomination could not be territorial; and in the individualistic society of the New World, it had great difficulty being confessional. Rather, it was (and is) primarily purposive, or missional, operating as "a voluntary association of like-hearted and like-minded individuals, who are united on the basis of common beliefs for the purpose of accomplishing tangible and defined objectives."[6] As it developed in America, the denomination was neither as inclusive as an established church nor as exclusive as a nonconformist sect. Each group was *denominated,* or named, according to certain characteristics peculiar to its historical provenance, but all groups were regarded as belonging to the one church of Jesus Christ. As Winthrop S. Hudson explained, denominationalism does not identify "the true Church" exclusively with any single ecclesiastical structure.

> No denomination claims to represent the whole Church of Christ.
> No denomination claims that all other churches are false churches.
> Each denomination is regarded as constituting a different "mode"
> of expressing in the outward forms of worship and organization
> that larger life of the Church in which they all share.[7]

Like every other product of the historical process, denominationalism has a prehistory (Hudson traced the theory back to seventeenth-century England). But it was in laissez-faire America that the denomination came to full flower as the standard form of religious organization. As remaining vestiges of church establishment were swept away, the experience of freedom and the impact of the revivals both pointed to denominationalism as the most feasible *modus vivendi* for church life in the new nation. By definition

---

[5]Philip Schaff, *History of the Christian Church,* 2d ed. (New York, 1910) 7:43n. Actually, the term *denomination* appears to derive from John Wesley; see Winthrop S. Hudson, *American Protestantism* (Chicago, 1961) 33.

[6]Sidney E. Mead, *The Lively Experiment: The Shaping of Christianity in America* (New York, 1963) 104.

[7]Hudson, *American Protestantism,* 34.

as well as necessity, denominations were voluntary associations; hence they could grow only by persuasion—and they did. The more "successful" ones effectively institutionalized the religious impulses described in the preceding chapter and thus became a visible framework of the social bonds created by such impulses. By the same token, however, in embracing more and more of the "grassroots" population, such denominations were unwittingly jeopardizing their ability to function as disciplined communities of faith and to exercise moral leadership on controversial issues without alienating their constituencies.

The associative impulse overflowed even the local congregations and national denominations. Freed from the restrictions of established state churches, evangelical faith inspired an impressive phalanx of voluntary organizations and movements to which thousands of men and women devoted their energies and resources. These included foreign-mission societies to carry Christian civilization to the "heathen"; domestic mission societies to sow Christianity on the unchurched frontier; Bible and tract societies to encourage personal devotional life; educational societies to establish colleges and subsidize the training of ministers; evangelistic societies to promote mass revivals; Sunday school "unions"—the term is significant—to educate the young; and a host of other societies to inculcate temperance, protect the Sabbath, suppress vice, reclaim "fallen women," minister to lonely seamen, help the poor, and promote numerous other good causes.

Though structurally unrelated to the churches, these interdenominational societies operated with the churches' full blessing. Each technically had only one purpose; but through their interlocking directorates, overlapping membership, simultaneous anniversaries, and use of common agents in the field, they constituted an "evangelical united front" dedicated to the mission of Christianizing the nation and, through it, the world. William G. McLoughlin surveyed these groups and concluded that through such combinations of resources the evangelical churches "retained the most important institutional role in the culture."[8]

---

[8]William G. McLoughlin, "The Role of Religion in the Revolution: Liberty of Conscience and Cultural Cohesion in the New Nation," in *Essays on the American Revolution*, ed. Stephen G. Kurtz and James H. Hutson (Chapel Hill, 1973) 253-55.

The voluntary societies, as Lois Banner noted, "offered an attractive solution to what many statesmen in the early republic saw
as three primary problems facing the new nation: first, how to make
the turbulent democratic element which had destroyed all previous
democracies into respectable citizens; second, how to pursue benevolent and reform objectives without involving the dangerous
power of the central state; and third, how to overcome the sectional
divisions which threatened the unity of the nation." In a subsequent essay, Banner commented further on the social role of the
societies as "workshops in republicanism." By bringing together in
harmony people of diverse classes and sections, and providing stable organizations and a sense of community for a society in flux,
they ensured that democracy would function effectively within the
republican framework.[9]

The energies of these groups were amazing. By 1828 they had
collected and distributed almost as much money as the federal government had spent on internal improvement, and their combined
annual receipts were approaching one-half million dollars. The next
year they launched a "saturation campaign" in the Great Valley of
the Ohio and Mississippi rivers to save the heartland of the continent—that "fair garden of the Lord"—from the evils of infidelity,
barbarism, and popery. The success of such expansive activities,
carried forward on the principle of free association, provided a major dimension of cultural cohesion in the new nation and served as
a spur to nationalism. Simply as a system of social organization, the
evangelical coalition helped to expand American consciousness
from localism to nationalism.[10]

At the end of the Revolution the three largest religious groups
were Congregationalists, Episcopalians, and Presbyterians. The first

---

[9]Lois W. Banner, "Presbyterians and Voluntarism in the Early Republic,"
*Journal of Presbyterian History*, 50 (1972): 195; Banner, "Religious Benevolence as
Social Control: A Critique of an Interpretation," *Journal of American History*, 60
(1973): 40.

[10]Charles I. Foster, *An Errand of Mercy: The Evangelical United Front, 1790-1837*
(Chapel Hill, 1960) 121; Hudson, *American Protestantism*, 84-90; Bertram Wyatt-
Brown, *Lewis Tappan and the Evangelical War Against Slavery* (Cleveland, 1969) 49-
51; Gregory H. Singleton, "Protestant Voluntary Organizations and the Shaping
of Victorian America," in *Victorian America*, ed. Daniel Walker Howe (Philadelphia, 1976) 48, 54.

centered almost exclusively in New England; and although "the expansion of New England" carried them through the Old Northwest to parts of Illinois and Iowa, they never developed a sizable Southern constituency—perhaps because the rigor of the Puritan spirit was incompatible with the less structured society and more easygoing mores of the Old South. Congregationalists thus did not become a truly national denomination. Episcopalians suffered four serious handicaps to national expansion: in spite of furnishing large numbers to the patriotic cause, they still carried the stigma of attachment to things English; the Great Awakening passed them by, and their unwillingness to adopt the methods of George Whitefield (an Episcopalian) and his followers shut them out of the "growth sector" of American religion; disestablishment cost them the support of government in states where they had enjoyed the favor of colonial legislatures; and they tended to draw mainly from the upper classes, which in a day of fading aristocracy and rising bourgeoisie almost inevitably consigned them to minority status.

Of the three largest churches in 1790, only Presbyterians were poised to develop into a nationwide popular denomination. Their center of strength was in the middle colonies, enhancing their development of close relations with New England Congregationalists (their first cousins in the Reformed tradition). They had also benefited to some extent from revivalism in the South and West. But Presbyterianism was at some disadvantage because of what one of its historians called its scholastic doctrinal system, rigid polity, and insistence on maintaining high standards of ministerial education.[11] Hence its post-Revolutionary growth was of modest proportions.

The groups whose fortunes were rising fastest were the more informal ones, especially Baptists and Methodists, who fully capitalized on their lowly origins as people's churches. At the time of the Revolution, these two bodies had been small sects on the fringe of American Christianity, but as products of the evangelical awakenings they were prepared to swell their membership by making effective use of techniques learned in the colonial revivals. Seizing

---

[11]Robert E. Thompson, *A History of the Presbyterian Churches in the United States* (New York, 1895) 70-71.

the opportunities afforded by full religious freedom, they evangelized so vigorously that shortly after the turn of the nineteenth century they outstripped every other denomination in the United States. Their sweeping gains testified to the efficacy of their adaptiveness to conditions of life in the new nation. With their simplified doctrines, folksy preaching, emphasis on immediate experience, efficient organization (especially the Methodists), energetic promotion of revivals, and above all, rapport with the common people, they had immense appeal to multitudes of Americans.

During the Revolution, a critic had scoffed that after the war Methodists would scarcely be numerous enough to fill a corn crib; but they reported 8,504 members in 1780 and 57,631 in 1790—a sevenfold gain in a single decade. Baptists increased from fewer than 10,000 before the Revolution to approximately 170,000 at the close of the century. In the early years of the National Period, the two groups continued to grow at a comparable rate while even Presbyterians were quadrupling. In 1820 Baptists and Methodists each reported 2,700 churches and Presbyterians 1,700, all three outnumbering the other denominations.[12]

Thus the evangelical Christianity that served as a major bond of union in post-Revolutionary America was finding its strongest institutional forms in these three popular denominations— churches of the people. They embraced constituencies widely distributed from Maine to Georgia, and from the Atlantic seaboard to the Mississippi River and beyond. Many of their preachers spoke with a powerful voice, and large numbers of people heard them gladly. They extended their influence beyond the pulpit through numerous printed periodicals and wide-ranging itinerant missionaries. But what is most impressive for the present purpose is their full national extent. This may be demonstrated best in a state-by-state comparison.

The following statistical picture enumerates local congregations rather than church members, the better to suggest geographic distribution. Since a local congregation is a discrete gathering point, a dozen such, however small, would indicate a

---

[12]These statistics are taken mainly from Edwin S. Gaustad, *Historical Atlas of Religion in America* (New York, 1962) 43, 52, 76.

wider dispersion of the denomination than two or three large congregations whose aggregate membership may exceed that of many smaller ones. The presence of one or more evangelical congregations in every settlement, moreover, served to enhance the pervasiveness of their influence throughout the country. To provide uniformity of comparison, all statistics are for the year 1850. Even though this is some time after the denominations separated into Northern and Southern factions, the national distribution and comparative strength of the denominational forces remained essentially the same.[13]

| | | | | TABLE ONE | |
|---|---|---|---|---|---|
| States in Which Both Baptists and Methodists Outnumbered Every Other Denomination: Number of Churches in 1850 | | | | | |
| STATE | METH-ODIST | BAPTIST | PRESBY-TERIAN | LARGEST OTHER DENOMINATION | |
| Maine | 199 | 326 | 7* | Congregational | 180 |
| New York | 1231 | 781 | 671 | Dutch Reformed | 233 |
| Virginia | 1025 | 649 | 240 | Episcopal | 173 |
| North Carolina | 784 | 615 | 151 | Episcopal | 50 |
| South Carolina | 484 | 413 | 136 | Episcopal | 72 |
| Georgia | 795 | 879 | 97 | Episcopal | 20 |
| Florida | 87 | 56 | 16 | Episcopal | 10 |
| Alabama | 577 | 579 | 162 | Episcopal | 17 |
| Mississippi | 454 | 385 | 143 | Episcopal | 13 |
| Louisiana | 125 | 77 | 18* | Roman Catholic | 55 |
| Texas | 176 | 82 | 45 | Roman Catholic | 13 |
| Arkansas | 168 | 114 | 52 | Roman Catholic | 7 |
| Tennessee | 861 | 646 | 363 | Episcopal | 17 |
| Kentucky | 530 | 803 | 224 | Roman Catholic | 48 |
| Missouri | 250 | 300 | 125 | Roman Catholic | 65 |
| Illinois | 405 | 282 | 206 | Roman Catholic | 59 |
| Indiana | 778 | 428 | 282 | Quaker | 89 |
| *States in which Presbyterians were not in third place behind Methodists and Baptists | | | | | |

---

[13]My tables were compiled from data in Gaustad's *Historical Atlas,* especially his table on "Number of Churches in 1850" on p. 168. Maps comparing the density of the churches by county are on 56, 77, and 89.

At mid-century the United States consisted of thirty-one states and the District of Columbia. In seventeen states both Methodists and Baptists reported more churches than any other denomination: Methodists leading in the twelve states where Baptists were in second place, and Baptists leading in the other five states where Methodists were second. In fifteen of these states Presbyterians were in third place. Methodists and Baptists enjoyed unchallenged preponderance in all twelve states south of the Potomac River, whereas Presbyterians ranked third in all these states except Louisiana.

In ten states and the District of Columbia, either Baptists or Methodists had more churches than any other denomination. In six of these eleven jurisdictions, Presbyterians were in second place and, in four of those six, Baptists were in third place.

| | | | | TABLE TWO | |
|---|---|---|---|---|---|
| States in Which Either Baptists or Methodists Outnumbered Every Other Denomination: Number of Churches in 1850 | | | | | |
| STATE | METH-ODIST | BAPTIST | PRESBY-TERIAN | LARGEST OTHER DENOMINATION | |
| New Hampshire | 103 | 193 | 13 | Congregational | 176 |
| Rhode Island | 23 | 106 | 0 | Episcopal | 26 |
| New Jersey | 312 | 108† | 149* | Dutch Reformed | 66 |
| Pennsylvania | 889 | 320 | 775* | Lutheran | 498 |
| Delaware | 106 | 12 | 26* | Episcopal | 21 |
| Maryland | 497 | 45 | 56 | Episcopal | 133 |
| Dist. of Col. | 16 | 6 | 6 | Episcopal | 8 |
| Ohio | 1529 | 551† | 663* | Lutheran | 260 |
| Michigan | 119 | 66† | 72* | Roman Catholic | 44 |
| Wisconsin | 110 | 49 | 40 | Roman Catholic | 64 |
| Iowa | 71 | 20† | 38* | Roman Catholic | 18 |
| *Presbyterians in second place          †Baptists in third place | | | | | |

In three New England states, the traditional center of Congregational strength, none of the nationwide popular denominations could claim a plurality; but the number of Methodist and Baptist churches combined was larger than the number of churches reported by the Congregationalists. In Vermont and Connecticut,

Methodists were in second place, Baptists in third. In Massachusetts, Baptists were in second place, Methodists in third. (Presbyterians had only forty-three churches in these three states, ranking them in fifth place behind the Episcopalians.)

| | | | TABLE THREE | |
|---|---|---|---|---|
| States in Which Baptists and Methodists Combined Outnumbered Every Other Denomination: Number of Churches in 1850 | | | | |
| STATE | METHODIST | BAPTIST | COMBINED TOTAL | CONGRE-GATIONAL |
| Vermont | 140 | 102 | 242 | 175 |
| Massachusetts | 262 | 266 | 528 | 448 |
| Connecticut | 185 | 114 | 299 | 252 |

Evangelicals were a minority among the churches in only one state—California—which was newly admitted to the Union in 1850. Here Roman Catholics outnumbered all other religious groups combined. But California was remote from the areas of the United States most affected by the Civil War, and this lonely statistic hardly changes the picture of nationwide evangelical dominance in the antebellum period.

The popular denominations, as the tables show, were especially strong in the South. W. J. Cash explained their rapid rise to cultural hegemony in that region in terms of an affinity between the characteristics of the people and the evangelicals' simplicity of doctrine and directness of approach.

These personal and often extravagant sects, sweeping the entire American country with their revivals in the first half of the nineteenth century, achieved their greatest success in the personal and extravagant South. And not only among the masses. Fully nine-tenths of the new planters—of the men who were to be masters of the great South—were . . . numbered among their adherents.

Cash added that by mid-century every non-Anglican educational institution in the South except the University of Virginia "was in the hands of evangelical faculties." The Southern success of the popular denominations is confirmed by closer statistical studies. Charles S. Sydnor, for example, found that "between 1820 and 1850 the membership of the Methodist church in Virginia, the Carolinas, and Georgia increased from 93,000 to 223,713 and of the Baptist church from 99,000 to 246,000, while the aggregate population of these four states increased [by] only one third."[14]

Viewing the same phenomenon from a slightly different angle, Edwin S. Gaustad observed that "the leading slaveholding states were Virginia, South Carolina, Georgia, Alabama, and Mississippi, in that order." He calculated that "Methodists and Baptists together accounted for 90 percent of all the churches in Georgia, and for over 80 percent in all of the other states."[15] This picture also can be tabulated, showing that in the eleven states that seceded from the Union in 1860-1861, Methodists claimed 45 percent of the total number of churches, Baptists 37 percent, and Presbyterians 12 percent—a stunning 94 percent of all the churches in the heavily churched Confederacy.

| | | | TABLE FOUR |
|---|---|---|---|
| Number of Churches in the Eleven States That Would Form the Confederacy: 1850 | | | |
| | METHODIST | BAPTIST | PRESBY-TERIAN | ALL OTHERS |
| Number of Churches | 5536 | 4495 | 1423 | 762 |
| Percent of Total | 45.3% | 36.8% | 11.7% | 6.2% |

It should not escape notice that large numbers of Southern church members were black. Missionary work among the slaves, pursued for purposes of social control as well as for Christian evangelism, had met with notable success. In Georgia and the Carolinas, for example, 40 percent of the Methodist membership was black. By the time of the Civil War, although only an estimated 12 percent of the total black population was enrolled in the churches, in some of the large urban congregations of the South black members far outnumbered the whites.[16]

---

[14]W. J. Cash, *The Mind of the South* (New York, 1941) 58-59; Charles S. Sydnor, *The Development of Southern Sectionalism, 1819-1848* (Baton Rouge, 1948) 294.

[15]Gaustad, *Historical Atlas*, 58.

[16]Cf. Donald G. Mathews, *Slavery and Methodism: A Chapter in American Morality, 1780-1845* (Princeton, 1965) 68; Winthrop S. Hudson, *Religion in America*, 3d ed. (New York, 1981) 225; Kenneth K. Bailey, "Protestantism and Afro-Americans in the Old South: Another Look," *Journal of Southern History*, 41 (1975): 458.

Whatever allowances one may need to make for inaccurate reporting on the part of the churches and for discrepancies between the number of churches and the size of active membership, it seems clear that the growth of the popular evangelical denominations, especially in the South, had been just short of phenomenal. Even though the total enrollment of three and one-half million people was still a small percentage of the entire population—approximately one-seventh in 1850—this should not mask the fact that nearly every minister preached regularly to congregations three or four times the size of the church membership. T. Scott Miyakawa compiled data on this point from a wide variety of sources:

> For the 1837-38 conference year, Allen Wiley, a pioneer Indiana Methodist presiding elder, gave roughly three thousand as the membership of the Crawfordsville District and twelve thousand as the total for those present at the services. A Baptist historian, J. Newton Brown, estimated the Baptist national membership at approximately six hundred thousand in 1840 and their "population" at three million. The figures on the proportion of nonmembers attending seem exaggerated, but a British Congregational delegate to America, Dr. Andrew Reed, reported in 1835 that the two Presbyterian churches in Lexington, Kentucky, had twelve hundred at the services and three hundred members, the two Baptist meetings about one thousand attendants and two hundred communicants, and the two Methodist societies about eleven hundred regular visitors and four hundred members. In any case, the denominational influence was far wider than the stated membership [might indicate].

Allan Nevins reported that on the eve of national disruption, "the Eighth Census showed that the country had one church for every 580 people, [and] the churches had facilities for seating three-fifths of the population at one time." Such data add up to more than a generally pervading "influence"; they document a massive social reality. These churches of the people constituted a powerful visible structure shaping the common experiences and folkways of large numbers of American citizens nationwide. No other organization in the country was in closer direct touch with more people. Most Americans most likely gained their first experience in cooperation from their church organizations. These bodies enrolled millions who knew no other club or company; they enlisted men and women "in active continuous work to an extent never equalled even by the political parties, and they touched life at more popular points than any other body."[17]

A specific illustration of how the popular churches with their far-flung organizations and multitudinous activities affected social bonding in the United States has been suggested by Donald G. Mathews. In his essay, "The Second Great Awakening as an Organizing Process," he developed Perry Miller's thesis about the revivals in terms of organizational results. The Second Awakening, Mathews wrote, was "a general social movement that organized thousands of people into small groups"—the various societies for evangelism, missions, benevolence, and reform, and most importantly, local churches. Describing the "epidemic of organization" that followed the Revolution, Mathews argued that in viewing independence "as an event which gave them control over their own destiny, many Americans could find it relatively easy to participate in the only organization which sought them out, made them responsible for ordering a new holy community, and built the entire structure upon their own personal experience."

The surging success of the churches, Mathews concluded, lay in their ability to organize people. By multiplying congregations throughout the nation, the churches created a national spirit that rested in significant measure "not on the power of a national institution so much as [on] the relevance, power and similarity of thousands of local organizations that helped to create 'a common world of experience.' " And even more important than organization, as Mathews affirmed in a later work, was participation: "the convert was offered a chance to participate with God in his own salvation; he was required to participate with his fellows in the disciplined life of the Christian community; and he was expected to participate with persons of other localities in strengthening the life of the denomination."[18]

---

[17]T. Scott Miyakawa, *Protestants and Pioneers: Individualism and Conformity on the American Frontier* (Chicago, 1964) 18; Allan Nevins, *Ordeal of the Union*, 2 vols. (New York, 1947) 1:58n.; Nevins, *The War for the Union*, 4 vols. (New York, 1959) 1:258.

[18]Donald G. Mathews, "The Second Great Awakening as an Organizing Process, 1780-1830: An Hypothesis," *American Quarterly*, 21 (1969): 30, 33, 35, 43; Mathews, *Religion in the Old South* (Chicago, 1977) 58.

As time went on, the maturing national institutions began to assume larger significance. The Methodist Episcopal Church in particular demonstrated impressive ability not only to create large numbers of local units but also to draw them together in an efficient connectional system. In 1838 George G. Cookman marveled at the genius of Methodist organization, which he compared to Ezekiel's vision of the wheels (Ezekiel 1:15-21):

> You will perceive that there are "wheels within wheels." First, there is the great outer wheel of episcopacy, which accomplishes its entire revolution *once* in *four* years. To this there are attached *twenty-eight smaller wheels*, styled *annual conferences*, moving around *once a year;* to these are attached *one hundred wheels*, designated *presiding elders*, moving *twelve hundred other wheels*, termed *quarterly conferences*, every *three* months; to these are attached *four thousand wheels*, styled *travelling preachers*, moving round *once a month*, and communicating motion to *thirty thousand* wheels, called *class leaders*, moving round *once a week*, and who, in turn, being attached to between *seven and eight hundred thousand wheels*, called *members*, give a sufficient impulse to whirl them round *every day*. O sir, what a machine is this! This is the machine of which Archimedes only dreamed; this is the machine destined, under God, to *move the world, to turn it upside down*.

Philip Schaff was mildly disdainful of such "artificial machinery"; but, reduced to more professional terms than Cookman's fanciful analogy, Methodism was simply a highly articulated structure capable of significantly influencing the lives of its large and growing constituency.[19]

The Methodist Episcopal Church was the most extensive national institution in antebellum America other than the federal government. The significance of its connectionalism was that it helped to impose a uniformity on the many local institutions it embraced and thus contributed to social bonding in the whole nation. Its traveling clergy developed among Methodists a common set of shared experiences, which led in turn to a wider sense of community. The network of itinerant ministers was nationwide, enabling

---

[19]George G. Cookman, "Centenary Address," in *Speeches Delivered on Various Occasions* (New York, 1840) 136-37; Philip Schaff, *America: A Sketch of Its Political, Social, and Religious Character* (1855), ed. Perry Miller (Cambridge MA, 1961) 97.

preachers to circulate news among their charges and disseminate ideas garnered at regional and national conferences. This helped to impress on the whole denomination a national outlook. The *Book of Discipline,* moreover, held before all members a single standard of moral expectation. As Methodism successfully moved its organizing impulse into the growing cities, it maintained at the same time an undiminished vigor in the rural regions and on the frontier. A Scottish visitor in the early 1830s could observe accurately that "throughout the whole Union . . . the Methodists have acquired a powerful influence."[20]

An illustration of how Methodist connectionalism worked may be seen in an experience of James A. Thome, a senior divinity student at Oberlin who was working as one of "The Seventy," agents sent out by the American Anti-Slavery Society in the spring of 1836. On the last day of March, Thome wrote to his mentor Theodore Dwight Weld that he had gone to Petersburg, Ohio, and had lectured five times on the urgency of immediate abolition.

> Citizens mostly turned out to hear. Last evening they all voted in favor of *immediatism,* but they were not willing to form a society [to oppose slavery] immediately. The reason was they were chiefly Methodists, and were afraid to move until their minister should say—*move.*[21]

One misses the full force of Thome's last comment if one reads it solely as a tribute to the power and influence of a single Methodist minister over a local congregation. The overriding factor was that the Ohio Annual Conference of the Methodist Episcopal Church in 1835 had unanimously adopted resolutions condemning anti-slavery agitation, which meant that the minister himself could not "move" on Thome's proposal without violating denominational discipline. Such a violation could be very costly in terms of one's standing in the Conference, with unpleasant consequences for one's professional career. The Petersburg congregation's unwillingness to act—even when they had been persuaded on the principle—

---

[20]Thomas Hamilton, *Men and Manners in America* (London, 1833; rev. 1843; rpt. New York, 1968) 406.

[21]Gilbert H. Barnes and Dwight L. Dumond, eds., *Letters to Theodore Dwight Weld, Angelina Grimké Weld, and Sarah Grimké,* 2 vols. (Gloucester MA, 1965) 1:284.

demonstrates the force and authority of the Methodist system at the local level. Disciplinary requirements, of course, could be ignored or resisted; and sometimes they were, but always at the risk of disrupting the whole church. This essentially meant that a major national issue like slavery could neither be confronted nor evaded without traumatic repercussions throughout the whole denomination.

The case for the bonding force of the Baptist churches is harder to make because of their congregational polity. Since their forebears had suffered considerable persecution for dissent and nonconformity, they cherished individual freedom and mistrusted authority. They also shared the traditional Calvinistic suspicion of centralized power and therefore were fearful of supracongregational structures that might usurp the "autonomy" of local churches. In some quarters an antimissionary movement had developed in opposition to the formation and/or functioning of denominational agencies. Jealous of individual freedom and congregational independence, some objected to missionary boards and agencies that had authority to send missionaries wherever they pleased.[22] But notwithstanding such obstacles, the majority of Baptists did join together in regional associations for purposes of fellowship, sharing of information, and mutual counsel. Although none of these bodies could invoke disciplinary sanctions beyond simple nonrecognition of a church or minister, they published annual circular letters on a variety of topics, exchanged fraternal messengers among their various organizations, and exercised a moral authority that was generally respected. Beginning in 1821, Baptists began to form state conventions, and rapid progress in this direction was evidence of their desire to articulate a growing denominationalism.

Baptist periodicals circulated widely and kept church members informed of the course of national and denominational events. *The Christian Watchman*, founded in Boston in 1819, furnished during the antebellum years a lively and varied fare to readers as far away

---

[22]See Byron Cecil Lambert, "The Rise of the Anti-Mission Baptists: Sources and Leaders, 1800-1840" (Ph.D. dissertation, University of Chicago, 1957); Walter Brownlow Posey, *Frontier Mission: A History of Religion West of the Southern Appalachians to 1861* (Lexington, 1966) 62.

as Charleston, South Carolina. *The Columbian Star* began in Washington, D.C., in 1822; it moved in 1827 to Philadelphia and in 1833 to Georgia, where it became *The Christian Index* and continued as the voice of Georgia Baptists. *The Religious Herald,* which has enjoyed continuous publication in Richmond since 1828, quickly earned a reputation as one of the most influential papers of the South. The weekly *New York Baptist Register* (published at Utica from 1824) claimed thirty thousand readers at mid-century, while others, such as *The Baptist Banner* (started at Louisville in 1834), also had sizable circulations. These papers all copied extensively from each other and thus helped to sustain a denominational consciousness among the widely dispersed Baptists.

Although loyalties to state and regional organizations were often stronger than to any national body, the fact remains that Baptists had moved very early toward wider cooperation for missionary action. Three national organizations drew their support: the General Missionary Convention, which was primarily a society for foreign missions dating from 1814; the Baptist General Tract Society, formed in 1824 (becoming the American Baptist Publication Society in the 1840s); and the American Baptist Home Mission Society, organized in 1832.

As *societies* composed mainly of contributing individuals rather than as *churches* connected together through a denominational constitution, these bodies aroused few fears of ecclesiastical centralization. The Home Mission Society was perhaps the most "denominational" in structure; its constitution provided that "any person may become a member of this Society by contributing annually to its funds," and also that "any Baptist Church, or Association, or State Convention, or Missionary Society, that contributes annually to the objects of this Society, shall be entitled to be represented by one or more delegates, in its annual meetings." The Tract Society, on the other hand, offered membership only to "any person . . . paying the sum of one dollar annually."[23]

All these national societies met regularly, published reports, and carried on their work between anniversaries through elected boards

---

[23]The constitutions are printed in Robert A. Baker, ed., *A Baptist Sourcebook, with Particular Reference to Southern Baptists* (Nashville, 1966) 62-75.

of managers and executive officers. In this way they supplied, albeit in a less formally connectional way, the same kind of network of denominational relationships as the more highly structured Methodists. The important point is that each of the Baptist societies embraced a national constituency, and in time each would reflect in the rising controversy over slavery the sectional interests that were to divide them—and ultimately the nation.

Presbyterians had emerged from the Revolution in a stronger position than any other church in America. They grew rapidly in the National Period—in the North largely through accessions of westering New Englanders who moved easily from their hereditary Congregationalism into Presbyterianism by virtue of the Plan of Union (an interdenominational compact dating from 1801), and in the South and West by exploiting several features of revivalism. In the first three decades of the nineteenth century, communicant membership in the Presbyterian Church jumped from less than twenty thousand to almost a quarter of a million and embraced more people in the center of the social spectrum than either Methodists or Baptists. A British visitor to antebellum America observed that Methodists and Baptists were the most numerous, "Episcopalians the most fashionable; and the Preeminence of wealth and intelligence was thought to lay [sic] with the Presbyterians."[24] The higher educational level of the Presbyterian clergy enabled them to appeal to the entrepreneurial and business classes; and as a result, Presbyterians became something of an elite church among the evangelical denominations. Having never enjoyed establishment anywhere in colonial America, this "untraditional" (dissenting) church was accustomed to the conditions of pluralism and furnished many leaders for interdenominational cooperation. Before the schism of 1837 Presbyterians dominated the boards of the American Bible Society and the American Sunday School Union, though they remained cordially open to the participation of representatives from other denominations.

Long accustomed to a highly articulated polity, Presbyterians had a smoothly functioning organization. Their regional presby-

---

[24]Max Berger, *The British Traveller in America, 1836-1860* (New York, 1943) 142.

teries, area synods, and national assembly constituted a graduated
hierarchy of ecclesiastical judicatories that gave the church a social
influence comparable to that produced by the Methodist connection. As the General Assembly gathered in Philadelphia in 1837, a
Cincinnati newspaper editor calculated that their actions would
have nationwide impact.

> The General Assembly of the Presbyterian Church may be re-
> garded as representing a million of people, including not only
> church-members, but all connected with their congregations. And
> it represents a class containing as much intelligence, and swaying
> as much of influence as any other body whatever of equal num-
> bers. . . . It is composed of religious teachers, who from the desk
> [pulpit] and in pastoral intercourse and supervision, have access
> to, and authoritative influence over a vast multitude of minds. The
> Assembly is held, not in a remote corner, but in a great and cen-
> tral city, and the eyes of the American people are upon it, and its
> voice goes into all the land. . . . For good or evil, it is indeed a body
> of immense power.[25]

Like the other denominations, Presbyterians took full advan-
tage of the print medium. Upwards of twenty weekly newspapers
kept church members abreast of religious news, current affairs, and
editorial opinion. One may safely assume that Presbyterians, though
the least numerous of the three popular denominations, were of
comparable significance as a national religious body because of their
slightly higher level of education and affluence.[26] Although they
were spread more thinly than either Methodists or Baptists, they
were distributed almost as widely. Conflicts over slavery in such a
body accurately reflected the sectional strife that was tearing at the
whole nation, and it was not illogical to regard the Presbyterian
schisms as a credible threat to political union.

In sum, during the antebellum years Methodists, Baptists, and
Presbyterians enrolled the preponderant majority of American
Christians and extended their influence through a much larger
constituency to become a decisive force in the shaping of American

---

[25]*Journal and Luminary* (Cincinnati), 15 June 1837.
[26]Walter Brownlow Posey judged Presbyterians the most influential church in
the trans-Appalachian South; see *Frontier Mission*, 142, 413.

society. Together these three popular denominations constituted much of the institutional strength of evangelical Protestantism, which, as noted in the preceding chapter, was the prevailing mood of antebellum America. They not only furnished millions of people with a primary relationship of belonging; they also afforded opportunities unmatched elsewhere for gaining experience in voluntary organization, developing lay leadership, and regulating human behavior. Their network of representative units gave ample occasion for communicating local concerns to their national leaders and for transmitting the authority of the leadership to the local units.

There was no more pervasive presence that touched the lives of more Americans at more points than these churches of the people. This is why the involvement of such churches in the increasingly acrimonious debate over slavery was significant on a national scale. Whatever happened in the churches' inner civil war over slavery would inevitably send shock waves throughout the entire nation. Since evangelicalism had been one of the major bonds of national unity since pre-Revolutionary times, it is easy to understand why persons anxious about the future of the Union should have regarded the division of the popular denominations as an exceedingly ominous portent.

CHAPTER THREE

# SECESSION SCENARIO

The drama of the war and its antecedents has long been viewed as high tragedy in the classic sense. What is less often noticed is that the controversy that would eventually sunder the Union was focused sharply in the churches more than fifteen years prior to moving to the larger stage of the entire nation. The consequent division of the popular denominations may be viewed as a scenario of what was to come. The division of the churches over slavery dramatized the yawning moral chasm between North and South; and because the schisms split asunder major national institutions, they riveted the attention of the whole nation on the differences between the two sections. Seeing leaders of the largest organizations in the land unable—or unwilling—to reconcile their differences over the moral issue posed by slavery made it difficult to believe that the sectional conflict was by any means repressible.

The sequence of events followed a logic that, in historical retrospect, should not be surprising. Since the abolitionist vanguard based its attack specifically on moral and religious values, the Southern defense would also have to be essentially moral and religious. This is why ministers of the South were among the first to attempt a justification of the "peculiar institution." The churches, moreover, were neither as pragmatically pluralistic nor as resilient under strain as were political parties; therefore they broke apart sooner. The same religious commitments that reinforced nationalism, described in chapter 1, also generated strong sectional loyalties. After 1830 slavery was largely confined to one section and condemned by another, making it inevitable that the churches would become embroiled in the sectional dispute and in the civil war that ensued. In the heat of conflict, church leaders easily transferred their nationalistic sentiments to their own region, confident that their region was capable of fulfilling the mission and destiny formerly envisioned for the whole nation.

That these divergent nationalisms had widened the gulf between North and South became dramatically clear in the year of national breakdown. Benjamin Morgan Palmer, Presbyterian pastor in New Orleans and a leading champion of an independent South as "the cause of God himself," hailed the secession of South Carolina in December 1860 by preaching: "We have vainly read the history of our fathers, if we failed to see that from the beginning two nations were in the American womb." An independent South, Palmer believed, would consummate the American dream in the wake of Northern apostasy.[1] On the other side, Samuel Gridley Howe, New England reformer whose wife was soon to write the "Battle Hymn" that would inspirit Northern warriors to trample out the grapes of wrath against the sinful South, viewed with grim satisfaction "the prospect that with so many sparks flying about in the powder magazine there may be a blow up. Well," he snorted, "the Lord will save the pieces, and we'll have a Northern Union worth saving."[2]

The first major move in the direction of national "blow up" was marked by nationwide divisions in the three large popular denominations. Presbyterians separated into Old School and New School

---

[1]James W. Silver, *Confederate Morale and Church Propaganda* (New York, 1967) 27.

[2]Samuel Gridley Howe to Theodore Parker, 22 January 1860, in George M. Frederickson, *The Inner Civil War: Northern Intellectuals and the Crisis of the Union* (New York, 1965) 48-49.

factions in 1837 after a series of quarrels in which sharply differing views of slavery figured significantly if not decisively. The New School split again in 1857 because of increasingly strident clashes over what position the national assembly should take toward slaveholders. The Methodist Episcopal Church sundered in 1844 and the national Baptist societies in 1845, explicitly because of sharp internal disputes about this same issue. Thus several years before political rupture and war, Americans saw their three largest national churches act out a full-dress scenario for the subsequent disruption of the nation.

It is not necessary here to recount in detail the dreary story of those denominational schisms.[3] The present purpose is rather to show that the leaders of the dividing churches were aware of the probable political consequences of what they were doing, and that even so dismal a prospect as the ruin of their cherished political union did not deter them. Public comment in secular newspapers and in various political forums also resounded with dire predictions of national tragedy should the churches array themselves into Northern and Southern factions. It also appears that the contending churchmen did not even cast the alternatives in any way so as to avoid further polarization of the country and thereby maintain a slim hope of saving the Union without war. The argument in the churches developed in essentially the same way it would in the political arena: moderates counseled silence for the sake of "peace" in hopes that the divisive issue would somehow go away; disunionists urged schism for the sake of freedom either to reject or to preserve slavery; and ultraists demanded precipitate action without regard for the social and institutional realities of the situation. Polarities in the churches sharpened during the 1830s, and soon the Christian community was strained to the breaking point. Each dispute evoked dread premonitions about political disunion, spreading fear that the division of the churches would lead ineluctably to civil war.

---

[3]Details may be found in the standard denominational histories. A competent narrative summary of the schisms that gives due attention to the overriding force of the slavery controversy is H. Shelton Smith, *In His Image, but . . .: Racism in Southern Religion, 1780-1910* (Durham, 1972) ch. 2.

## I

The Presbyterian schism of 1837 opened the first major North-South cleavage in American institutions, although the line of division was not drawn strictly according to Mason and Dixon's famous survey. In most contemporary reports, as in the reading of some modern historians, the split was due primarily to controversies over doctrine and missionary method. An insurgent "New School," whose strength centered in New York and Ohio, had been aggressively promoting "new measures" in revivalism, new interpretations of the Westminster standards, and new forms of cooperation with other denominations, even when this required modifications of traditional Presbyterian polity. The New School, more than incidentally, also harbored most of the abolitionists in the Presbyterian Church. Resistance to deviations from the strict Reformed heritage came from an "Old School" coalition of traditionalists and moderates; with major strength in Pennsylvania and New Jersey, it embraced most of the Princeton Seminary faculty and several outspoken leaders in the South.

The New School, being the faster growing wing of the church, tended to dominate the General Assembly for several years prior to 1835, but in that year the Old School mustered a majority and repudiated a number of New School programs. The following year, however, the latter turned out in full strength to recapture control of the Assembly and reverse the actions of the previous year. Also in 1836, New School leaders in New York established a new theological seminary (Union) as a progressive counterweight to Princeton. Old School leaders, now thoroughly aroused, determined that the only way to preserve the Presbyterian heritage as they understood it was to exclude the New School from the church.

Following a carefully conceived strategy, they gained control of the General Assembly of 1837 and proceeded remorselessly to exscind the four New School synods, thus ridding themselves of "heresy," extra-denominational entanglements, and abolitionism at a single stroke. Within a year, the excluded synods had organized a General Assembly of their own, and by the time hesitant neutralists had declared their allegiance to one or the other side, it appeared that American Presbyterianism had rent itself almost in half. The New School claimed approximately 100,000 communicants in 1,200 churches and 85 presbyteries; the Old School reported 127,000 members in 1,763 churches and 96 presbyteries.[4]

The exscinding actions could not have been carried out without the support of the Southern presbyteries. Generally conservative but staunch supporters of Westminster, Southerners probably would have gravitated toward the Old School in any case. But the rapidly rising abolitionist advocacy of many New School adherents aroused the Presbyterians of the South. According to Lyman Beecher, the Southerners acted at the urging of Senator Calhoun of South Carolina.

> They got scared about abolition. . . . John C. Calhoun was at the bottom of it. I know of his doing things—writing to ministers, and telling them to do this and do that. The South finally took the Old School side. It was a cruel thing—it was an accursed thing, and 'twas slavery that did it.[5]

While there is little evidence that slavery was a divisive issue before 1836, delegates from the slave states and abolitionists both held separate caucuses at the General Assembly that year. The moderator, John Witherspoon of Camden, South Carolina, reported to Thomas Smyth of Charleston a rumor that 150 abolitionists were on the floor of the Assembly. "I can scarcely believe this," Witherspoon wrote, "and yet I am convinced *they be very many*. . . . I say, Sir, let the *South look well to her interests*." Other Southern delegates were equally disturbed. "The whole General Assembly is secretly heaving under the apprehension that slavery may divide this body before its close," wrote one commissioner. "It is the prevalent opinion among southerners," reported still another, "that we are to be unchurched by a considerable majority. If so, we can retire south of *Mason's and Dixon's line*, and . . . dwell in peace and harmony."[6]

---

[4]Cf. George M. Marsden, *The Evangelical Mind and the New School Presbyterian Experience: A Case Study of Thought and Theology in Nineteenth-Century America* (New Haven, 1970) 65-66.

[5]Lyman Beecher, *The Autobiography of Lyman Beecher*, ed. Barbara M. Cross, 2 vols. (Cambridge MA, 1961) 2:323.

[6]Ernest T. Thompson, *Presbyterians in the South*, 3 vols. (Richmond, 1963–1973) 1:386, 391.

The South Carolina Presbytery had already registered its belief that "the Old School 'and the New have got so wide apart, in sentiment and feeling, that for the future there can be no hope of friendly co-operation united in one body"; they urged that "for the sake of peace, and the better promoting [of] the interests of Christ's kingdom, the parties ought to separate." Lyman Beecher recoiled from such a thought. Taking the floor in the 1836 Assembly, he pleaded for harmony for the sake of a larger Union: "These silken ties, these soft but mighty bands which have held Christians of the North and of the South together are beginning to break. Well may panic go through the hearts of those who love the land." Beecher, however, was hardly the one to dissuade the Old School partisans, who were still fuming over his acquittal in a heresy trial the preceding year. It goes without saying that he had little influence in the South.[7]

As matters resolved, the Southerners had little to fear. Within a year they found themselves holding the balance of power in the Assembly and were able to trade their swing vote to exclude the New School synods in return for assurances from the Old School leadership that all discussion of slavery in the General Assembly would cease. William S. Plumer, pastor of the First Presbyterian Church in Richmond, stated the South's terms bluntly: "All we ask is that the Supreme Judicatory [the General Assembly] do nothing in the way of legislation on . . . slavery." Even though he insisted that the South's peculiar institution was purely political in character and not a proper subject for ecclesiastical consideration, he nevertheless felt constrained to deliver a lengthy defense of slavery on biblical and moral grounds. Plumer made his point, the Southerners received the assurances they wanted, the Old School got their vote, and the church was divided. As a historian of Southern Presbyterianism put it, "the Old School party won the victory over the New School party only by virtue of an almost 'solid South.' "[8]

---

    [7]Ibid., 1:391; Gilbert H. Barnes, *The Antislavery Impulse, 1830-1844* (Washington, D.C., 1933) 95; Stuart C. Henry, *Unvanquished Puritan: A Portrait of Lyman Beecher* (Grand Rapids, 1973) 209-22.
    [8]Thompson, *Presbyterians in the South*, 1:393; Thomas C. Johnson, *History of the Southern Presbyterian Church* (New York, 1894) 359.

The Cincinnati *Journal and Luminary* had no doubts about the real issue at stake:

> The question is not between the new and the old school—is not in relation to doctrinal errors; but it is *slavery and anti-slavery*. It is not the [doctrinal] *standards* which were to be protected, but the *system of slavery*.

One of the paper's correspondents wrote from Philadelphia that the Southern delegates "seem to have felt that their business in the Assembly was to cut off in the face of the constitution enough Northern Synods to render slaveholding impregnable in the Presbyterian Church." Old School stalwarts dismissed such charges as canards of an "abolitionist paper."[9] The next year Zebulon Crocker, a delegate to the Assembly from Connecticut, assigned less importance to slavery than to issues of doctrine and polity but supplied considerable evidence for suspecting "a mutual understanding between the abolitionists of the Old School and their southern brethren of the majority, that, letting this exciting topic [of slavery] alone, they should march in unbroken ranks against heresy; while the South would in a measure gain its objective, by excluding New England influence from the Presbyterian Church."[10] Contemporary observer John Quincy Adams declared unequivocally that "this question of slavery" was agitating several church bodies and "has already completed a schism in the Presbyterian Church."[11]

In the 1840s, as Methodists and Baptists divided over slavery, Presbyterians examined their feelings on the issue more candidly. A pseudonymous writer in the *New York Observer*, an Old School paper, reflected in 1845 on the "unhappy separation" that his church had suffered eight years previously. "Altho' doctrinal discrepancies were the alleged grounds of the division, and probably had a principal influence in producing them, yet it is well known that the

---

[9]*Journal and Luminary* (Cincinnati), 15 January 1837; *Biblical Repository and Princeton Review*, 9 (1837): 479.

[10]Zebulon Crocker, *The Catastrophe of the Presbyterian Church in 1837* (New Haven, 1838) 68. Crocker had been a delegate from Connecticut to the General Assembly of 1837.

[11]Charles Francis Adams, ed., *Memoirs of John Quincy Adams*, 12 vols. (Philadelphia, 1874–1877) 9:544.

subject of slavery was one of the principal and most exciting topics of discussion, which fired the breasts of the disputants, and eventually formed one of the lines of the final separation." The fact that the New School harbored—and heeded—many voices of antislavery, while the Old School refused to discuss the issue, seemed to the writer abundant proof of his point.

There is further confirmation of decisive Southern influence: during the twenty-five years from 1837 to 1861, the Old School Assembly elected as many moderators from the South as in the entire preceding forty-seven years that the Presbyterians had existed as a united national church. Whatever else it meant, the Old School action of 1837 was for the Southern presbyteries a welcome victory over abolitionism. Professor George A. Baxter of Union Theological Seminary in Richmond rejoiced that if the course of the General Assembly should be sustained and carried out by the churches, "it will put an end to the abolition question and disturbance in the Presbyterian church." For Baxter, the victory lay in the fact that "by getting clear of the New School," the church would at the same time "get clear of abolition."[12]

The extent to which slavery was a decisive cause of the Presbyterian schism remains a matter of some dispute. C. Bruce Staiger argued that the slavery question was "closely interwoven" with the doctrinal disputes of the 1830s, concluding that if New School abolitionism had not aroused the fear and resentment of Southern presbyteries, throwing them into the arms of the Old School, "the break would never have occurred." Elwyn A. Smith responded to Staiger's argument with an attempt to "offer a somewhat more precise judgment on the role of the South in forming the two Presbyterianisms which emerged after 1838." His conclusion was that while the slavery issue alone might not have "tipped the balance toward schism," the support that proslavery Southerners gave to the Old School in exchange for "an explicit understanding that there would be no subsequent church declaration on slavery was crucial

---

[12]"Pro patria Deoque," *New York Observer*, 21 June 1845, 98, and 15 July 1837, 26. Cf. also Lewis G. Vander Velde, *The Presbyterian Churches and the Federal Union, 1861-1869* (Cambridge MA, 1932) 26.

for the Old School victory in exscinding the four New School synods."

Ernest T. Thompson, a careful historian who combined sympathetic understanding with critical judgment, prepared the fullest account. "Slavery was an issue in this division of the church only in the South," he wrote, though he was not certain that it was the decisive issue. "The theological conservatism of the South would have aligned it naturally with the Old School," while at the same time, Old School leaders in the North had a natural disposition to maintain a discreet silence on the slavery question. Thompson had no reason to doubt that the Old School's agreement to forbid discussion of slavery in the Assembly "helped to solidify Southern support for the Old School 'reforming measures' and thus to ensure the resultant division of the church."[13]

What is rarely noticed is that throughout the controversy prominent Presbyterians confessed their awareness that a division of the church could precipitate a crisis in the political compact. As tempers were warming in the early 1830s, Amasa Converse tried to focus the issue in the columns of the *Southern Religious Telegraph,* which he edited in Richmond. Slavery was an evil, he admitted—going farther than many of his coreligionists were then willing to go—but the South was not initially responsible for it. Since neither North nor South could find an acceptable solution to the problem, and abolitionism was only making things worse, Converse counseled Presbyterians to keep quiet about the whole business. "[R]ailing accusations against the South" must be kept from the floor of the Assembly, because "to condemn slavery as sin under all circumstances would divide the church, and to that extent the nation," which must by all means be avoided.

However, Converse then proceeded to fly in the face of his own advice. So long as he feared that the General Assembly might vote

---

[13]C. Bruce Staiger, "Abolitionism and the Presbyterian Church Schism, 1837-38," *Mississippi Valley Historical Review,* 36 (1949): 391, 414; Elwyn A. Smith, "The Role of the South in the Presbyterian Schism of 1837-38," *Church History,* 29 (1960): 45, 58, 60; Thompson, *Presbyterians in the South,* 1:411, 394; cf. also 397-99. Marsden, *The Evangelical Mind and the New School Presbyterian Experience,* 250-51, summarizes the historiography of this debate; his own views, which are not significantly different from Thompson's, are on 98-99.

any disapproval of slavery, he kept urging Southern Presbyterians to form their own Assembly. Charles Hodge, staunch defender of Old School orthodoxy, also warned that the breakup of the churches could lead to the dismembering of the Union. Like Converse, he blamed the abolitionists; their stigmatizing of slavery as a sin and a crime "must operate to produce the disunion of the states, and the division of all ecclesiastical societies. . . . We shall become two nations in feeling, which must soon render us two nations in fact."[14]

On the eve of the pre-Assembly caucus in 1837, William S. Plumer set forth the issue in apocalyptic terms:

> Should the Assembly . . . legislate and decide that slaveholding is a sin . . . the Southern churches would all feel themselves instructed by the Apostle Paul to "withdraw from such" [1 Tim. 6:5]. . . . Thus our church would be rent asunder. . . . Then nothing is left . . . except to . . . rend the star-spangled banner in twain. . . . Soon the hostile forces will be marshalled against each other, and the Potomac will be dyed with blood. . . . Can it be that the righteous Judge of all the earth has so dreadful a controversy with the Presbyterian Church of the United States as to give her up to the folly and madness of being the first to hoist the gate and let the flood of desolation roll in?

This dire prediction notwithstanding, Plumer made the most persuasive speech of the Assembly advocating division of the church and was rewarded by being chosen as first moderator of the Old School faction.[15]

The Southerners may have sensed that their victory with the Old School would be costly. As Methodists and Baptists divided in the following decade, evincing a further fraying of the bonds of political union, misgivings multiplied among Presbyterians. The disruption of the churches, in the minds of apprehensive ecclesiastics, raised the haunting specter of an imminent breakdown of the Union. Southern Presbyterians' leading theologian James Henley Thornwell, "the Calhoun of the southern church," voiced the

---

[14]*Biblical Repertory*, 2d ser., 8 (1836): 301. Hodge, the presumed author of this piece, was reviewing William Ellery Channing, *Slavery* (Boston, 1835).

[15]*Southern Religious Telegraph*, 8 August 1837, 124, quoted in Thompson, *Presbyterians in the South*, 1:393-94; see also Henry Alexander White, *Southern Presbyterian Leaders* (New York, 1911) 289.

group's forebodings in a widely distributed pamphlet of 1851. Again, the fault lay with agitators who would not let the question of slavery alone.

> We are solemn and earnest, not only because we deplore a schism in the body of Christ, but because we deplore a schism among the confederated States of this Union. We . . . declare our deliberate conviction, that the continued agitation of Slavery must sooner or later shiver this government into atoms. . . . If Slavery be indeed consistent with the Bible, their responsibility is tremendous, who, in obedience to blind impulses and visionary theories, pull down the fairest fabric of government the world has ever seen, rend the body of Christ in sunder, and dethrone the Saviour in His own Kingdom. . . . Are our country, our Bible, our interests on earth and our hopes for heaven to be sacrificed on the altars of a fierce fanaticism? . . . Slavery is implicated in every fibre of Southern society; it is with us a vital question, and it is because we *know* that interference with it cannot and will not be much longer endured we raise our warning voice. We would save the country if we could.[16]

Thornwell was precisely correct—almost clairvoyant—on one point: the unity of the country was tied closely to the unity of the churches. By the time these words were published, Methodists and Baptists had broken over slavery; and their separate, hostile factions stood in many minds as a proleptic sign of the imminent rupture of the Union.

Meanwhile the New School Presbyterian Church tried to maintain an unstable peace with its slaveholding members. The division of 1837 had not been along strictly North-South lines, and a few Southern presbyteries claiming some ten thousand members had gone with the New School because they were convinced that the exscinding acts had been unconstitutional. But slavery continued to agitate the Constitutional Assembly, as the New School called itself, by virtue of a constant stream of overtures from antislavery presbyteries demanding that slavery be declared a sin and that slaveholding members be subjected to church discipline. Never as

---

[16]James Henley Thornwell, "Relation of the Church to Slavery" (1851) in *The Collected Writings of James Henley Thornwell*, ed. John B. Adger and John L. Girardeau, 4 vols. (Richmond, 1871–1873) 4:394-96.

solidly abolitionist as Southerners had suspected, the Assembly customarily remanded such petitions back to the initiating presbytery for further discussion on the ground that an affirmative response would disrupt the entire church. In 1845, as Methodists and Baptists were dividing, the Slavery Committee of the General Assembly reported its apprehension that continued agitation would have a tendency "evidently to separate the Northern from the Southern portion of the Church; a result which every good citizen must deplore as tending to dissolution of the Union of our beloved country."[17]

But Presbyterians above the Mason-Dixon line repeatedly condemned slavery—which was easy enough for them to do, since their state laws forbade it anyway—and the petitions kept coming. In 1850 the Assembly responded to the extent of reaffirming the verbal condemnation of slavery which the General Assembly of the undivided Presbyterian Church had enacted in 1818: "We consider the voluntary enslaving of one part of the human race by another, as a gross violation of the most precious and sacred rights of human nature; as utterly inconsistent with the law of God, which requires us to love our neighbour as ourselves, and as totally irreconcilable with the spirit and principles of the Gospel of Christ, which enjoins that, 'all things whatsoever ye would that men should do to you, do ye even so to them.' "

Although the statement went on to declare that "it is manifestly the duty of all christians . . . as speedily as possible to efface this blot on our holy religion, and to obtain the complete abolition of slavery throughout christendom," the only concrete actions recommended by the Assembly of 1818 had been that Presbyterians support the Colonization Society, provide religious instruction for their slaves, and seek to prevent cruelties in the treatment of slaves. But now the New School Assembly added a stinger: while noting the restrictions imposed by state laws, it went on to designate slaveholding as a breach of ecclesiastical discipline. "The holding of our fellow-men in the condition of slavery, except in those cases where it is unavoidable by the laws of the State, the obligations of guard-

---

[17]Reported in the *Nashville Whig*, 27 May 1845.

ianship, or the demands of humanity, is an offence in the proper import of that term as used in the Book of Discipline . . . and should be regarded and treated in the same manner as other offences"— that is, made a matter of church discipline.[18]

Even though the 1850 Assembly left disciplinary jurisdiction to the presbyteries, the Southerners were offended. After six more restive years, the Presbytery of Lexington, South (in Mississippi), declared flatly that some of its members and ministers held slaves "from principle" and "of choice" and believed this "to be according to the Biblical right." In 1857 the General Assembly condemned the declaration by a vote of 169 to 26 and affirmed solemnly that "such doctrines and practices cannot be permanently tolerated in the Presbyterian Church." Twenty-one Southern and border presbyteries with about fifteen thousand communicants promptly severed their connection with the New School Assembly, protesting that its actions effectively exscinded them from the church and were "unrighteous, oppressive, uncalled for . . . destructive of the unity of our branch of the Church . . . and adding to the peril of the union of these United States." The seceders organized themselves the following year at Knoxville, Tennessee, as The United Synod of the Presbyterian Church in the United States of America.[19]

The sectional division of Presbyterianism was now almost complete. The only remaining body that embraced both Northern and Southern members was the Old School Assembly, which maintained its peace and unity by declaring in 1845: "The church of Christ is a spiritual body, whose jurisdiction extends only to the religious faith, and moral conduct of her members. She cannot legislate where Christ has not legislated, nor make terms of membership which he has not made." Since the Scriptures do not

---

[18]The 1818 statement is printed in H. Shelton Smith et al., eds., *American Christianity: An Historical Interpretation with Representative Documents*, 2 vols. (New York, 1960–1963) 2:179-82. Minutes of the (New School) General Assembly, 1850, are printed in Maurice Whitman Armstrong et al., eds., *The Presbyterian Enterprise: Sources of American Presbyterian History* (Philadelphia, 1956) 203.

[19]Minutes of the (New School) General Assembly, 1857, in Armstrong, *Presbyterian Enterprise*, 204; Hiram Mattison, *The Impending Crisis of 1860* (New York, 1858) 106. (Mattison was a Methodist, and his title refers to the "crisis" expected to erupt at the 1860 General Conference of the Methodist Episcopal Church.)

teach anywhere that slaveholding, "without regard to circumstances, is a sin, the renunciation of which should be made a condition of membership," the proper thing for the church to do is remain silent on the subject.[20] The peace purchased by such a statement, however, was not to endure long. The lines had already been drawn, by Methodists and Baptists as well as Presbyterians, and William S. Plumer's prophecy was drawing closer to fulfillment.

## I I

In Scene Two of the scenario, the Methodists followed essentially the same script as the Presbyterians, except that they adopted a Plan of Separation with votes from both sides of the "continental divide" between antislavery and proslavery. Although the fundamental issue was irrefutably the question of slavery, with no doctrinal differences intruding between North and South, the dispute leading to rupture assumed the shape of a contention over polity and procedure. The close connectionalism of the Methodist Episcopal Church meant that matters affecting polity and procedure received intense scrutiny, and any significant dispute had to be dealt with—usually in some annual conference, and if not settled satisfactorily there, in General Conference.

The slavery dispute was especially crucial, because its existence in only one region compromised the uniformity of Methodist discipline and threatened the integrity of the connectional system. This meant that if the question of slaveholding should ever become a matter of moral judgment at the highest level of the church, one part or another of Methodism's national constituency would have to be censured. Despite the efforts of centrist ecclesiocrats to suppress the issue, slavery was too all-encompassing to keep off the agenda of the General Conference forever. When the question did come squarely before the General Conference, by a certain perverse logic it was almost predictable that Methodists should react to unreconciled conflict by separating; and given the national extent of their connection, it was equally logical that their separation

---

[20]Minutes of the (Old School) General Assembly, 1845, in Armstrong, *Presbyterian Enterprise,* 200.

should set off alarming repercussions throughout the entire political union.

Peter Cartwright, well-known Methodist preacher from Illinois, attended the General Conference of 1844, when the church broke into Northern and Southern factions. Reflecting twelve years later on the course of events leading to schism, he wrote:

> All the time of the protracted debates I knew, if the Southern preachers failed to carry the point they had fixed, namely, the tolerance of slaveholding in the episcopacy, that they would fly the track, and set up for themselves. And in that event . . . war and strife would prevail among brethren that once were united as a brotherly band, and that they must of necessity become a slavery Church. And I the more deeply regretted it because any abomination sanctioned by the priesthood, would take a firmer hold on the country, and that this very circumstance would the longer perpetuate the evil of slavery, and perhaps would be the entering wedge to the dissolution of our glorious Union; and perhaps the downfall of this great republic.[21]

Cartwright had good reason to be apprehensive. The Methodists had not developed the largest voluntary organization in the United States by challenging the social system very sharply, and they had learned as early as 1785 that John Wesley's denunciation of slavery as "that execrable sum of all villainies"—and American slavery as "the vilest that ever saw the sun"—would not find a universally sympathetic hearing in America. Antislavery preaching was unwelcome because it disturbed the ecclesiastical peace and hindered the growth of the church. Early disciplinary rules to limit or proscribe slaveholding had foundered on the rocks of popular prejudice, civil law, and economic greed. By 1834 the New York *Christian Advocate*, which took in $25,000 a year from its twelve thousand Southern subscribers, was opposing abolitionism on the ground that it conflicted "with the best interest of the country." The only safe course for Methodists to follow was evangelistic work among the slaves and half-hearted support of the colonization scheme. Had not

---

[21]Peter Cartwright, *The Autobiography of Peter Cartwright* (1856), ed. Charles L. Wallis (Nashville, 1956) 276.

even the great Mr. Wesley admonished his preachers, "You have nothing to do but save souls"?

Formidable opposition notwithstanding, abolitionism was on the rise in the Methodist Episcopal Church, causing many of its leaders to share the fears expressed by Cartwright. As early as 1835, bishops Elijah Hedding and John Emory were rebuking antislavery activists in New England, where Methodist abolitionism was growing more and more strident, warning that their agitations had "already been productive of pernicious results, and tend to the production of others yet more disastrous, both in the Church and in the social and political relations of the country." The General Conference of 1836, meeting in Cincinnati at the very edge of the slaveholding region, acknowledged the evils of slavery but rejected proposals for any new legislation on the matter. Instead, the delegates voted themselves "decidedly opposed to modern abolitionism, and wholly disclaim[ed] any right, wish or intentions to interfere in the civil and political relation between master and slave as it exists in the slave-holding states of this Union." From the balcony of Wesley Chapel's new brick edifice, where the General Conference was convened, James G. Birney cast a sorrowful eye over the proceedings and concluded that the Methodist Episcopal Church was "staggering more and more under the life-destroying influence of the pestilent atmosphere with which [slavery] has enveloped her."[22]

The following June, the Georgia Annual Conference resolved unanimously that "slavery, as it exists in the United States, is not a moral evil." At the same time Bishop Beverly Waugh, presiding at the New England Annual Conference, refused to entertain any abolitionist petitions. He admonished antislavery activists not to "hazard the unity of the Methodist Episcopal Church . . . by agitating those fearfully exciting topics" in opposition to the deliberate decision of the last General Conference. "Are you willing," the bishop

[22]Elijah Hedding and John Emory, "Address to the Ministers and Preachers of the Methodist Episcopal Church . . . September 10, 1835," in Charles Elliott, *History of the Great Secession* (Cincinnati, 1855) 898-99; Journal of the General Conference, 1836, in *Journals of the General Conference of the Methodist Episcopal Church,* 1796-1836 (New York, 1855) 447; *The Philanthropist,* 27 May 1836, quoted in Betty Fladeland, *James Gillespie Birney: Slaveholder to Abolitionist* (Ithaca, 1955) 134-35.

asked reproachfully, "to contribute to the destruction of our beautiful and excellent form of civil and political government, after it has cost the labor, treasure, and blood of our fathers to establish it?"[23]

At the time Waugh spoke, the Presbyterian schism was but a fortnight old, and ominous forebodings were already abroad. By December the *Southern Christian Advocate* was even more explicit about the dangerous consequences:

> In the present state of the country we believe it to be of the utmost importance to the country itself, that the churches be kept together. Let the bonds be once severed which hold the churches of the North and South together, and the Union of these states will be more than endangered, it will presently be rent asunder.[24]

But hostile parties were crystallizing rapidly in the church. William A. Smith of Virginia had already devised a plan of separation that he was prepared to push relentlessly unless General Conference "would agree to expunge everything from the Discipline of the Methodist Church on the subject of slavery."[25] He had no need to unveil his plan, however; the next General Conference (1840) managed to maintain the stalemate, endorsing the Colonization Society but ruling ambiguously on the rights of black members in church trials. By the time the delegates gathered on 1 May 1844 at the Greene Street Church in New York City for what was to be the last General Conference of the undivided Methodist Episcopal Church, the bishops' attempts to suppress antislavery activity—while at the same time evincing little disfavor toward slaveholding—had already provoked the withdrawal of a sizable abolitionist group in 1843 that formed the Wesleyan Methodist Church under the lead-

---

[23]*Zion's Herald* (Boston), 28 June 1837, quoted in John Nelson Norwood, *The Schism in the Methodist Episcopal Church, 1844: A Study of Slavery and Ecclesiastical Politics* (New York, 1923) 35-36.

[24]William Capers, in the *Southern Christian Advocate* (Charleston), 8 December 1837, quoted in Henry S. Stroupe, *The Religious Press in the Southern Atlantic States, 1802-1865; An Annotated Bibliography with Historical Introduction and Notes* (Durham, 1956) 22.

[25]Cartwright, *Autobiography of Peter Cartwright*, 238.

ership of Orange Scott.[26] Some six thousand Methodists residing from New England to Michigan soon switched their allegiance to the Wesleyans, and the number would grow to fifteen thousand by the end of 1844. These losses and the fear of further defections in the same direction stiffened antislavery sentiment among the leaders of the church, so much so that their refusal to yield to Southern demands for retaining a slaveholding bishop became the occasion for a sectional division of Methodism.

The bishop in question was James O. Andrew of Georgia, who had been elected to the episcopacy in 1832, in part because he was not a slaveowner. Since then, however, he had become "connected with slavery" when his deceased wife bequeathed him a young mulatto woman, Kitty, and a black boy. The boy had been separated from his family and was too young to send away; Kitty refused to migrate to a free state or to join the new colony of free blacks in Liberia; and Georgia state law prohibited manumission. In addition, Andrew's second wife had inherited several slaves from her former husband, although Andrew himself had promptly executed a quitclaim deed forgoing any interest in his wife's slaves as common property. In a candid report to the Conference Committee on Episcopacy, the bishop truthfully declared that he had neither bought nor sold a slave, that he was only an unwilling trustee, and that there was no legal or practical way of emancipating either his slaves or those of his wife. Andrew offered to resign his episcopal office, but his fellow Southerners would not hear of it. This was a test case, and both Northern and Southern factions were determined to press the question to its issue, even if that meant fracturing the church.

In the protracted debate that ensued, no one disputed the facts or charged Bishop Andrew with violating any civil law or standing rule of the church. Because the Methodist *Discipline* allowed ministers to own slaves in states where the law forbade manumission, Andrew's opponents were left with the choice of focusing directly on the moral issue or arguing their case on the ground of expe-

---

[26]See Donald G. Mathews, "Orange Scott: The Methodist Evangelist as Revolutionary," in *The Antislavery Vanguard: New Essays on the Abolitionists*, ed. Martin Duberman (Princeton, 1965) 71-101.

diency. In the tangle of motives driving the protagonists on each side, the moral issue was fundamental; but once again, the nature of Methodist polity turned much of the debate into a procedural dispute.

The procedural arguments focused on the nature of the episcopacy. According to the constitution by which Methodists were then operating, a bishop was a general superintendent for the entire church, but under the tensions of the 1840s a slaveholding bishop would have found little acceptance in much of the North. Nor would Andrew's Southern supporters consent to a geographical limitation of his superintendency. After almost two weeks of strenuous debate, the decisive vote came on a resolution stating that since Bishop Andrew's "connection" with slavery "will greatly embarrass the exercise of his office . . . if not in some places entirely prevent it," he should "desist from the exercise of his office so long as this impediment remains." The resolution was adopted by a vote of 110 to 68 along manifestly sectional lines.

The Southerners took this as a signal that they must withdraw from the national church and began making immediate preparations to organize their half million members into the Methodist Episcopal Church, South. The majority went on to adopt a report from the Conference Commission on Slavery which resolved in part that "the General Conference would take measures entirely to separate slavery from the church"—an action that gave the Southerners grounds for claiming that they had been forced out of the Methodist Episcopal Church.[27] An agreement for the equitable division of the church property concluded the General Conference and inaugurated a century-long division of American Methodism.

What is striking about that oft-told story is the persistence with which predictions of the political consequences intruded into the debate. William Winans of Mississippi was the first to voice the ominous possibility of national rupture, though he could not bring himself to pronounce the word of disunion—an indication of both the intensity of the forebodings and the dread with which they were held. Such reluctance to verbalize an event too awful to contem-

---

[27]Journal of the General Conference (1844), 83-84, 112.

plate seems to have been a common phenomenon of the period, for in 1850 James J. Pettigrew of North Carolina marveled at a recent rapid rise of disunion talk: "No one considers it at all startling to discuss the matter in a calm tone, whereas a few years ago it was necessary to be worked up into a furious passion before the word could be uttered."[28] But Methodists, like other evangelicals, were no strangers to "passion"; if Winans shrank from explicit reference to secession, others did not. Elias Bowen of the Oneida Conference entertained a similar dread of ecclesiastical rupture and its probable political impact, yet he stated candidly that he would prefer a peaceful division of Methodism into two parts rather than increasingly exacerbated conflict in one church.

> We deprecate the idea of division, sir. We know that our great republic is connected together by the twofold ties of civil and ecclesiastical union. We are aware, that to dissolve one of these ties would weaken the union of the whole, and, viewed under a civil aspect exclusively, we start back from the very idea; but sir, it must be allowed that secession is preferable to schism.[29]

The last clause is somewhat puzzling. Since Bowen was a New Yorker, he probably meant that the church should allow the South to secede in peace rather than risk further schism by impatient abolitionists. In any case, neither this nor any conceivable alternative explanation would weaken Bowen's point that division of the church would endanger the national union.

Though he was on the other side of the controversy, Thomas Crowder of Virginia shared the same fear, warning that if Bishop Andrew were not permitted to exercise his episcopacy throughout the church, "the division of our Church may follow—a civil division

---

[28]James J. Pettigrew, letter of 8 January 1850, quoted in David M. Potter, *The Impending Crisis, 1848-1861* (New York, 1976) 124. On 13 March 1850, the Philadelphia *Christian Chronicle* (Baptist) editorialized on "The Dissolution of the Union," noting that the phrase was "the theme of conversation in all the walks of life." James Henley Thornwell, justifying the secession of the Southern states, wrote in 1861: "Few men, in all the South, brought themselves to pronounce the word DISUNION without sadness of heart" (*The State of the Country* [New York, 1861] 25).

[29]Robert A. West, ed., *Report of Debates in the General Conference of the Methodist Episcopal Church* (New York, 1855) 90.

of this great confederation may follow that, and then hearts will be torn apart, master and slave arrayed against each other, brother in the Church against brother, and the north against the south—and when thus arrayed, with the fiercest passions and energies of our nature brought into action against each other, civil war and far-reaching desolation must be the final results."[30]

William A. Smith of Virginia, who had been urging division since 1836, rose to argue that whereas ecclesiastical union "ought to exert a happy effect on our political union," the opposite was becoming true and "our separation becomes necessary to preserve our political union." Turning the case for political disaster on its head, Smith contended that by permitting antislavery activity within the church, the General Conference had allowed the abolitionists to undermine the Union. "By years of departure from the plain duties which appertain to you as a council of Christian ministers," he reproached the delegates, "to discuss and settle the great and perplexing question of American slavery—*a question which belongs exclusively to our national councils, and one which statesmen of the greatest distinction touch with a trembling hand*—you are rendering yourselves odious to the political union." The remedy, he declared, would be to divide the church—in effect sacrificing ecclesiastical unity for the sake of the political Union.[31]

This reasoning had a powerful appeal to the politically sensitive Southerners. William Capers went home to editorialize in his *Southern Christian Advocate*:

> The prospect for peace and amicable relations, is infinitely better with a separation than under a forced and nominal union. And if so, the safety of the country is to a much greater extent bound up with a division of the church, than a continued union. The division of the Methodist Church will demonstrate this fact to the country, that Southern forbearance has its limits, and that a vigorous and united resistance will be made at all costs, to the spread of the pseudo-religious phrenzy called abolitionism. Thus a check will be put upon a movement which, more than all other causes of discord put together, threatens the political union.

[30]Ibid., 95.
[31]Ibid., 144.

But Capers's counterpart in New York City, Thomas E. Bond, wrote in the *Christian Advocate and Journal:* "We believed a division of the Methodist Episcopal Church, especially on the question of 'Southern institutions,' would sever an important ligament of our political union, and this opinion very generally obtains."[32]

As the General Conference debate lengthened and temperatures warmed, the pressing moral question of what the church should do about slavery became more and more entangled with contentions over the locus of authority and who controlled the church. The authority question had rumbled like a not-quite-dormant volcano in the Methodist Episcopal Church since 1808, when a new constitution was framed making the quadrennial General Conference a delegated assembly. Controversy had erupted periodically over whether the episcopacy possessed authority coordinate to that of the General Conference or was subordinate to it. Division of opinion, significantly, had often fallen along geographical lines, with Southern delegates arguing for the "strict constructionist" view of coordinate authorities, while Northern delegates customarily upheld the supremacy of General Conference over the bishops, whom they regarded simply as elected officers.

This issue now burst forth with new intensity during the dispute over the slaveholding bishop and in 1844 became the ostensible occasion of schism. Five days after Bishop Andrew was instructed to "desist from the exercise of his office" as long as the "impediment" of his slaveholding remained, a minority of the conference, including a sprinkling of Northern delegates along with all the Southerners, brought a lengthy protest against the action as "extra-judicial" and lawless. Their statement concluded:

> By pressing the issue in question the majority virtually dissolve the government of the Methodist Episcopal Church, because in every constitutional aspect it is sundered by so crippling a co-ordinate branch of it as to destroy the itinerant general superintendency altogether. . . . The law of union, the principle of gravitation, binding us together, is dissolved, and the general superintendency of the Methodist Episcopal Church is no more! . . .

---

[32]Capers's editorial appeared on 22 November 1844, Bond's on 25 December 1844.

*The South cannot submit, and the absolute necessity of division is already dated.*[33]

Donald G. Mathews, correctly arguing for the primacy of the slavery issue as the overriding reason for the Methodist schism, nevertheless dismissed the constitutional dispute too lightly: "prior to the General Conference of 1844 there were no widespread debates over episcopal powers. . . . Only after the question of Bishop Andrew's slaves came up did anyone raise the constitutional question of who could do what to whom." This is not quite the case. An old but perceptive *Constitutional History of American Episcopal Methodism* described earlier controversies that, in the 1820s, "radically divided the northern and southern sections of the Church on the nature of our ecclesiastical government." The author then commented: "In our Church, as in our nation, the division was along the line of strict construction of the powers delegated by the constitution, on the one hand, and a loose and broad interpretation of those powers, on the other."

This dispute over polity and authority had been so sharp that a sizable group of "democratic reformers" broke away in 1830 to form the Methodist Protestant Church. A recent historian of that movement remarked that even at that early date the pattern of differences on constitutional opinion was "curiously sectional." In the 1840s the nexus of causes leading to all the major denominational schisms closely paralleled that in the nation at large: slavery was the "cause" of the conflicts in a quite fundamental sense, but there were also sharp differences of constitutional interpretation that polarized the geographical sections.[34]

The intensely political character of the controversy leading to the division of Methodism in 1844 may help to explain why that event evoked concern throughout the nation as being an ominous portent of what the future might hold for the national union. Wor-

---

[33]Journal of the General Conference (1844), 197-98.

[34]Donald G. Mathews, *Slavery and Methodism: A Chapter in American Morality, 1780-1845* (Princeton, 1965) 250 n.; John J. Tigert, *A Constitutional History of American Episcopal Methodism* (Nashville, 1894) 371; Douglas R. Chandler, "The Formation of the Methodist Protestant Church," in *The History of American Methodism,* ed. Emory S. Bucke, 3 vols. (Nashville, 1964) 1:646.

ried observers noted that the Methodist debates paralleled, politically as well as morally, the rising dispute over slavery in the nation at large. Since the Congress had no constitutional power to abolish slavery directly, it had to approach the nation's most pressing problem through peripheral cases like whether slavery should be allowed in the territories and newly admitted states. Given the South's fear of becoming a political minority in an expanding Union, every territorial question became a sectional issue. And the primary argument in each case involved authority: Who had the right to deal with slavery? Was it a matter of local judgment, to be dealt with under the rubric of states' rights and popular sovereignty, or was it a national issue to be legislated by the Congress? Shall the Constitution's provisions with respect to slavery be interpreted "strictly" or "broadly"?

Questions of this nature were woven inextricably into the Methodist debates of 1844, and that is perhaps why so many participants and observers feared that the separation of the churches—and particularly of the Methodist Church—possibly presaged national disruption. Viewed in this light, the ordeal of the Methodists was a painful rehearsal for the political deadlock of 1846-1850, the mounting tensions of the 1850s, and the crisis of the Union in 1861.

Shortly after the General Conference of 1844 adjourned, John P. Durbin of Philadelphia traveled westward through Pittsburgh to Cincinnati, testing Methodist sentiment at each intermediate point. En route home in August, he wrote to Matthew Simpson, then president of Indiana Asbury College (now DePauw University) and destined to become a bishop in the Northern church in 1852, predicting that the schism would become permanent unless the Southerners became alarmed at the political consequences of separation—"provided they object to the separation of the Union." The most critical danger would arise, Durbin thought, if slaveholders in the border conferences decided to go with the Southern faction of the church, drawing the fault line of the ecclesiastical dispute precisely where the political fissure was about to open. "I fear most of all the effect of this movement on the Union—I see it has already been the subject of resolutions at political meetings." Simpson was equally apprehensive. After attending the Louisville Convention, where Southern Methodism organized itself in May 1845, he wrote to his wife his opinion that "the South will go pretty much *en masse,* and slavery will be the cause of ultimately severing the Union as well as the Church. Winans avows that if voting for dividing the Church should divide the Union, he would still do it."[35]

Such fears as Durbin and Simpson expressed were not unrealistic. The South was not bluffing (as some Northern politicians thought as late as 1861), and the solid determination of the Methodists at Louisville illustrated this. Winans reported that he had canvassed all of Southern Methodism to assess the opposition to separation. "In New Orleans there is 1 member of the whole church opposed to division. In the Natchez district there is 1.—In the whole Mississippi Conference 3. And 12 out of 15 conferences represented here present about the same state of things."[36] Winans was clearly a "fire-eater," as aggressive secessionists would later be called, and his course of action established a precedent that the entire South would follow all too soon. The Methodist Episcopal Church was the largest religious body in a country that still drew many of its values from the Christian religion; its membership was widely distributed throughout the nation, and its organization was as tightly connectional as any ecclesiocracy could be in a voluntary society. When the Methodist Church showed itself unable or unwilling to come to terms on the moral issue of slavery and divided sectionally over the question, little clairvoyance was needed to discern that the political impact could be disastrous.

Peter Cartwright reflected in 1856 that

this dreadful rupture in the Methodist Church spread terror over almost every other branch of the Church of Christ; and really, disguise it as we may, it shook the pillars of our American government to the center, and many of our ablest statesmen were alarmed, and looked upon it as the entering wedge to political disunion, and a fearful step toward the downfall of our happy republic; and it is greatly to be feared that the constitutional agitation and unscrupulous anathemas indulged in by frenzied preachers

---

[35]John P. Durbin to Matthew Simpson, August 1844, in Matthew Simpson Papers, Box 4, Library of Congress; Matthew Simpson to Mrs. Simpson, 7 May 1845, printed in George R. Crooks, *The Life of Bishop Matthew Simpson of the Methodist Episcopal Church* (New York, 1891) 243.

[36]*Louisville Journal,* 5 May 1845.

and unprincipled demagogues, that seek more for the spoils of office than the freedom of the slave or the good of the country, will so burst the bonds of brotherly love and the real love of country, that all the horrors of civil war will break upon us shortly, and firebrands, arrows, and death, be thrown broadcast over the land, and anarchy, mobs, and lawless desperadoes reign triumphant; and then the fair fabric of our happy republic will be tumbled into ruins, and the liberties that our fathers fought for, and that cost the blood and treasure of the best patriots that ever lived, will be lost forever.[37]

Within five years Cartwright's predictions were coming true.

## III

Baptists had neither a central governing authority nor a supreme judicatory. Reflecting the congregationalism of their polity, their chief denominational organizations were two national missionary societies and a tract society, each of which functioned in the same manner as any other benevolent society in antebellum America. Each society was an extra-church organization supported by interested contributors, and each served one purpose only. If an extrinsic matter were introduced, a society's officers could plausibly plead responsibility only for carrying forward the society's single enterprise and refuse petitions to use its resources for anything else. By this device the Baptist General Tract Society maneuvered itself away from the slavery controversy early on and in 1835 even instructed its agents not to "agitate the question of slavery."

When some English Baptists, gratified by the abolition of slavery throughout the British Empire in 1833, wrote to the Board of the General Missionary Convention (the foreign mission society) in Boston urging a more active advocacy on behalf of American slaves, the board cautiously resolved that while "their love of freedom, and their desire for the happiness of all men, are not less strong and sincere than those of their British brethren, they cannot, as a Board, interfere with a subject that is not among the objects for which the Convention and the Board were formed."[38] Baptist abolitionists in

---

[37]Cartwright, *Autobiography of Peter Cartwright*, 286-87.

[38]This exchange, which occurred in 1833-1834, is printed in Arthur T. Foss and Edward Mathews, comps., *Facts for Baptist Churches: Collected, Arranged, and Reviewed* (Utica, 1850) 17-23; the quoted words are on p. 21 n.

New England were offended by such a noncommittal response, but a denominational editor in Cincinnati publicly commended the board for exercising "a wise precaution in respect to subjects irrelevant to the single and grand purpose of the Baptist General Convention, which is the publication of the gospel to the heathen world."[39]

This attitude was typical of most Baptists outside the abolitionist camp. In the incident just cited, the Board of the General Convention rejoiced at the *"pleasing degree of union among the multiplying thousands of Baptists throughout the land"* and refused "to use language or adopt measures which might tend to break the ties that unite [slaveholders] to us . . . and to array brother against brother, church against church, and association against association, in a contest about slavery."[40] The opposition to slavery that had surfaced earlier among Baptists soon declined to the point that slaveowners were not seriously discomfited in the Baptist fellowship. Indeed, the General Convention had had a slaveholder as president for twenty-one of its first thirty years of existence, and the rising voice of abolitionism after 1830 provoked more displeasure toward the "agitators" than toward slavery.

At the general meetings of the societies throughout the 1830s, pleas were often heard that the governing boards should attend solely to missions and not threaten Baptist cooperation by opening the agenda to controversial matters. Discussion of slavery, as everybody knew, would alienate Southern supporters. But as Methodists and Presbyterians—indeed, all Americans—were discovering, the slavery issue ramified in so many directions that nobody could evade it. A policy of silence to preserve harmony could suppress the question for only so long. When proslavery Baptists in the South forced Northern-based executives of the national societies to admit that they could not in good conscience appoint slaveholding mission-

---

[39]*The Cross and Baptist Journal*, 27 March 1835, 210. The publisher of the *Cross and Journal* was "a colonizationist who was outspoken enough [in his antislavery views] to be accused by the *Cincinnati Gazette* of being 'half or more an abolitionist'—a charge which [the publisher] regarded as an insult" (Wesley Norton, *Religious Newspapers in the Old Northwest to 1861: A History, Bibliography, and Record of Opinion* [Athens OH, 1977] 114).

[40]Foss and Mathews, *Facts for Baptist Churches*, 22-23.

aries, the offended Southerners withdrew from participation, and Baptists acted out Scene Three of the churches' scenario for secession.

There had been earlier occasions on which sectional disagreements had ruffled the smooth surface of Baptist cooperation. These occurred mainly when Baptists in the South complained that the Home Mission Society was spending less money to evangelize the South than the Southerners were contributing to the society, which in turn gave rise to sporadic calls for Baptists in the South to organize their own society for domestic missions. The records show that these complaints were largely unfounded, but Southerners continued to feel exploited.[41]

Another source of tension was the preference of some Baptist leaders in the South for a different method of organizing their cooperative efforts. The society method that had emerged in the North, they thought, was not as effective as a more comprehensive structure that would bring together all denominational work—foreign missions, domestic missions, education, publication, and benevolences—in a single organization. The Southern Baptist Convention, formed in 1845, actually was such an overarching body, whereas Baptists in the North continued to cooperate through separate societies until these were merged (somewhat loosely) in the Northern Baptist Convention in 1907. The centralizing ecclesiology of Southern Baptists was perhaps somewhat analogous to the "strict constructionist" perspective of Southern Methodists. But even though such long-standing differences helped aggravate the dissatisfaction of Baptists in the South and strengthen their resolve to depart the national societies, they lacked the compelling force of the all-encompassing issue of slavery. Among the Baptists, as in the other denominations and in the nation at large, slavery inexorably enveloped all other issues to become the overpowering force of division, stimulating and reinforcing all other sectional disputes.

As Scene Three unfolded, the script once again revealed the same essential plot, the *dramatis personae* differing only in name from those in the first two scenes. Northern abolitionists organized the

---

[41]Cf. Robert A. Baker, *Relations Between Northern and Southern Baptists* (Fort Worth, 1948) 35-41.

American Baptist Anti-Slavery Convention in New York City in April 1840 and promptly issued "An Address to Southern Baptists," denying the now standard biblical justification for slavery, exhorting the Southerners to confess the sinfulness of holding slaves, and urging them to initiate immediate steps for legal emancipation. Should the Southerners refuse, the abolitionists declared, "we cannot and we dare not recognize you as consistent brethren in Christ . . . and we cannot, at the Lord's table, cordially take that as a brother's hand, which plies the scourge on woman's naked flesh,—which thrusts a gag into the mouth of a man,—which rivets fetters on the innocent,—and which shuts up the Bible from human eyes." Baptists in the South, smarting under the charge that they were unfit for Christian fellowship, warned that "unless aspersions upon their character ceased they would cut off their benevolent funds to the general Baptist agencies, and, if necessary, even separate from them altogether."[42]

Taking note of the rising conflict over slavery and hoping to forestall its divisive effects, the Executive Committee of the American Baptist Home Mission Society issued a position paper in February 1841. This circular warned of evil consequences that might come from dragging "secular conflicts" into the church's arena and pled for "a union of hearts, even where there may not be entire union of views." Once again, the premise was that the society was chartered for only one purpose. "It would be traveling out of the record to allow the introduction of the question [of slavery], or admit it even as a subject of conference in the Society." The committee remarked *en passant* that "as patriots, we must cherish religious union as one among the strongest, although not the most prominent, of the bonds that hold together the Union of these States."

A review of the circular by the editor of the *Christian Reflector* (published in Worcester, Massachusetts) picked up the last point and retorted that compromise with evil was a far greater threat to the Union than division of the church.

If *we* were to express our sincere opinion on the bearing of slavery

---

[42]*Christian Watchman* (New York), 19 June 1840, 97; Smith, *In His Image, but,* 119.

on our national union, we should say that it is this very thing, more than anything else, which by its moral and political influences, threatens to *sunder* the union of these States, instead of tending to its perpetuation. How strange, then, to urge a compromise on this question, for the sake of preserving the union of slaveholders and Abolitionists in the church, as essential to national union!

There were many antislavery Baptists, especially in New England, who could cheerfully see the proslavery churches go their separate way.[43]

When the Home Mission Society met in Philadelphia in April 1844, the widening fissure between Northerners and Southerners was painfully evident. Rev. Richard Fuller, a pastor from South Carolina, spoke of the danger of division: "A separation or rupture in the Baptist denomination would not only be disastrous to the church, but also to the nation." Yet "if the [Southern] brethren thought it better to separate, he would not object."[44] Upon his return home, Fuller addressed to the *Christian Reflector* a long letter explaining his position.

> My chief hope for the Union is in the conservative power of religion, and the day is not far when that power will be required in all its stringency. Look at the distracted condition of this land; reflect on the appalling character of a civil war; and if you love the country, or the slave, do not sever the bands which unite the Baptist churches.[45]

Fuller's letter appeared in print just before the Methodists announced the "mutual and friendly division" of their church. Several weeks later a Southerner in New England wrote to a Richmond paper to express dire forebodings that if the churches of the North separate from those of the South, that division "must act as an entering wedge to a dissolution of our political bonds." The writer feared that

---

[43]Foss and Mathews, *Facts for Baptist Churches,* 70-71, 74.

[44]Minutes of the American Baptist Home Mission Society, 23 April 1844; ibid., 90.

[45]Reprinted in *Domestic Slavery Considered as a Scriptural Institution: In a Correspondence Between the Rev. Richard Fuller . . . and the Rev. Francis Wayland* (New York, 1845) 3.

the Methodist Church will be divided into two great parties, with mutual jealousies and antagonistic measures. The Presbyterians are in danger of the same evil. And if the Baptists, unmindful of their duty to Christ and their country, shall bite and devour one another, and array themselves into two great parties, the Northern and the Southern, what conservative principles, what salt of the earth will be left to restrain and modulate the madness of political strife and ambition and save from ruin our Republic?[46]

None of these cautions prevailed.

In the tense mood of its triennial meeting in April 1844, the General Convention made a last-ditch attempt to declare neutrality on slavery: "We disclaim all sanction, either expressed or implied, whether of slavery or antislavery; but as individuals we are perfectly free both to express and to promote our own views on these subjects *elsewhere*, in a Christian manner and spirit." Alabama Baptists were still suspicious, and in November they addressed a formal resolution to the Acting Board of the General Convention (a small executive committee located in Boston) demanding "the distinct, explicit avowal that slaveholders are eligible, and entitled, equally with non-slaveholders . . . to receive any agency, mission, or other appointment" under the Convention. The board demurred at "being compelled to answer hypothetical questions" but maintained its right to judge "the competency or fitness of an individual to receive an appointment." No slaveholder had ever applied for appointment, they declared, but then—not to be "evasive or timid"—they added:

> If, however, any one should offer himself as a missionary, having slaves, and should insist on retaining them as his property, we could not appoint him. One thing is certain, we can never be a party to any arrangement which would imply approbation of slavery.

Whatever their personal sentiments, the board's members were now fearful that antislavery Baptists would begin to defect in growing numbers, causing a rift in the North that might be more serious for

---

[46]*Religious Herald* (Richmond), 24 October 1844.

the future of the denomination than loss of the proslavery Southerners.[47]

Since the General Convention had just reaffirmed a neutral position on the explosive issue, the Southerners declared that the board had overstepped its authority. The decision could not be appealed until 1847, and events were hurrying too fast to wait that long. The Virginia Baptist Foreign Mission Society immediately issued a call for a consultative convention to consider forming a new missionary organization. They explicitly disavowed a sectional purpose by offering to unite with "all our brethren, North and South, East and West," who were "aggrieved" by the Boston board's refusal to appoint slaveholders. They wanted to avoid separating along strictly geographic lines, stating pointedly that to do so would increase the danger of political disunion. One Virginian asked uneasily, "Should religious bodies be divided by the line that separates slave from free states, who can tell what might be the tendency of such a split to sever the United States?" But when proslavery Baptists assembled in Augusta, Georgia, on 8 May 1845, no one from north of Baltimore or west of New Orleans attended. There was only one representative from Kentucky, none from Tennessee. The sparse attendance from outside the deep South may have been due less to nonsympathy with the purpose of the meeting than to inadequate communications and insufficient time for more states to choose delegates. The local newspaper noted that "owing to the short notice of the meeting of the Convention, the States of Mississippi, Tennessee, Arkansas, and Florida were represented only by letters." At the time of this report, delegates were still arriving, and the meeting proceeded with the confidence that Baptists in unrepresented states would approve of their actions.[48]

A standard history of the Southern Baptist Convention asserts that "Baptists in the South were almost unanimous for separation." Of the 293 delegates (from eight states and the District of Colum-

---

[47]Minutes of the General Missionary Convention (1844) in Foss and Mathews, *Facts for Baptist Churches*, 94. The other documents are in Peter G. Mode, *Source Book and Bibliographical Guide for American Church History* (Menasha WI, 1921) 589-92.

[48]Eli Ball, letter in *Religious Herald*, 10 April 1845; Augusta *Chronicle and Sentinel*, 9 May 1845.

bia) who attended the called meeting, 139 were from Georgia and 102 from South Carolina.[49] Included were "governors, judges, congressmen, and other functionaries of highest dignity," who demonstrated their solidarity with the ministers by electing Wilson Lumpkin of Georgia, a former governor and United States senator, first as chairman of the preliminary consultation and then as vice president of the newly organized convention. Geographically, the Baptists schism drew the sectional line approximately where the Methodists had. After unanimously adopting a resolution expressing "a profound sense of responsibility" in view of the contemporary crisis, and "as the integrity of the nation, the institutions of truth, and the sacred enterprize of converting the heathen, are all involved in [our] deliberations," the delegates proceeded to organize the Southern Baptist Convention. As the meeting drew to a close, they all joined hands and sang "Blest Be the Tie That Binds."[50]

Many Baptists openly expressed their apprehensions about the impact of their schism on the political union. A Baptist ministers' meeting in Washington, D.C., in April 1845 had urged people going to Augusta "not to adopt any measures tending to a dissolution of the Union of the General Convention" because "division would have an unhappy bearing not only upon the cause of Christ but upon our National Union." If religious bodies divide over slavery, they asked, "how can we expect political parties to bear the excitement?" Jeremiah Bell Jeter, pastor of the First Baptist Church in Richmond, felt the same way. A month before traveling to Augusta, he attended a meeting of the General Board of the General Missionary Convention at Providence, seeking a reversal of the Acting Board's decision. Although he failed, he still found the thought of separation very painful. "When I think of the disastrous influence of division on our denominational prosperity, the mission enterprise and (may God avert the evil) the perpetuity of our happy political Union, my heart sinks within me."[51]

---

[49]William Wright Barnes, *The Southern Baptist Convention, 1845-1953* (Nashville, 1953) 28. Delegates are listed by states on 311-13.

[50]*Baptist Memorial and Monthly Record* (New York), July 1845, 216; *Proceedings of the Southern Baptist Convention* (1845) 2; *Baptist Banner* (Louisville), 5 June 1845, 1.

[51]Mary P. Putnam, *The Baptists and Slavery, 1840-1845* (Ann Arbor, 1913) 59-69.

One week before the Southerners gathered in Augusta, a lengthy editorial appeared in the *Baptist Banner and Pioneer* (Louisville) warning that a "state line division" of Northern and Southern Baptists "will not only separate those brethren, churches and Associations, that now hold sweet intercourse and fellowship, across these lines, but it will tend to gender sectional strifes and divisions; it will produce alienation of heart, and lead to contentious turmoil and warfare, along the whole line of division." The Kentucky editor identified the various "ligaments" that bound together the United States as "political, mercantile, and social relations," and underscored the "social"—in which he included ecclesiastical—as the strongest. Pointing uneasily to the Methodist rupture about to be consummated in his own city and at continuing strains among Presbyterians, he wrote: "Let the three great denominations of christians be divided, by State lines, upon the subject of abolitionism, and who does not see that all social intercourse between the parties will be sundered, and the parts continually recede?" The editor disagreed with those who thought that trade and commerce would suffice to hold the nation together.

> The policy of the Northern manufacturers and that of the Southern planters are antipodes, and have been the fruitful cause of half the strife and debates in Congress for the last fifteen years; so that we can hope for but little resistance to a separation from the mercantile interests by which the North and the South are bound. Who does not see, therefore, that if the religious and consequently the social interests of the country are divided by State lines, that more than half of the bonds which hold the political compact in harmony are dissolved, and that the ground work is laid for the ultimate dissolution of the Union, and the destruction of the fairest fabric of civil and religious liberty the world ever saw?

His aim, the editor vowed, was "TO PRESERVE THE UNION."[52]

## IV

After the church schisms had become *faits accomplis*, comment continued to focus on possible political repercussions. The Presbyterian *Watchman of the South* (Richmond) was deeply apprehen-

---

[52]*Baptist Banner and Pioneer* (Louisville), 1 May 1845.

sive because the Methodist and Baptist divisions had both fallen along sectional lines.

> The churches once divided, North and South, Demagogues will have but little [more] to do to dissolve the Union of the States. That done, then we shall see war and horrible contests. Brother will slay brother. The father and the son will stand in opposing battle lines, and tyrants, and demons will clap their hands at the blighting of the last hopes of Man, for a fair fabric of well established liberty, for a scale of imposing magnitude.

A Boston editor rehearsed at length the history of the Baptist rupture, and after defending the Acting Board's reply to the Alabama queries, he observed somberly that the severance of long-standing ties between Northern and Southern Christians was "a solemn and momentous act. . . . No man can calculate the extent of the influence which this single act may exert, not only upon the great work of imparting Christianity to the heathen, but upon the institutions, or even the existence, of our common country." In Philadelphia the *Christian Observer,* a Presbyterian paper, reprinted an editorial from the *Charleston Courier,* noting that "the die has been cast" against the Union and asking, "If a union cemented by all the finer influences of the gospel could not last, what can?"

Three years later the anxiety had not subsided. In 1848 John Lightfoot Waller of Kentucky expressed the continuing apprehension of the western border states:

> Who can expect that our country will remain united when the bonds of religious concord are broken? If the ties of Christian love are sundered, what bands can bind this nation together? He, therefore, that encourages religious strife and division between the Northern and Southern sectors of the United States, is contributing to the disruption of our Federal Union.[53]

---

[53]*Watchman of the South,* 4 July 1845, 182; *Christian Review* (Boston) 10 (1845): 487; *Christian Observer,* 23 May 1845; Foss and Matthews, *Facts for Baptist Churches,* 342. Waller was no abolitionist (he was elected to the Kentucky constitutional convention in 1849 on a proslavery ticket), but like many other Southerners, he vowed to remain in the Union until "driven out—that the guilt may rest on other heads than ours."

If church leaders and the religious press were fearful of the political impact of ecclesiastical schism, politicians and editors of secular newspapers were not less so. The whole nation was watching with more uneasiness than has been commonly recognized. There were some twelve hundred newspapers in the United States in the 1840s, and they covered the disruption of the churches closely, quoting copiously from each other to pass the disquieting news along and offering frequent editorial comment.

The Cincinnati *Journal and Luminary* reported extensively on the Presbyterian schism of 1837, warning that "principles have been avowed, and acts have been done by the General Assembly of the Presbyterian church, which, if tolerated, and followed out, will shake this country to the centre, and involve in one common ruin all the free institutions of the land." In Philadelphia the *Public Ledger* for Monday, 27 May 1844 (quoting from the New York *Journal of Commerce*), gave half of its front-page news coverage to the Methodist General Conference debates about the slaveholding bishop—and this at the same time the Democratic national convention was in session selecting its presidential candidate! The *Charleston Mercury,* edited by the South Carolina "fire-eater" Robert Barnwell Rhett, on 14 and 20 June 1844, declared the division of the Methodist Church to be "the most ominous event of the times . . . the first dissolution of the Union."[54]

As Southern Methodists planned their separatist church, the Reverend William A. Booth of Somerville, Tennessee, wrote to former (and future) Senator Henry Clay of Kentucky asking his opinion on the questions, "Will the division of the Methodist Episcopal Church into two separate organizations (slavery being the cause of division, and the dividing line) be likely to affect the civil connection between the slave and non-slaveholding States? If so, will it strengthen or weaken the bonds of their Union?" Clay answered at length, confessing his deep concern over that "unfortunate controversy . . . all of which I have attentively perused"; his reply was widely reported in the secular and religious press. A division of the

---

[54]*Journal and Luminary* (Cincinnati), 15 June 1837; Laura A. White, *Robert Barnwell Rhett: Father of Secession* (New York, 1931) 73.

church on account of slavery, Clay thought, would be deplorable not only for the church's sake but for its political impact.

> Indeed, scarcely any public occurrence has happened for a long time that gave me so much real concern and pain as the menaced separation of the Church, by a line throwing all the Free States on one side, and all the Slave States on the other.
>
> I will not say that such a separation would necessarily produce a dissolution of the political union of these States; but the example would be fraught with imminent danger, and, in co-operation with other causes unfortunately existing, its tendency on the stability of the Confederacy [the Union] would be perilous and alarming.

His whole letter makes it plain that Clay's overriding concern was "the political aspect of the subject."[55]

The year 1845, when both Southern Baptists and Southern Methodists organized, saw a large outpouring of concern in the columns of the nation's newspapers. In fact, the quantity of comment itself became noteworthy. The *New York Observer* noted that

> the progress of separation in different denominations of Christians, occasioned by the vexed question of slavery, is exciting universal attention, and awakening various emotions in the public mind. The religious newspapers and secular journals of a respectable character, alike influenced by a spirit of pure patriotism, are expressing their serious apprehension of the influence of these divisions on the integrity of the Union.

Watching the spirit of schism gather momentum, the *Richmond Enquirer* predicted gloomily: "This will be followed, we fear, by ill will and jealousy, weakening the bonds of union between the two grand divisions of the country, and, (which Heaven forbid!) resulting in a dissolution of our political Union."

---

[55]Henry Clay, letter to William A. Booth, 7 April 1845, in *The Works of Henry Clay*, ed. Calvin Colton, 6 vols. (New York, 1857) 4:525. Clay was temporarily out of the United States Senate, having campaigned unsuccessfully the previous year as the Whig candidate for president. Not a professing Christian at this time, he joined the Protestant Episcopal Church in 1847.

As Southern Baptists gathered in Augusta, "Publius," correspondent for the *Charleston Mercury,* wrote a too-optimistic prognosis:

> If there is one hope left of preserving the *Union* of the Baptist Churches, which we hope there is, we doubt not they will avail themselves of it. They cannot be rash or fanatical. They love the church too much; they love the political Union too much; the State, the Government, with all its glorious associations. They know too well how deep an impression these religious divisions make. They know how little is to be expected from any other *Union,* if the union of Christians fail.

At the close of the first day's deliberations, however, "Publius" was much less sanguine.

> From all appearances a separation of the Church is inevitable. We could hope otherwise; but so it is, and we must submit. When we are forced out of the Church by Northern fanatics we shall next be forced out of the Union by the same nefarious acts.[56]

After the organization of separate denominations for both Southern Baptists and Southern Methodists was announced, the *Mercury* editorialized grimly:

> In this contest of religions, we have an entire and remediless severance of the Union—a division that henceforth creates in the two most numerous denominations of the country *a Northern and a Southern religion*—and this separation brought about by no accident, nor heat of the moment, but after much deliberation and unwearied efforts to reconcile the dissension—efforts that yielded only to a settled conviction that reconciliation was impossible. . . . Mr. Clay sees it in the true light—a dissension that turns one of the strongest bands of the political union into a destroying sword.[57]

As news of the Southern Baptist and Southern Methodist organizations was telegraphed across the country, the *New York Jour-*

---

[56]*New York Observer,* 21 June 1845; *Richmond Enquirer,* 16 May 1845; *Charleston Mercury,* 9, 10 May 1845.

[57]This piece was printed also in *Niles' National Register,* 24 May 1845. The widespread copying of such "exchange items" greatly increased their circulation and thus their impact.

*nal of Commerce* published a somber assessment. Recalling that Presbyterians had divided earlier over "the same questions," the editor spoke ominously of "a line of demarcation" that was now drawn "between almost the entire body of Northern and Southern Christians." This, he warned, could not but heighten sectional tensions. The political consequences were impossible to foresee, but "it is obvious that the bonds of our national union are weakened thereby." The voluntary societies were still operating on a national basis, and they furnished "to some extent a bond of union, but the strongest bond—that which united the more than a million Methodist church members throughout the Union in a compact mass, and the half a million Baptists—is broken." The *New York Evangelist,* a Presbyterian paper, editorialized in a similar vein on "Rupture of the Methodist Church," concluding that "the rupture, one after another, of the ties which have bound the different sections of our country together, and the growing distrust between the North and the South, are unpleasant symptoms." The editor cited the widespread fears that the same forces that had sundered the churches could easily "proceed to disunion and civil war."[58]

Thoughtful people continued for the next five years to ponder the possible consequences of the denominational schisms. By the end of the decade other portents of sectional rift—the Wilmot Proviso (1846), disputes over the introduction of slavery into newly annexed territories, changes in tariff policy, the weakening of the Democratic party, and the increasing stridency of the abolitionists—had deepened the sense of crisis. But whereas the North was still fragmented by a welter of conflicting opinions, Southern sentiment had been consolidated by the example of the separated churches, whose leaders walked in lockstep with the rest of the South's molders of public opinion. By 1850 every medium of Southern expression was sending the same message. "From the pulpit, from the editorial sanctum, from state legislatures, from party conventions, from mass meetings, [and] from southern congressmen there poured out a steady stream of sermons, editorials,

---

[58]*New York Journal of Commerce* editorial, printed also in the (Louisville) *Baptist Banner,* 5 June 1845; *New York Evangelist,* 29 May 1845, 86.

resolutions, speeches, and joint statements, all warning of the immediate possibility of disunion."[59]

As debates over the Compromise of 1850 brought national controversy to fever pitch once again, the denominational schisms were recalled with the same forebodings as in 1845. The most famous and articulate reminder came in the United States Senate on 4 March 1850 from John C. Calhoun, who made a compelling analysis of the cords that had bound the Union together and described how, one by one, they were snapping. The "cast-iron southerner" was too feeble to deliver the speech himself—he would die before the month was out—but the words read for him by Senator James M. Mason of Virginia had been written with perception and passion. Though some points are often quoted out of context, the whole passage evinces a progression in logic and rhetoric that propels the reader, even at this distance, inexorably toward its prophetic conclusion. This section of Calhoun's speech, therefore, is given here entire, omitting only a few non-essential sentences.

> The cords that bind the States together are not only many, but various in character. Some are spiritual or ecclesiastical; some political; others social. . . . The strongest of those of a spiritual and ecclesiastical nature, consisted in the unity of the great religious denominations, all of which originally embraced the whole Union. All these denominations, with the exception, perhaps, of the Catholics, were organized very much upon the principle of our political institutions. Beginning with smaller meetings, corresponding with the political divisions of the country, their organizations terminated in one great central assemblage, corresponding very much with the character of Congress. At these meetings the principal clergymen and lay members of the respective denominations, from all parts of the Union, met to transact business relating to their common concerns. It was not confined to what appertained to the doctrines and discipline of the respective denominations, but extended to plans for disseminating the Bible—establishing missions, distributing tracts—and of establishing presses for the publication of tracts, newspapers, and periodicals, with a view of diffusing religious information—and for the support of their respective doctrines and creeds. All this combined contributed greatly to strengthen the bonds of Union. The

---

[59]Potter, *The Impending Crisis*, 96.

ties which had held each denomination together formed a strong cord to hold the whole Union together; but, powerful as they were, they have not been able to resist the explosive effect of slavery agitation.

The first of these cords which snapped, under its explosive force, was that of the powerful Methodist Episcopal Church. The numerous and strong ties which held it together, are all broken, and its unity gone. They now form separate churches; and instead of that feeling of attachment and devotion to the interests of the whole church which was formerly felt, they are now arrayed into two hostile bodies, engaged in litigation about what was formerly their common property.

The next cord that snapped was that of the Baptists—one of the largest and most respectable of the denominations. That of the Presbyterians is not entirely snapped, but some of its strands have given way. That of the Episcopal Church is the only one of the four great Protestant denominations which remains unbroken and entire. . . .

If the agitation goes on, the same force, acting with increased intensity, as has been shown, will finally snap every cord, when nothing will be left to hold the States together except force.[60]

Calhoun, who certainly had done his part to pave the road to secession, seems to have recognized with somber finality that the example of the popular churches had established some sort of *nihil obstat* for the final breach of Union.

"Sigma," a writer in the *New York Daily Tribune* (6 June 1850), charged Calhoun with deploring schisms that he "did all he could to bring about." Rumors in several places nurtured the suspicion that the separation of the Southern churches had been planned as a prelude to political secession, and that Calhoun was at the bottom of this scheme. Available evidence indicates that he was more than simply an interested spectator, but that he engineered a Machiavellian conspiracy is extremely doubtful.[61]

Henry Clay, whose final years were devoted to efforts of pacification and compromise, seems to have brooded frequently over the political consequences of the church schisms. A few weeks be-

---

[60]Richard K. Crallé, ed., *Speeches of John C. Calhoun, Delivered in the House of Representatives, and in the Senate of the United States* (New York, 1968) 556-58.

[61]See Norwood, *Schism in the Methodist Episcopal Church,* 194.

fore his death in 1852, he was interviewed by the editor of the *Presbyterian Herald*. Like Calhoun, he regarded the splintering of the denominations as having severely weakened the Union.

> I tell you this sundering of the religious ties which have hitherto bound our people together, I consider the greatest source of danger to our country. If our religious men cannot live together in peace, what can be expected of us politicians, very few of whom profess to be governed by the great principles of love? If all the Churches divide on the subject of slavery, there will be nothing left to bind our people together but trade and commerce. . . . That is a very powerful bond, I admit, but when the people of these states become thoroughly alienated from each other, and get their passions aroused, they are not apt to stop and consider what is to their interest.

Clay had grown to maturity in a day when the Union was "so powerful a concept that Americans looked with horror on the violence, desolation, and darkness which dismemberment would bring." This made it all the more unthinkable that the churches, flying in the face of their own private premonitions and the public apprehensions of observers, should be willing to risk a rupture of the Union rather than "to be governed by the great principles of love" in their unreconciled conflict over slavery.[62]

Following the churches' three-scene scenario, the Union finally broke on 20 December 1860, when the South Carolina legislature met in the First Baptist Church of Columbia and at 1:15 P.M. passed without dissent an ordinance declaring that "the union now subsisting between South Carolina and other States, under the name of the 'United States of America,' is hereby dissolved." On the day following South Carolina's secession, the *Cleveland Daily Plain Dealer* sadly reminded its readers of the whole process leading to the breakdown.

> For years the Union has, in fact, been dissolving. Political parties first divided. The union Whig party was first rent asunder. Then the churches North and South divided. Then our Bible, Tract, and

---

[62]Chester F. Dunham, *The Attitude of the Northern Clergy Toward the South, 1860-1865* (Toledo, 1942) 21; Paul C. Nagel, *One Nation Indivisible: The Union in American Thought, 1776-1861* (New York, 1964) 218.

Missionary Societies, and finally the social relations to an alarming extent. . . . The Secession of South Carolina, yesterday, was
but the culmination of events which had been progressing for
years.[63]

If there was one condition *sine qua non* leading to the final disruption, according to many, many commentators, it was the severing
of ecclesiastical ties. As the Civil War began, a Southern Presbyterian editor surveyed the event with grim satisfaction: *"This present
revolution,"* he declared, is nothing less than an "uprising" of Southern Christians. "Much as is due to many of our sagacious and gifted
politicians, they could *effect nothing* until the religious union of the
North and South was dissolved, nor until they received the *moral
support and co-operation of Southern Christians."*[64] There was much
truth to his claim. The popular churches had begun to script a
scenario for secession almost a quarter of a century before Sumter.

---

[63]Howard C. Perkins, ed., *Northern Editorials on Secession* (New York, 1942) 695-
96. The slavery controversy in the national benevolent societies did not produce
separations as clear-cut as in the popular denominations. Abolitionists provoked
several defections from regional Bible societies, installed sympathetic officers in
the American Home Missionary Society, and organized a separatist antislavery tract
society—all in the late 1850s. See Clifford S. Griffin, *Their Brothers' Keepers: Moral
Stewardship in the United States, 1800-1865* (New Brunswick NJ, 1960) ch. 10; also
John Wells Kuykendall, " 'Southern Enterprize': The Work of National Evangelical Societies in the Antebellum South," (Ph.D. dissertation, Princeton University,
1975).

[64]A. A. Porter, editorial in the *Southern Presbyterian,* 20 April 1861, in Robert
Livingston Stanton, *The Church and the Rebellion* (New York, 1864) 198.

# CHAPTER FOUR

# THE BROKEN UNION

Shortly after the United States Congress enacted the series of laws known as the Compromise of 1850, Iveson L. Brookes, a South Carolina Baptist writing pseudonymously as "A Southern Clergyman," protested what he felt was the law's inequity, using language that exactly paralleled the charges made by aggrieved Southern Methodists and Baptists against their national organizations in 1844-1845. The actions of the Congress, Brookes complained, had "put the South into a predicament, where she must either leave the Union or be ruined."[1] As alienation between North and South deepened during the 1850s, the controversy leading to political rupture replicated to a remarkable degree the ones that had led to the denominational schisms of the preceding decade. In each case the apprehensions, accusations, arguments, and sometimes even the personnel were the same.

On the Northern side, evangelical abolitionists made no secret of their conviction that the antislavery crusade was of one piece in church and nation. As James G. Birney put it, they were "laboring

---

[1]"A Southern Clergyman," *A Defense of Southern Slavery Against the Attacks of Henry Clay and Alex'r Campbell* (Hamburg SC, 1851) preface.

zealously to banish Slavery, and the spirit of Slaveholding from our American churches; not only with a view to their purification, but as . . . an indispensable preliminary, to the extermination of Slavery from the whole land."[2] Against such threatening purposes, Southern church leaders could easily think of themselves as the first line of defense for the South and its way of life. As the nation became increasingly polarized, Southerners were convinced that they were being forced to a crucial, destiny-determining choice: "they must somehow stabilize their position in the Union, with safeguards to preserve the security of the slave system, or they must secede before their minority position made them impotent."[3] The Southern churches had already resolved this dilemma by separating from their national organizations, and now they were prepared to transpose the ecclesiastical arguments of the 1840s to the political conflicts of the 1850s.

The South's religious leaders, like most of its political theorists, customarily thought of the United States as a confederacy and regarded the Constitution as a compact among "sovereign" states. Many of them had freely imbibed John C. Calhoun's doctrines designed to protect Southern interests from Northern encroachment. Calhoun advocated, for example, a dual executive for the United States, that is, a "president" for the South and one for the North. That idea appeared in ecclesiastical garb in the Methodist General Conference of 1844 immediately after Bishop James O. Andrew was ordered to desist from all episcopal functions as long as he remained a slaveowner. William Capers of South Carolina, soon to be elected bishop in the Methodist Episcopal Church, South, offered on 3 June a series of resolutions that, if adopted, would have created two General Conferences, one in the slave states and one in the free, each with power to elect its own bishops. The Conference promptly rejected the plan. On 4 June Calhoun wrote to Capers in New York:

My dear Sir:—I have felt a deep interest in the proceedings of your

---

[2]James G. Birney to Will Jay (a London minister), 5 October 1840, in *Letters of James G. Birney, 1831-1857*, ed. Dwight L. Dumond, 2 vols. (New York, 1938) 2:605.

[3]David M. Potter, *The Impending Crisis, 1848-1861* (New York, 1976) 94.

conference in reference to the case of Bishop Andrew. Their bearings, both as it relates to Church and State, demand the gravest attention on the part of the whole Union and the South especially.

I would be glad if you and Judge [Augustus B.] Longstreet, and other prominent members of the conference, would take Washington in your route home, and spend a day or two with us, in order to afford an opportunity of exchanging ideas on a subject of such vital importance.[4]

Capers declined the invitation so as to forestall charges that he was in collusion with the politicians, but he and Calhoun did confer on many other occasions.[5]

Another of Calhoun's devices was the doctrine of the "concurrent majority," an arrangement whereby every group in the body politic could have a veto over actions of an absolute majority whenever it considered such actions inimical to its own interests. This proposal, first advanced during the nullification crisis of 1832, also found ready resonance in Southern ecclesiology. In 1837 a South Carolina presbytery, happy enough to see the General Assembly exscind four abolitionist synods, still expressed apprehension about the strategy that secured the action: "Let the principles involved in the doings of the late Assembly be carried out, and as a minority in the Assembly our rights as Presbyterians . . . are held in suspense, at the mercy of the non-slaveholding states. . . . The majority decide our fate."[6]

Southern Methodists had even greater reason to fear "tyranny of the majority." At the beginning of denominational life in 1784,

---

[4]Capers later gave the letter to the *Richmond Christian Advocate*, which printed it on 7 August 1851.

[5]See Charles Elliott, ed., *History of the Great Secession* (Cincinnati, 1855) 1008; and George R. Crooks, *The Life of Bishop Matthew Simpson of the Methodist Episcopal Church* (New York, 1891) 240-45. On Calhoun's correspondence with the Southern delegates to the General Conference of 1844, see John P. Durbin to Matthew Simpson, August 1844, in Simpson Papers, Box 4, Library of Congress; and William M. Wightman, *The Life of William Capers* (Nashville, 1858) 514. Lyman Beecher also reported Calhoun's contacts with Southern churchmen; see Lyman Beecher, *The Autobiography of Lyman Beecher*, ed. Barbara M. Cross, 2 vols. (Cambridge MA, 1961) 2:323.

[6]*Southern Religious Telegraph* (Richmond), 4 August 1837, quoted in Ernest T. Thompson, *Presbyterians in the South*, 3 vols. (Richmond, 1963–1973) 1:401.

ninety percent of Methodist church members lived below the Mason-Dixon line, mostly in Maryland and Virginia. By 1812, however, the North had overtaken the South, so that in the General Conference of that year there were 42 Northern delegates and 35 Southern. (Thirteen more came from the Western Annual Conference, which at the time embraced churches on both sides of the Ohio River.) Four years later General Conference seated 60 Northern delegates and 45 Southern. By 1844 the sectional representation of elected delegates was 118 to 58 in favor of the North, causing a frustrated Mississippian to sigh, "We can out-speak them, but they will always be able to out-vote us."[7] Such imbalance is precisely what Calhoun had foreseen in the political sphere, and he hoped to prevent the disadvantage to the South by his concept of the concurrent majority. Southern Methodists were acting in harmony with Calhoun's perspective when in 1845 they rejected "the *proscription and disability* under which the Southern portion of the Church must of necessity labour . . . unless some measures are adopted to free the minority of the South from the oppressive jurisdiction of the North."[8]

Virginia Baptists were thinking along the same lines in March 1845 as they issued their call for the "consultation" that would result in the formation of the Southern Baptist Convention. The Virginians declared that Baptists of the South "indignantly refuse to co-operate with [the General Convention] on any terms implying their inferiority."[9] Failing to win adequate concessions from the Northern majority and finding no effective way to veto statements that displeased them, the Southerners simply withdrew. The logic of secession was the same throughout the South, whatever the institution. As the Confederacy was organizing, Southern Presbyterians declared that North/South differences regarding slavery were so radical and fundamental that "it is becoming every day more and more apparent that the religious, as well as the secular, interests of

---

[7]William Winans, quoted in *The Christian Advocate and Journal* (New York), 21 May 1845, 162.

[8]"Proposal for a Separate Denomination, Signed by Fifty-One Southern Methodist Ministers," in R. Sutton, *The Methodist Church Property Case* (Richmond, 1851) 90.

[9]*Religious Herald* (Richmond), 13 March 1845.

both will be more effectually promoted by a complete and lasting separation."[10]

The significant point here, with enormous implications for the secession crisis of 1860-1861, is that it was in the churches that Southerners first acted to free themselves from "the oppressive jurisdiction of the majority of the North" by the simple expedient of seceding. As the crisis grew, there was a striking congruency between earlier arguments for splitting the churches and those for breaking the federal Union. This should not be surprising, seeing that the same divisive forces that had torn the churches apart were tearing also at the nation. The religious covenant dissolved prior to the political compact, not only because the bonds of political union were diffused over a broader cultural spectrum, but also because in the churches the moral issue of slavery was focused more sharply, absolutes were affirmed more dogmatically, and moral ambiguity was impossible to tolerate indefinitely. But the same passions were at work in both arenas, and in each case the seceders thought it more important to preserve slavery than to maintain unity.

At the close of the 1844 Methodist General Conference, the separating Southerners justified their withdrawal: "The opinions and purposes of the Church in the north on the subject of slavery, are in direct conflict with those of the south, and unless the south will submit to the dictation and interference of the north . . . there is no hope of any thing like union or harmony."[11] At the same time, a Baptist in the South, distracted by the slavery controversy in his own denomination, was advising an identical course of action: "Depend on it, brethren, if we desire peace and quietness, we should separate from these Northern societies."[12] The Southern religious press chorused in unison that separation was the South's only way to escape from "Christless abolitionism" and "political tyranny,"

---

[10]"Address of the General Assembly of the Presbyterian Church in the Confederate States of America" (1861) in *The Presbyterian Enterprise: Sources of American Presbyterian History,* ed. Maurice Whitman Armstrong et al. (Philadelphia, 1956) 213.

[11]Document in Charles Elliott, *History of the Great Secession from the Methodist Episcopal Church* (Cincinnati, 1855) 1045.

[12]*A Calm Appeal to Southern Baptists in Advocacy of Separation from the North in All the Works of Christian Benevolence* (n.p., n.d. [1845?]) 7.

neatly merging the arguments for ecclesiastical schism and civil secession.

Thus the *Sumter Banner* was simply echoing the earlier arguments of seceding churchmen when it screamed in 1849: "The only remedy which will free . . . [the South] from Northern oppression . . . is the SECESSION OF THE SLAVEHOLDING STATES IN A BODY FROM THE UNION AND THEIR FORMATION INTO A SEPARATE REPUBLIC."[13] The following year, in his last major speech (4 March 1850), Senator Calhoun stated flatly that "the South will be forced to choose between abolition and secession."[14] As the choice drew nearer, Mississippi newspapers urged, "Let every Southern man insist on his rights IN the Union, or let him seek them OUT of it."[15] William Gilmore Simms, romantic novelist of South Carolina, asked, "Of what . . . value to a Christian man is that sort of union which persists in keeping men in the same household who hate and blaspheme each other?"[16] Throughout the region Southern nationalists argued forcefully, as their church leaders had done earlier, that the strife over slavery could be ended only by withdrawing to pursue an independent course free from Northern interference with their peculiar institution.

Southerners were not the only ones speaking of separation as the most appropriate solution of the sectional conflict. The number of Northerners willing to let the South go its own way was far more than a noisy band of radical abolitionists. In April 1845 the *New York Baptist Register,* as weary of controversy as Southerners were of criticism, had been ready to accept a peaceful parting of the ways.

> For ourselves, we deplore the necessity of the division, but when things reach such a crisis as they appear to have done, deplore it

---

[13]*Sumter Banner,* 21 March 1849, quoted in Avery O. Craven, *The Coming of the Civil War,* 2d ed. (Chicago, 1957) 244.

[14]Richard K. Crallé, ed., *Speeches of John C. Calhoun* (New York, 1968) 556.

[15]The admonition appeared first in the *Mississippi Baptist* and was reprinted in the *Eastern Clarion* (Jackson) on 5 December 1860; see Percy Lee Rainwater, *Mississippi: Storm Center of Secession, 1856-1865* (Boston, 1938) 175.

[16]William Gilmore Simms to John Jacob Bockee, 12 December 1860, in *The Letters of William Gilmore Simms,* ed. Mary C. Simms et al., 5 vols. (Columbia SC, 1952-1956) 4:288.

as we may, there is no prospect of peace or comfort in the contin-
uance [of the united missionary organizations]. . . . Why is it not
best that our southern brethren take their position on one side of
the line, and we take ours on the other, and engage in the various
departments of benevolent effort with renewed zeal and increased liberality?[17]

Francis Wayland, president of Brown University and one of the
most prominent Baptists in the antebellum North, accepted that
reasoning and in May 1845 serenely told the departing Southern
Baptists, "You will separate, of course. I could not ask otherwise."
By 1854, however, Wayland was profoundly disturbed by the Kan-
sas-Nebraska Bill and wanted to let the whole South go, lest its intransigent slavocracy corrupt the entire continent. "I value the
Union as much as any man. I would cheerfully sacrifice to it everything but truth and justice and liberty. When I must surrender these
as the price of the Union, the Union becomes at once a thing I
abhor." Wayland could pass easily from ecclesiastical schism to political separation, relying on the same logic in both cases. So could
Daniel D. Whedon, a Methodist professor of philosophy at the
University of Michigan. Although he earlier opposed abolitionism,
Whedon had accepted the division of his denomination; now he saw
in the secession movement many compensations. "Countless will be
the blessings of a full emancipation from the dread evils not only
of slavery domination but of union with slaveholders."[18]

By 1860 there was substantial agreement within the Northern
churches to permit the South to depart in peace. In November of
that year, the *New York Observer* announced:

If any one of the States of this confederacy is so mad on its idols,
so blind to its interests, so deaf to the lessons of wisdom, so dead
to the holy and lofty spirit of *patriotism* . . . we say, *let her go*. . . . Let
us arrange the terms of separation amicably, as did Abraham and
Lot, and may God bless the right and save us all.[19]

---

[17]*New York Baptist Register* (Utica), 4 April 1845, 34.
[18]Francis Wayland to Jeremiah Bell Jeter, printed in the *Daily Chronicle and
Sentinel* (Augusta GA), 10 May 1845; *Dr. Wayland on the Moral and Religious Aspects
of the Nebraska Bill* (Rochester NY, 1854) 5; Daniel D. Whedon, "The State of the
Country," *Methodist Quarterly Review*, 43 (1861): 321.
[19]*New York Observer* (Old School Presbyterian), 22 November 1860, 370.

Northern readiness to accept disunion, like that of the Southern secessionists, fed on the example of the agreements whereby the divided churches had already eased themselves away from further controversy over slavery. Allan Nevins commented:

> So jangling had the national household become that not a few sincere lovers of concord believed that disunion would actually promote peace. The perpetual brawling over the slavery question was like some chronic dispute between husband and wife which only divorce could heal. The history of the Methodist Church seemed to illustrate the possibility of gaining harmony by a choice of separate ways. Before the church split, the General Conference was always a scene of disgraceful bickering; after the separation, Southern and Northern wings went forward peaceably and happily.[20]

The same could be said of Baptists and Presbyterians as they "went forward" on their separate ways.

But "peaceably and happily"? That was a fateful illusion. The myth of peaceable secession that was embraced by disunionists of both South and North seems to have been nurtured largely by the apparent success of the divided denominations. During the nullification crisis of 1832, when South Carolina was rattling the saber of secession, President Andrew Jackson had threatened the state not only with the full power of the federal government but with the judgment of Almighty God. The Great Ruler of Nations, Jackson warned, would invoke a dreadful curse on any people so wicked as to disrupt the Union.[21] But after 1845, if anyone asked how the South could survive outside the Union, or how the Union could go on without the South, the question could be answered by pointing to the divided denominations. They had been demonstrating for several years that they could be viable as sectional independents. Schism had stilled internecine strife, and national meetings no longer provided a stage for wrangling over slavery. Just after the Baptist division was consummated, a Southerner wrote confidently

---

[20]Allan Nevins, *The Emergence of Lincoln*, 2 vols. (New York, 1950) 2:332.
[21]Paul C. Nagel, *One Nation Indivisible: The Union in American Thought, 1776-1861* (New York, 1964) 264-65.

to a Boston paper that the distressing periodic "collisions" would occur no more.

> [Separation] will prevent the annual and especially the triennial collisions betwixt Northern and Southern Baptists. For some years past in every such meeting, some of the worst passions of our nature have been excited. Many ministers for the time being have appeared to forget their sacred calling and to lend themselves to animosity and strife. How can two walk together except they be agreed [Amos 3:3]? Whilst one party has been engaged in asserting most earnestly, slavery to be a sin, and the other party has earnestly engaged in denying the assertion, peace has been expelled. Every meeting of those holding such antagonistic views must be anything but lovely. By our present arrangement we meet no more.—This will give us peace.[22]

The intersectional "peace" was illusory, as the subsequent account will show, but for the moment the institutional life of all the separated churches appeared to be healthy.

The division of the national church bodies had been easy—deceptively so—and the reasons for this reach far back into history. Sectarian Protestantism had long ago breached the barriers to fundamental schism, so that a sense of continuity with the historic Christian tradition rested very lightly if at all on their shoulders. Antichurchly bias aroused in the Reformation had flourished in migration to the freer atmosphere of the New World. In seventeenth-century England, moreover, the feathering out of left-wing Puritanism had produced a plethora of new sects; although some of these had become mainline denominations in the United States, they remained notoriously contemptuous of tradition and authority. Two centuries of experience in America had given them a high regard for individualism, experimentation, and local autonomy, which further eroded their sense of history. Their formal religious authority was still the Bible—the *sola scriptura* of the Reformers— though unlike the Reformers, they interpreted it less according to the norms of classical Christianity than through the presumed competence of private reason and individual experience.

---

[22]"Communication" from Gainesville, Georgia, dated 22 May 1845, in *The Christian Watchman* (Boston), 6 June 1845.

The ignoring of historical development and tradition in a "back-to-the-Bible" approach is often designated *primitivism,* and its mood comported easily with the ahistorical temper of revivalism. Revival conversions came in the immediacy of the moment, usually suddenly, and with little relation to the traditioning nurture of the church. Primitivism and revivalism confirmed the popular churches in a reductionist ecclesiology that accorded less importance to the church than to the experience of salvation. The church, in this perspective, was simply a place to gather the converts of the revivals. The word "church" itself usually signified a local congregation (or even its building!), not the whole company of the faithful, and congregations might be multiplied or divided easily according to shifting local needs and preferences.

Disestablishment placed the American churches in the framework of a voluntary society, which meant that, legally, churches were only private groups of private individuals. This made it even even easier for them to splinter without excessive trauma, and splinter they did—frequently—sometimes for rather trivial reasons, though the schisms were mostly local or regional rather than national. Such behavior appears to contradict the claim that the churches constituted a force for cultural cohesion, but it was their way of expressing the vaunted American individualism. The evangelical bond was still intact, however, and what saved the churches from total chaos was that most of their burgeoning branches remained more or less attached to the trunk of the common evangelical tree. They could be organizationally separate and even competitive up to a point, but they could still cooperate on certain enterprises which they understood to be their common mission in Christianizing the nation.

This easygoing ecclesiology suggested a simple way for people influenced by such churches to dissolve their political compact, for the belief that converted people create the church is exactly parallel to the idea that consenting people create the state. That is to say, the political version of evangelical voluntaryism appears in the doctrine of states' rights, a notion that Horace Bushnell labeled in 1861 as "the crowning mischief." In a sermon preached to his Hartford congregation on the Sunday after the first battle of Bull Run, Bushnell declared:

Our political theories never gave us a real nationality, but only a copartnership, and the armed treason is only the consummated result of our speculations. Where nothing exists but a consent, what can be needed to end it but a dissent? And if the states are formed by the consent of individuals, was not the general government formed by the consent of the states? What then have we to do but give up the partnership of the states when we will? If a tariff act is passed, displeasing to some states, they may rightfully nullify it; if a president is elected not in the interest of slavery they may secede; that is, withdraw their consent and stand upon their reserved rights.[23]

Bushnell, a Congregationalist, was probably oblivious to the parallelism between the doctrine of states' rights and the idea of the voluntary church. But the low-church localism that characterized the functioning polity of the popular denominations and the Enlightenment assertion that government rests solely on the consent of the governed clearly matched and reinforced each other. Each idea could lead easily toward fragmentation in its own sphere and by synergism could augment the centrifugal forces in the other.[24]

The peaceable division of the churches was not only easy, it was also deceptive. Those who tried to transpose the tactic to the political arena rarely stopped to consider that even though the national government was formed originally "by consent," as an ongoing polity for a whole people, it was inescapably an organic unity, and breaking it apart would be exceedingly more traumatic than dividing the churches. The churches were already disunited denominationally, even within denominational families; their "unity in diversity" rested on the more intangible ground of common feeling and experience, and such subjectivities were hard to absolutize. The

---

[23]Horace Bushnell, *Reverses Needed, a Discourse Delivered on the Sunday after the Disaster at Bull Run* (Hartford, 1861) 20. Bushnell's organicism is examined by Howard A. Barnes, "The Idea that Caused a War: Horace Bushnell versus Thomas Jefferson," *Journal of Church and State,* 16 (1974): 73-83; and Daniel Walker Howe, "The Social Science of Horace Bushnell," *Journal of American History,* 70 (1983): 305-22.

[24]The doctrine of states' rights originally meant much more than the right to withdraw from the Union. Arthur Bestor noted that "secession itself was responsible for reducing the argument over state sovereignty to such simple terms" ("The American Civil War as a Constitutional Crisis," *American Historical Review,* 69 [1964]: 350).

nation, on the other hand, had long been gathering to itself more of the traditional "churchly" attributes than the various denominations could ever display. Paul C. Nagel's perceptive study, *One Nation Indivisible,* has shown how Union ideology moved decisively from concept and experiment to the more formidable categories of Spirit and Absolute; and many other scholars have demonstrated how nationalism flourished as a profoundly religious *faith* in the period of the Revolution and afterwards. Abraham Lincoln, member of no church and yet deeply religious, has been described accurately enough as revering the Union with a sense of awe approaching religious mysticism.[25] He was not alone. If there was any "high-church" sense of visible unity, catholicity, mission, and destiny in antebellum America, it attached more to the nation itself than to any of its various churches. Thus the churches might agree to "multiply by dividing," but that option was not open to the nation without wrenching trauma.

John C. Calhoun had few illusions about the approaching necessity to maintain the Union—if it were to be maintained at all—by force. Daniel Webster had none. In his famous Seventh of March (1850) speech, Webster declared that the undivided Methodist Church had been "one of the great props of religion and morals throughout the whole country." Its rupture had given him "great concern . . . about the [political] result." Webster traced other signs of widening cleavage between North and South, and then cried:

> Peaceable secession! Sir, your eyes and mine are never destined to see that miracle. The dismemberment of this vast country without convulsion! The breaking up of the fountains of the great deep without ruffling the surface! Who is so foolish, I beg everybody's pardon, as to expect to see any such thing? . . . Peaceable secession is an utter impossibility. . . . Sir, I see as plainly as I see the sun in heaven . . . that disruption . . . must produce war, and such a war as I will not describe.[26]

---

[25] The observation was made by Alexander H. Stephens, vice-president of the Confederacy. See Edmund Wilson, *Patriotic Gore: Studies in the Literature of the American Civil War* (New York, 1961) 97, 422.

[26] *The Works of Daniel Webster,* 16th ed., 6 vols. (Boston, 1872) 5:331, 361.

But the temporarily flourishing state of the separated churches in the South gave the lie to such dire predictions. Their membership was growing, their financial status was sound, their missionary and benevolent work was expanding, and best of all, they were free from embarrassments previously suffered under antislavery attacks in their national assemblies. If the churches could solve their problems by peaceable secession, why not the whole South? James Chesnut of South Carolina scoffed at Webster's warning and promised to drink all the blood that might be shed as a result of secession. A flippancy current throughout the South claimed that "a lady's thimble will hold all the blood that will be shed," while Augustus B. Longstreet, jurist, clergyman, and president successively of major universities in Georgia, Louisiana, and South Carolina, proposed in 1859 to "stake everything I am worth" on the proposition that the South could secede peaceably.[27] Had not the churches shown the way?

The Southern churches also outfitted the argument that remaining in union with the North was costing more than the benefits returned. As noted in the previous chapter, a long-standing grievance of Baptists in the South against the American Baptist Home Mission Society was that they contributed more to the society than the society expended for missionary work in their region. Although such complaints had small basis in fact, prevalent suspicions gave currency to the suggestion that a Southern missionary society would be more cost-effective and also more sensitive to needs in the South. The political parallel to this was the South's objection to federal tariff policies, which Southerners complained were designed to favor Northern industry at their expense. Feelings of being financially exploited served in both disputes to heighten Southern indignation. Not surprisingly, in 1860 some Southern churchmen refurbished the old complaint of missionary neglect into an argument for secession.

> Basil Manly claimed that for years the South had borne the chief financial burdens of the government without receiving its proportional share of the benefits. . . . James C. Furman argued that

---

[27]Potter, *The Impending Crisis,* 490, cites several such boasts.

the unjust practice of converting the wealth of the South into building up the North should cease. A Baptist editor pointed out the economic disadvantages of the South by showing that the tariff laws placed two-thirds of the cost of government on one-third of the people, who, in return, received only one-fourth of the disbursements of governmental revenue.[28]

Methodist leader William M. Wightman, chancellor of Southern University at Greensboro, Alabama, had no doubts in 1861 that the Confederacy would have adequate resources to "stand against the world" because the millions of Southern dollars that had gone to build up Northern cities could now be used to "build up our own commerce, manufacturers, [and] literature."[29]

The rhetoric of secession sometimes outdid that of the earlier denominational schisms, even in turgid biblical allusions. In 1848, for example, Senator Thomas Hart Benton (D-Mo.) compared the ubiquity of the slavery question to the plague of frogs in ancient Egypt (Exodus 8:1-14): "You could not look upon the table but there were frogs, you could not sit down at the banquet but there were frogs, you could not go to the bridal couch and lift the sheets but there were frogs!" It was the same way with "this black question, forever on the table, on the nuptial couch, everywhere!"[30] Governor John J. Pettus of Mississippi preached his state into the Confederacy by comparing the South's course to the flight of the Christ-child.

> Mississippi must go down into Egypt [join the Confederacy] while Herod rules in Judea [Lincoln in Washington]. . . . And when in after years it shall be told you that they [Republicans] who sought the life of this Prince of Peace [slavery] . . . are dead, you may come

---

[28]W. Harrison Daniel, "Southern Protestantism and Secession," *The Historian,* 29 (1967): 405. Basil Manly was president of the University of Alabama 1837-1855 and afterwards a Baptist minister in South Carolina. James C. Furman, also a Baptist minister, was professor and president at Furman University 1844-1879; an outspoken advocate of secession, he was a member of the South Carolina Secession Convention in December 1860.

[29]"Baccalaureate Address of W. M. Wightman, D.D., LL.D.," *Quarterly Review of the Methodist Episcopal Church, South* (October 1861): 527-28.

[30]*Congressional Globe,* 30th Congress, First Session, 686.

up out of Egypt [rejoin the Union] and realize all the fond hopes of . . . peace on earth and good will among men.[31]

Southern church folk could respond to that with a resounding "Amen!" because they had already fled to their ecclesiastical Egypt. Living as they did in tight symbiosis with Southern culture, they found their attitudes and those of their region resonating easily together.

By 1860 there was a rising crescendo of voices urging the South to file for divorce with full benefit of clergy. The *New Orleans Bee* put in political context exactly the same argument that the Southern churches had framed fifteen years earlier when separating from their national organizations:

> As long as slavery is looked upon by the North with abhorrence; as long as the South is regarded as a mere slave-breeding and slave-driving community; as long as false and pernicious theories are cherished respecting the inherent equality and rights of every human being, there can be no satisfactory political union between the two sections. If one-half the people believe the other half to be deeply dyed in iniquity; to be daily and hourly in the perpetuation of the most atrocious moral offense, and at the same time . . . conceive themselves authorized and in some sort constrained to lecture them, to abuse them, to employ all possible means to break up their institutions, and to take from them what the Northern half consider property unrighteously held, or no property at all, how can two such antagonistic nationalities dwell together in fraternal concord under the same government? Is not the thing clearly impossible?[32]

The logic and language of the political crisis was precisely parallel to that of the ecclesiastical disputes. Conditioned by the earlier schisms, Southern church folk, especially in the lower South, advocated secession before it came, applauded when it did, and in the resulting war gave unqualified support to the Southern cause.

In so doing, they were following powerful opinion-makers like Basil Manly, Sr. Prominent Baptist minister, president of the Uni-

---

[31]Quoted in David M. Potter, *Lincoln and His Party in the Secession Crisis* (New Haven, 1942) 226.

[32]*New Orleans Bee*, 14 December 1860, in *Southern Editorials on Secession*, ed. Dwight L. Dumond (New York, 1932) 336.

versity of Alabama for eighteen years, a founder of Furman University and of the Southern Baptist Theological Seminary, owner of much land and many slaves, Manly persuaded his fellow Alabamians that God ordained slavery and approved secession. Since the 1830s he had wanted Baptists in the South to sever their ties with all national organizations infected with abolitionism. Three weeks after his state withdrew from the Union, he wrote to his son, "I thank God that I have lived, after thirty years of waiting, to see [secession]."[33] The Southern churches, having already broken fellowship with Northern Christians, felt few restraints against political cleavage. Indeed, the heady experience of having crossed that Rubicon added to the stridency of their regionalism. The separation of the whole South would vindicate their church schisms, and they could then regard the forming of the new Confederacy as a surpassing moral victory.

The central question remains: To what extent did the denominational schisms influence the rupture of the nation and the coming of the Civil War? Did the forebodings of church leaders, expressed at the very time they were driving Northern and Southern Christians asunder, become self-fulfilling prophecies? Did such forebodings simply reflect an estrangement already far advanced in the nation at large? Were the ominous predictions merely rhetorical hyperbole to calm sporadic tempests in ecclesiastical teapots? Perhaps, as one scholar ventured, the separation of contending factions in the churches may have decreased occasions for sectional friction and thus "delayed rather than hastened national disunion."[34]

This last idea was recognized by some contemporary thinkers. Shortly before the group that formed the Southern Baptist Convention gathered in Augusta, an anonymous Southern Baptist pro-

---

[33]Daniel, "Southern Protestantism and Secession," 393n. Southern Baptists who opposed secession before the event included James P. Boyce and John A. Broadus of the theological seminary at Greenville, South Carolina, and J. M. Pendleton, editor of *The Tennessee Baptist* (H. Shelton Smith, *In His Image, but . . .: Racism in Southern Religion, 1780-1910* [Durham, 1972] 173n., 186).

[34]Mary B. Putnam, *The Baptists and Slavery, 1840-1845* (Ann Arbor, 1913) 92. Walter Brownlow Posey, *Frontier Mission: A History of Religion West of the Southern Appalachians to 1861* (Lexington, 1966) 370, also accepted this supposition.

posed that "for the welfare of the political union of these States, it is expedient to dissolve all religious connection with the North. . . . Our ecclesiastical connection serves rather to weaken than to strengthen the political bonds" because it provides a ready focus for Northern abolitionists to agitate the slavery issue and engender sectional animosities.[35] Henry B. Bascom, president of Transylvania University and soon to become a bishop in the Methodist Episcopal Church, South, likewise argued that the South's withdrawal from the abolitionist faction in the church would demonstrate its law-abiding nature, put a stop to controversy, and thus strengthen the political union.[36]

More common, however, were comments such as the one in the Presbyterian *New York Observer* on 7 June 1845: "We have deeply regretted that the ties of union should be sundered between Christians at North and South on the question of slavery, apprehending that differences of opinion might, in consequence, increase rather than diminish." Of the several conceivable suppositions, the one most strongly supported by available evidence is that the church splits produced a portentous acceleration of estrangement between the two sections of the country. On 28 May 1845, with both Southern Methodists and Baptists now organized as separate denominations, the *New York Journal of Commerce* prophesied that "as in cases of divorce between those most closely allied in domestic relations, the alienation of feeling will increase, and error on both sides [will] become more inveterate."

According to a growing consensus among Civil War scholars, a major factor in the nation's breakdown was this deepening sense of alienation, even isolation, that distanced North and South from each other in the 1850s. David Potter described it: "As they became isolated, instead of reacting to each other as they were in actuality, each [section] reacted to a distorted mental image of the other—the North to an image of a southern world of lascivious and sadistic slave drivers; the South to the image of a northern world of cunning Yankee traders and of rabid abolitionists plotting slave insurrec-

---

[35]*A Calm Appeal to Southern Baptists,* 10.
[36]Henry B. Bascom, *Methodism and Slavery* (Frankfort KY, 1845) 96-97, 115-17.

tions." Avery O. Craven, "the scholar who has wrestled most persistently with the problem of why the American nation broke apart," likewise argued that the differences between North and South were never great enough to make war necessary; sectional antagonism arose not from fundamental differences so much as "from the creation of false images with a high, unreasoning emotional content." Craven concluded that the war came "more because of psychological attitudes than objective conditions."[37]

It is undeniable that the churches played a crucial role in creating and sustaining those distorted images and psychological attitudes. The churches' role, in fact, may even have been determinative, for in spite of advancing secularism throughout western civilization, ministers in antebellum America were still of strategic importance in molding public opinion and influencing emotional responses. One should beware of claiming too much on this point, of course, for diagnosing human motivation is difficult even for a psychiatrist with a single living subject; it is enormously more so for a historian dealing with group behavior on the basis of fragmentary and often skewed materials from the past.[38] But available evidence in the present case suggests that after the popular denominations split, each side of what was formerly a far-flung network of relationships was left to nurture its grievances against the other with few opportunities to check its deepening suspicions in fraternal encounter. As the *Christian Advocate and Journal* declared only three months after the Methodist schism, no further "charitable friendship" was possible.

> [The Southerners] have made . . . the specific charge, that the majority are tyrants, oppressors, covenant-breakers, and false accusers. . . . If the authors of this charge believe their brethren to be

---

[37]Potter, *The Impending Crisis,* 43. Craven's work is summarized in David M. Potter, *The South and the Sectional Conflict* (Baton Rouge, 1968) 94-95; see also Don E. Fehrenbacher, "Disunion and Reunion," in *The Reconstruction of American History,* ed. John Higham (New York, 1962) 117.

[38]For an old but still suggestive statement of the problems of psychological interpretation in Civil War historiography, see Howard K. Beale, "What Historians Have Said about the Causes of the Civil War," in *Theory and Practice in Historical Study: A Report of the Committee on Historiography,* Bulletin No. 54 of the Social Science Research Council (New York, 1946) 83-92.

thus guilty, all confidence in them must have already been with-
drawn, and the majority, if conscious of their own integrity, must
of course forego all fellowship with men by whom they are thus
accused.[39]

And so it came to pass. Estranged churches North and South regarded their sectional counterparts as apostate and assiduously
reinforced their respective region's twisted perceptions of the other.
From both sides came repeated accusations of malevolence, which
widened the gap of alienation, provoked some to extreme posi-
tions, and thrust the strained nation closer to an open break.[40]

One of the more decisive factors in sharpening the lines of sectional conflict was the sharp divergence in religious perspectives that
grew out of the bitter dispute over slavery. Many Northern clergy
thought that connivance with slavery corrupted both the gospel and
the preachers who claimed to represent it. Southern theologians
insisted that slavery was an ordinance of God fully sanctioned in
Scripture and that all who denied the plain meaning of the texts
were obtuse, perverse, and heretical. The texts were plain enough:
Abraham and the patriarchs held slaves, obviously with God's approval; Jesus lived in a world where slavery was rampant and never
condemned it; Paul wrote explicit instructions for the duties of
masters and slaves, and he even sent a fugitive slave back to his
master.

The proslavery apologetic thus encapsulated the Southern
churches in a rigid biblicism supported by the literal language of
selected proof texts unrelieved by any appreciation of changed historical circumstances. On the other hand, the antislavery attack relied more on ideas like the requirements of Christian love and the
"spirit of Jesus," a progressive type of interpretation that gave more
weight to the "principles of Christianity." If the South refused to
allow the leaven of the gospel to spread throughout the society,
producing freedom and the application of the Golden Rule to all
of life's relationships, then its religion was suspect in the North. If

---

[39]*Christian Advocate and Journal,* 4 September 1844, 14.
[40]James H. Moorhead, *American Apocalypse: Yankee Protestants and the Civil War,
1860-1869* (New Haven, 1978) 29-32, describes the hardening of Northern attitudes toward the South.

the North rejected the literal and strict construction of the church's "constitution," its religion stood condemned in the South. Their conflicting attitudes toward slavery set the religions of the two regions on divergent courses, which in turn conditioned each region's estimate of the other's character.

Visiting the Louisville Convention, where Southern Methodism organized itself in 1845, Matthew Simpson, then president of Indiana Asbury College, heard "Young Pierce of Georgia" castigate Northern apostasy. As Simpson recalled the diatribe:

> Pierce tried to show reconciliation hopeless and impossible, because the North would not concede. Charged ignorance of the Bible in Northern Abolitionists, and declared that they did not appeal to the Bible for the justness of their cause but to the writings of Jefferson. And that after all the movement of the Northern church was not so much against *Slavery* as against *Episcopacy*. That the North were radicals—that they had ceased to use bread and water in lovefeasts, and their speeches were somewhat like those of Fourth of July toasts—and that in ten years there would not be a vestige of the peculiarities of Methodism among them.[41]

Peter Cartwright retorted for the North that the Southern secession was "not a 'division,' but an APOSTASY FROM THE GOOD AND RIGHT WAY OF METHODISM."[42] Thus the ground of controversy shifted from the morality of slavery to the question of which section's religious faith was the more authentic.

The Southern strategy, as Presbyterian Robert Lewis Dabney articulated it, was to "push the Bible argument continually, drive Abolitionism to the wall, compel it to assume an anti-Christian position." James Henley Thornwell, another Southern Presbyterian protagonist for the literal word of Scripture, accused the antislavery churches of following a "higher law" than the Bible.

> Rationalism . . . lies at the foundation of modern speculation in relation to the rights of man. Opposition to slavery has never been the offspring of the Bible. It has sprung from visionary theories

---

[41]Journal, 8 May 1845, Matthew Simpson Papers, Box 1, Library of Congress. George Foster Pierce was thirty-four years old; nine years later he would be elected a bishop of the Methodist Episcopal Church, South.

[42]*Western Christian Advocate*, 4 July 1845, 46.

of human nature and society; it has sprung from the misguided reason of man. . . . [Christians who oppose slavery] are striking at the foundation of our common faith. They are helping the cause of Rationalism.

Thomas Smyth, a Scottish Presbyterian now in Charleston, joined the chorus, preaching that abolitionists "have perverted and prostituted the Bible . . . by subjecting it to the private interpretations of men; to the developments in philosophy, falsely so called; to the licentious and atheistic spirit of a liberty which knows no restraint and no authority, human or divine." Smyth went on to attack the Declaration of Independence as an "infidel, atheistic, French Revolution, Red Republican principle."[43]

After the churches broke apart, the war of words escalated into what Thornwell called in 1861 "the dialect of Billingsgate." Among the Methodists, for example, the restrained rhetoric of 1844 soon gave way to harsh invective, inflamed by a litigious dispute over church property that went all the way to the Supreme Court. In 1848 Kentucky's Henry B. Bascom charged that Northern Methodism was a "prominent engine" for the "invasion of southern rights." The Northern church, he fumed,

> is so mixed up with the whole machinery of abolition and anti-slavery agitation and invasion . . . that its own chosen colors will not allow us any longer to distinguish it from the common enemy. . . . [Its members] have no fixed principles or settled views. They are the victims of a mania, constantly involving them in contradiction and inconsistency. . . . The firmness, consistency, moderation, and dignity of strong moral conviction—of fixed religious principle—are no where to be found among them; all is agitation, caprice, passion, and resentment.

Charles Elliott, editor of the *Central Christian Advocate* in St. Louis, observed that to be a member of the (Northern) Methodist

---

[43]Robert Lewis Dabney to Charles William Dabney (a brother), 15 January 1851, in *The Life and Letters of Robert Lewis Dabney,* ed. Thomas C. Johnson (Richmond, 1903) 129; "The Relation of the Church and Slavery" (1851), in *The Collected Writings of James Henley Thornwell,* ed. John B. Adger and John L. Girardeau, 4 vols. (Richmond, 1871-1873) 4:393; "The Sin and the Curse; Or, The Union and the True Source of Disunion" (1860), in *The Complete Works of Thomas Smyth,* 10 vols. (Columbia SC, 1910) 7:543, 545.

Episcopal Church in the western border states during the 1850s "was the greatest crime known . . . as membership in that Church was synonymous with *negro thief,* incendiary, insurrectionist, and the like." George F. Pierce of Georgia, a bishop of the Southern church, denounced all Northern Methodists as "abolitionists [who] can not and ought not to be tolerated in the Southern States." Their principles and doctrines, he declared, constitute them as "disturbers of the peace" and "enemies of the institutions of the people." In a typical diatribe, published in the *Southern Christian Advocate,* Pierce railed without restraint:

> On their own theory, they can not be faithful to God without aiding and abetting runaway slaves. They must sympathize with arson, blood and murder, insurrection and carnage. . . . No quarantine will justify their admission [to the South], no fumigation can disinfect them. Rank, rotten with the foul virus of an incurable disease [abolitionism], foes of God and man, spies and traitors to their country and their kind, let them stay where they belong![44]

Sectional partisans in other denominations were equally bitter. Southern Baptists condemned the "lawless reign of terror" in the North which threatened "to wage upon the South a warfare of savage barbarity, to devastate our homes and hearths with hosts of ruffians and felons, burning with lust and rapine." Thomas Smyth lumped all Northerners into a conglomeration of "atheists, infidels, communists, free-lovers, rationalists, Bible haters, anti-Christian levellers, and anarchists."[45] Benjamin Morgan Palmer, popular pastor of the First Presbyterian Church in New Orleans, also linked the "atheistic spirit" of the North with the French Revolution: "Its banner-cry rings out already upon the air—'Liberty, equality, fraternity,' which, simply interpreted, mean bondage, confiscation, and massacre. With its tricolor waving in the breeze, it waits to inaugurate its reign of terror." Palmer's dramatic sermon, re-

---

[44]James Henley Thornwell, "Our National Sins" (1860), in *Fast-Day Sermons; Or, The Pulpit on the State of the Country* (New York, 1861) 40; Henry B. Bascom, *A Brief Appeal to Public Opinion* (Louisville, 1848) 61-62; Charles Elliott, *South-Western Methodism: A History of the M. E. Church in the South-West from 1844 to 1864* (Cincinnati, 1868) preface; *Southern Christian Advocate* (Charleston), 4 October 1860.

[45]Southern Baptist Convention, *Annual* (1861) 63; "The Sin and the Curse," in *Works of Thomas Smyth,* 7:542.

produced many times and circulated in more than thirty thousand pamphlets, won him instant fame across the South and was a decisive factor in coagulating secession sentiment.[46] According to a common opinion during the war, Palmer did "more for the Confederate cause than a regiment of soldiers."[47]

Northern preachers hurled comparable vituperations against Southerners as moral degenerates and apostates, "traitors, rebels, thieves, plunderers, cowards." During the 1850s a growing number of regional Baptist associations in the North renounced all fellowship with slaveholders. To treat a slaveowner as any different from a kidnapper or a robber, declared Jacob Bailey in Wisconsin, "is to connive at his guilt and become a partaker of his evil deeds." The *Western Christian Advocate* condemned the creed of the Southern Methodist Church as "based upon a brutal licentiousness lower than that of polygamous Mormonism." Such attitudes, openly voiced and printed, could only drive the two sections farther and farther apart. On the eve of secession John B. Minor, professor of law at the University of Virginia and an active Presbyterian layman, concluded that

> Christians have a fearful responsibility for the present exasperation. . . . Forgetful that the "wrath of man worketh not the righteousness of God," they are so far from exercising . . . any wholesome restraint upon the passions of their neighbors and associates, that they are amongst the foremost, frequently, in kindling resentment . . . by inflammatory representations.[48]

---

[46]"Slavery as a Divine Trust," in *Fast-Day Sermons,* 70. Cf. Wayne C. Eubank, "Benjamin Morgan Palmer's Thanksgiving Sermon, 1860," in *Antislavery and Disunion, 1858-1861: Studies in the Rhetoric of Compromise and Conflict,* ed. John Jeffrey Auer (New York, 1963) 291-309; and Haskell Monroe, "Southern Presbyterians and the Secession Crisis," *Civil War History,* 6 (1960): 355.

[47]"Secesh Lady," letter to the *Philadelphia Presbyterian,* 16 August 1862. Cf. Lewis G. Vander Velde, *Presbyterian Churches and the Federal Union, 1861-1869* (Cambridge MA, 1932) 31; and Robert E. Thompson, *History of the Presbyterian Churches in the United States* (New York, 1895) 156, where a similar statement is attributed to a Confederate general (probably Thomas R. R. Cobb).

[48]*Central Presbyterian* (Richmond), 11 May 1861, 74; John R. McKivigan, "The American Baptist Free Mission Society: Abolitionist Reaction to the 1845 Baptist Schism," *Foundations,* 21 (1978): 35-51; *The Christian Times* (Chicago), 26 August 1857, 1; *Western Christian Advocate* (Cincinnati), 31 August 1854; John B. Minor to Robert Lewis Dabney, 14 January 1861, in Johnson, *Life and Letters of Robert Lewis Dabney,* 219.

Thus the denominational schisms not only severed a bond of national union and set a deceptive example for the states to follow; they also cast the sectional churches in an adversary relationship that actively exacerbated the alienation of North and South until sectional differences were *felt* to be irreconcilable. As early as 1868, historian Jesse T. Peck noted that "the *feeling* of difference [was] always stronger than the reality."[49] That is a highly significant perception, for feelings were preeminently the springs of action for evangelicals. Their stress on the personal response of deep moral feeling equipped them to make a crusade out of abolitionism or slaveholding with equal ease. Both sides portrayed the controversy in cosmic terms—eternal right against eternal wrong, God against Satan, the "conflict of the ages"—until mutual recriminations drove the estranged factions beyond the possibility of reconciliation. After their division, the churches became almost completely identified with their respective section's interests—so much so that the Whig party, itself under severe strains of sectional conflict, could not even agree on "a reverend gentleman" to offer the opening prayer at its 1852 convention.

Politicians invoked the polarization of the churches in order to sway public sentiment. The address of Justice Henry L. Benning of the Georgia Supreme Court to the Virginia Secession Convention is one example.

> With us, you will have concord on the slavery question, and fellowship in the pulpit and at the communion table. . . . With the North you will have increased discord on the slavery question; you will be repelled from pulpit and communion-table as being, by countenancing slavery, as foul as Brigham Young or any other polygamist.

As war broke out, a Presbyterian editor observed sadly that "politics and religion had become so mixed up that their hates and antagonisms were interchanged."[50]

---

[49]Jesse T. Peck, *History of the Great Republic, Considered from a Christian Stand-Point* (New York, 1868) 693.

[50]Henry L. Benning, Address to the Virginia Secession Convention, 18 February 1861, in *Rebellion Record: A Diary of American Events*, ed. Frank L. Moore, 12 vols. (New York, 1861-1868) Supplement 1, p. 154; *The Presbyterian* (Philadelphia), 21 September 1861, 150.

The bitterness of estrangement among those who once had regarded themselves as one in the family of God and in the Union of
God's own making may be gauged by the belligerence of a Louisiana minister who defied Northern ministers to set foot in the South:

> I am one of five ministers, of three different denominations, in a
> single company [of the Confederate army], armed for the de-
> fence of our rights and liberties, three of whom are between 50
> and 60 years old. And I tell you in candor, and in the fear of God,
> that if you or any of the *brethren* who have urged on this diabolical
> war, come on with the invading army, I would slay you with as
> hearty a good will, and with as clear a conscience, as I would the
> midnight assassin. . . . You are my enemy, and I am yours.

One Mr. Black, a Northern Methodist minister in Newport,
Kentucky (opposite Cincinnati), reciprocated the hostility. On one
Sabbath he decorated his church with United States flags and brass
eagles, and led the congregation in singing "The Star-Spangled
Banner," "The Red, White, and Blue," and "Hail, Columbia." He
prayed that God would preserve the Union, "even though blood
may come out of the wine-press even unto the horses' bridles" (Rev.
14:20). In his sermon he said:

> I trust our troops will rally and wipe out the disgrace of Manassas,
> though it cost the life of every rebel under arms. Let Davis and
> Beauregard be captured to meet the fate of Haman [Esther 7].
> Hang them up on Mason and Dixon's Line, that traitors . . . may
> be warned. Let them hang until the vultures shall eat their rotten
> flesh from their bones; let them hang until the crows shall build
> their filthy nests in their skeletons; let them hang until the rope
> rots, and let their dismembered bones fall *so deep into the earth that
> God Almighty can't find them on the day of resurrection.*[51]

It must not be forgotten that the all-transcending provocation
of the denominational schisms, as of the Civil War itself, was slavery and the giant contradiction it presented to the most basic of
American values. It was the consuming controversy over slavery that
rent much of the Christian community, and it was a sectional Christianity that exacerbated the national struggle over slavery. The

---

[51]Moore, *Rebellion Record*, 3:P-13, 4:P-22.

churches were critical agents in a reciprocal process of cumulating alienation. In the onrushing tragedy, it became evident that evangelical Protestantism, a powerful cultural force in both sections, had been turned to the purposes of regional identity and defense, that equally earnest expositors could draw from the same scriptures diametrically opposite conclusions about the most distinctive feature of the Southern way of life, and that the common faith that had once undergirded national unity had itself become an instrument of division.

This might lead one to ask legitimately whether the nonseparating churches—those communions that did not divide until political rupture made it expedient if not inevitable—exerted any countervailing influence in the increasing polarization of the United States. The answer is simply that since 82 percent of all churches in the eleven states that formed the Confederacy were either Methodist or Baptist, no other church embraced a national constituency numerous enough to make much difference one way or the other. The churches that remained united until forced apart by political secession and war simply avoided all discussion of the inflammatory issue of slavery.

The Protestant Episcopal Church maintained an official neutrality and avoided schism until 1861, although there were several articulate activists on both sides of the slavery dispute. The Roman Catholic Church did likewise; in the decrees and pastoral letter issued from its first Plenary Council (Baltimore, 1852), there was no reference whatsoever to slavery, abolition, or the sectional controversy. The chief periodical of Lutherans, *The Lutheran Observer*, assured its readers that they need not "fear that we are going to agitate the turbid and muddy stream of abolition or slavery."[52] In each of these communions the paramount aim was to prevent ecclesiastical disturbance, and this strategy was successful until political breakdown and war forced a temporary sectional division.

The Disciples of Christ embraced both abolitionists and defenders of slavery, with a large body of moderates "who united around the central conviction that the slavery question ought not

---

[52]Quoted in Chester F. Dunham, *The Attitude of the Northern Clergy Toward the South, 1860-1865* (Toledo, 1942) 23.

to disturb the unity of the church." Northern abolitionists bolted the fellowship in the late 1850s, but the Disciples' center of strength was in the critical border states, where their churches held together by virtue of their decentralized polity and Alexander Campbell's teaching that "one's opinion on slavery was a matter of 'opinion' rather than 'faith' and should not become a test of Christian fellowship."[53]

The Old School Presbyterian Church was the most significant national Protestant organization to avoid division prior to 1861. Before the whole country broke apart, Cyrus McCormick thought that the Presbyterian church and the Democratic party, to both of which he belonged, were "the two hoops which hold the Union together." After the General Assembly expelled the New School presbyteries in 1837, the Old School was able to retain its Southern members by suppressing the few remaining abolitionist voices. Its official position was that slavery was an acceptable part of Southern society and should be regulated only by civil law.

George Lewis, a minister of the (Presbyterian) Free Church of Scotland visiting the General Assembly at Louisville in 1844, was distressed when the commissioners rejected an overture from some of the free-state presbyteries to take up the question of slavery. The Southern members, Lewis reported, threatened to hold a caucus to plan their withdrawal; "one of them, the most popular preacher in the slave States, declared privately to a friend, that if slavery were abolished he would go to Texas." Lewis spoke privately with a prominent Northern minister and asked him whether the state governments, in forbidding churches to teach slaves to read, did not "interfere with your liberties as a Church of Christ." The minister admitted as much but added lamely, "we cannot presently help ourselves." Lewis reminded him that he had "the duty of teaching the negro how to obey the command, 'Search the Scriptures!' The Government has plainly invaded your province as a Church. . . . In the sight of God and all good men, you are called to tell the civil power to go back to its own place." The minister replied:

---

[53]David E. Harrell, *Quest for a Christian America: The Disciples of Christ to 1866* (Nashville, 1966) 126-38; William E. Tucker and Lester G. McAllister, *Journey in Faith: A History of the Christian Church (Disciples of Christ)* (St. Louis, 1975) 191.

> At present we must be content to acquit our consciences by dis-
> obeying privately, and doing our duty as it were in a corner. . . .
> The Assembly is not itself prepared for speaking out. Our people
> are still less prepared, and our hearts are terrified by the conse-
> quences of a separation from the churches of the South, and the
> breaking up of the Union.[54]

The only substantive pronouncement coming from the Old
School Assembly was a statement in 1845 that slavery was biblically
sanctioned and that the means of grace should be extended to the
slaves; masters were exhorted to treat them according to the Golden
Rule. To declare slaveholding in itself a sin and thus a part of ecclesiastical discipline, the Assembly declared, would virtually require the church to dissolve itself. The Southern part of the church
would surely separate, "a result which every good citizen must deplore as tending to the dissolution of the union of our beloved
country, and which every enlightened Christian will oppose as
bringing about a ruinous and unnecessary schism between brethren who maintain a common faith."[55]

Having once again forestalled controversy by what one observer called "boundless concessions to the South for the sake of
denominational unity," the Old School kept an uneasy peace until
1861, when the secession movement prompted the Northern majority to declare support for the Union, which in turn provoked the
Southerners to withdraw. At the General Assembly in that critical
year, Charles Hodge, whose loyalty to the Union and to the church
never wavered, noted apprehensively that all other nationwide denominations had sundered and "we alone retain, this day, the proportions of a National Church." But unwilling as he was to "sever
this last bond which holds the North and South together in the fellowship of the Gospel," he could not escape the dilemma that over-

---

[54]George Lewis, *Impressions of America and the American Churches* (Edinburgh,
1848; rpt. New York, 1968) 297-98.

[55]*A Collection of the Acts, Deliverances, and Testimonies of the Supreme Judicatory of
the Presbyterian Church*, ed. Samuel J. Baird (Philadelphia, 1855) 824. Commonly
called *Assembly Digest*, this collection followed the Old School after 1837. See also
*Watchman of the South* (Richmond), 29 May 1845.

took those who had hoped that suppression of the slavery issue would preserve the ecclesiastical peace.[56]

The same policy of silence was pursued by the Methodist Episcopal Church in its desperate attempt after 1844 to prevent the border conferences in Maryland, Virginia, Kentucky, and Missouri from following their fellow slaveholders into the Southern church. Northern Methodism, even after the loss of thirteen Southern conferences, was still the largest Protestant denomination in the United States. According to Robert D. Clark, it remained "the church which most effectively bound together the border and the North." But that bond was extremely tenuous.

> Abolitionists feared that further concession to the slave power would doom the moral stature of both nation and church. Border Methodists foresaw a struggle which could devastate their area worst of all. And conservative leaders became all the more concerned to suppress controversy for the sake of both church and nation. To them, national unity and church unity now went hand in hand, and it was their patriotic as well as Christian duty to calm the storm and prevent the controversy from reaching destructive proportions.

The *Christian Advocate and Journal* (New York), which still had a sizable circulation in Virginia and Maryland, spoke very cautiously, warning that any agitation would bring about another division of the Methodist church and probably of the nation as well. John P. Durbin, who had voted with the majority against Bishop Andrew in 1844 and was now denominational Missions Secretary, published in 1856 an open letter advising that the best way to end slavery would be to keep slaveholders in the church and try to influence them to favor emancipation. But the *Northwestern Christian Advocate* (Chicago) retorted: "Our fathers hoped to hasten [slavery's] extirpation in the country by proscribing it in the church. And it is what the church of today must do if she wishes to do her duty."[57]

---

[56]"The Assembly in Philadelphia," *American Presbyterian*, 23 May 1861; *New York Evangelist*, 30 May 1861; *Philadelphia Presbyterian*, 25 May 1861. Cf. Vander Velde, *The Presbyterian Churches and the Federal Union*, 54-75.

[57]Robert D. Clark, "Methodist Debates and Union Sentiment on the Border, 1860-1861," in *Antislavery and Disunion*, 153; Ralph A. Keller, "Methodist Newspapers and the Fugitive Slave Law," *Church History*, 43 (1974): 321; *Christian Advocate and Journal*, 9 January 1851, 6; Richard M. Cameron, *Methodism and Society in Historical Perspective* (Nashville, 1961) 180.

In response to insistent demands from antislavery Methodists, the Northern General Conference of 1860 extended its proscription from slavetrading to slaveholding—and then added an ambiguous admonition that led to uncertainty as to whether the new chapter was advisory or statutory. In any event, mildness of interpretation and lack of enforcement allowed the church to avoid schism while it nurtured Union sentiment in the border states. But it did little for the moral stance of the church in regard to slavery, which illustrates again the painful quandary of all the churches. To say nothing about slavery would alienate abolitionist members and leave the slaves to the questionable mercy of their masters; to condemn the system on moral grounds would drive out Southerners and their sympathizers and invite civil disaster without promising any guaranteed benefit to the slaves.

Thus churches that retained any relationship with Southerners simply acquiesced in the South's refusal to permit any discussion of slavery. A growing fear of insurrection and resentment of abolitionism which began in the 1820s had combined to create in the South a social pathology that effectively eliminated criticism and bound the region's molders of public opinion to a monothematic dirge in support of the peculiar institution and its basic purpose of racial separation and control. In such a situation most ecclesiocrats either parroted a party line or tried to maintain a discreet silence. A modern historian shrewdly related this unhappy situation to the operation of the voluntary principle:

> These divisions within the churches reflected the fundamental dilemma of broadly representative denominations within a free society. On controversial issues, these bodies could move neither too far ahead nor lag too far behind their constituencies lest disaffected minorities secede. In a time of general agreement, the problem might be minimal, but in an era of contradictory commitments, unity could be purchased only by moral platitudes and purity by schism. The inability of Protestants to agree whether the American promise was a sacred polity to be preserved or a higher law to be obeyed represented the impotence of moral suasion in face of the crisis besetting the nation.[58]

---

[58]Moorhead, *American Apocalypse*, 16.

The same dilemma, of course, impaled the major political parties, which also dared not alienate proslavery interests in the South or racist supporters in the North. As the churches' scenario for secession had portended, the political controversy over slavery caused party allegiances to divide ominously along sectional lines. For the sake of unity, the political parties tried to suppress all discussion of slavery, just as the churches had. But political parties live or die not by moral suasion, but by how well they can balance competing interests. It is—or should be—otherwise with churches.

"The impotence of moral suasion." To unpack that phrase is to reach the heart of the matter in probing the churches' role in the crisis of the Union.

# CHAPTER FIVE

# A FAILURE
# OF LEADERSHIP

Peter Fontaine, an Anglican rector in colonial Virginia, concluded early that slavery was "the original sin and curse of the country."[1] Similar language surfaced occasionally in congressional debates over slavery, as in the speech of Representative John W. Taylor of New York. Opposing the introduction of slavery into Missouri, Taylor exclaimed in 1819: "How often have [the advocates of slavery] disclaimed the guilt and shame of that original sin, and thrown it back upon their ancestors!"[2]

It is indeed tempting to think of the system of human bondage as the "original sin" of the American nation, but suggestive as such language may be, it belongs to the realm of theological affirmations that lie beyond the reach of historical method either to sustain or refute. Whether or not Fontaine and Taylor were correct *coram deo*, it does seem clear that slavery was a "curse" to the extent that its miasma of evil infected all of America's institutions, compromised its most fundamental values, and jeopardized its aspirations

---

[1]Quoted in David Brion Davis, *The Problem of Slavery in Western Culture* (Ithaca, 1966) 143.

[2]*Annals of Congress*, 15th Congress, 2d Session (February 1819) 1174.

as a "redeemer nation." Most telling, perhaps, is the fact that none of America's major Christian churches was able to deal redemptively with the issue, even within its own ranks. Yet the uncomfortable feeling persisted in many quarters that the churches, as moral interpreters and guides seeking to realize America's destiny as a free Christian republic, should be able to do something to eradicate the monstrous evil in their midst.

The churches and their leaders did not lack for critics of their temporizing on the moral anomaly of slavery. As early as 1816 George Bourne, an English immigrant who was to exert a profound influence on William Lloyd Garrison, wrote in *The Book and Slavery Irreconcilable* that "every man who holds Slaves and who pretends to be a Christian or a Republican, is either an incurable Idiot who cannot distinguish good from evil, or an obdurate sinner who resolutely defies every social, moral, and divine requisition." In Bourne's judgment,

> the most obdurate adherents of Slavery are Preachers of the Gospel and Officers and Members of the church. . . . Had this compound of all corruption no connection with the church of Christ . . . the redress of the evil would have been committed. But *Slavery* is the *golden Calf*, which has been elevated among the Tribes, and before it, the Priests and the Elders and the *nominal* sons of Israel, *eat, drink, rise up to play, worship and sacrifice.*

Harriet Martineau, who during her travels in the United States (1836) identified readily with the abolitionist movement, arrived at the same conclusion. "The most guilty class of the community in regard to the slavery question at present," she wrote, "is not the slaveholding, nor even the mercantile, but the clerical." It shocked her to hear the Southern clergy "boasting at public meetings, that there was not a periodical south of the Potomac which did not advocate slavery." She castigated such clergy as being the "rearguards of society."[3]

Beriah Green preached to New York Presbyterians in 1836 that judgment had to begin at the house of God: unless the church

---

[3]George Bourne, *The Book and Slavery Irreconcilable* (Philadelphia, 1816) 1, 8, 18-19; Harriet Martineau, *Society in America,* 2 vols. (London, 1837) 2:320, 356-57.

turned "back from the grave of infamy, which is even now yawn-ing, impatient to swallow its prey," it would perish. And the church was not alone—"the republic must rot with her in the same dishon-ored tomb!"[4] James G. Birney, ex-slaveholder turned abolitionist, drove home the charge in 1840 with a widely circulated pamphlet entitled *The American Churches the Bulwarks of American Slavery*, which made its point merely by quoting extensively from leading minis-ters and church resolutions, both Northern and Southern, as well as from professedly Christian slaveowners and nonslaveowners, all defending slavery as biblically approved and socially acceptable.[5]

Stephen S. Foster became so disillusioned with the churches be-cause of their refusal to condemn slavery as immoral that he for-sook divinity studies and became an active abolitionist. In 1843 he blasted church and clergy generally as a "brotherhood of thieves" that repelled every assault on "the bloody slave system." Their close identity with slavery, Foster declared, is proof of "their deep and unparalleled criminality . . . and is fully adequate to sustain the gravest charges, and to justify the most denunciatory language, that have ever fallen from the lips of their most inveterate opponents." The Methodist Episcopal Church in particular was "more corrupt and profligate than any house of ill fame in New York."[6]

Gerrit Smith charged the clergy with being "the most guilty and corrupting body of men in the land. . . . With comparatively few exceptions, they are unworthy and dangerous spiritual guides. It is not too much to say, that the minister who does not plead for God's poor is a minister of Satan, not of Jesus Christ."

George Lewis, a Scottish minister who visited the United States in 1844, suggested that the American churches should rid them-

---

[4]Beriah Green, *Things for Northern Men to Do; A Discourse Delivered Lord's Day Evening, July 17, 1836, in the Presbyterian Church, Whitesboro', N. Y.* (New York, 1836) 20, in *The Antislavery Argument*, ed. William H. Pease and Jane H. Pease (India-napolis, 1965) 182-91.

[5]The pamphlet was published originally in England as part of Birney's con-tribution to the London World Antislavery Conference; an American edition ap-peared in 1842.

[6]Stephen Symonds Foster, *The Brotherhood of Thieves; Or, A True Picture of the American Church and Clergy* (New London CT, 1843) 7, in Pease and Pease, *The Antislavery Argument*, 135-42. Foster's book, which went through five editions, pro-voked an uproar in the churches.

selves of slavery by the same tactic that earlier churches had employed against polygamy, namely proscription, beginning with church officials.

> Were the Churches of America, throughout the slave States, to take this step with office-bearers, and insist on all pastors being free from this sin, it were a most valuable declaration of their moral sentiments upon this great question, and a step of the most important character in the right direction—a step surely entirely competent for any Church to take without intruding into the province of the civil power.[7]

John Greenleaf Whittier cast aside all concern for literary polish and wrote fierce doggerel assailing the churches for supporting the Fugitive Slave Act. In "A Sabbath Scene" he depicted a minister interrupting divine worship to recapture a runaway slave girl who had come to implore the congregation for sanctuary:

> *I saw the parson tie the knots,*
> *The while his flock addressing,*
> *The Scriptural claims of slavery,*
> *With text on text impressing.*
>
> *"Although," said he, "on Sabbath day,*
> *All secular occupations*
> *Are deadly sins, we must*
> *Fulfill our obligations;*
>
> *And this commends itself as one*
> *To every conscience tender:*
> *As Paul sent back Onesimus,*
> *My Christian friends, we send her!"*[8]

No truth or mercy in *that* church, and Whittier was outraged.

Harriet Beecher Stowe, as recent scholarship has concluded, wrote from her conviction that the continuing existence of slavery was "largely the result of beliefs and actions stemming from the influence of the Presbyterian Church." William Lloyd Garrison, more

---

[7]*New York Observer,* 4 May 1844, 69; George Lewis, *Impressions of America and the American Churches* (Edinburgh, 1848; rpt. New York, 1968) 98.

[8]*Platform of the American Anti-Slavery Society and Its Auxiliaries* (New York, 1855) 34-35, printed in Pease and Pease, *The Antislavery Argument,* 124-28.

faithful to the libertarian heritage of his Baptist forebears than many of his contemporaries of that faith, kept insisting that "the vitality, the strength, the invulnerability of slavery are found in the prevailing religious sentiment" of the churches.

> More than half a million of slaves at the South are owned by ministers, office-bearers, and church members, who buy, sell, bequeath, inherit, mortgage, divide, and barter slave property, as they do any other portion of their personal or real estate. At the North, every section [of the church], desirous of national extension, can secure it only by acknowledging slaveholders as brethren in Christ. All the great, controlling ecclesiastical bodies and religious denominations in the land . . . are one in sentiment on the subject.[9]

Accusations of massive complicity in the whole system of human bondage naturally angered and alienated many church people. But some of them became convinced that despite hyperbole, the charges were essentially correct. Baron Stow, no radical (he was recording secretary of the Board of the Baptist General Convention), wrote privately in 1839 to a friend in London: "It would not be difficult to show that *the influence of the American Church is, at present, the main pillar of American slavery.*"[10] Several antislavery advocates asserted forthrightly that if the churches would quit supporting slavery, it would soon disappear. Albert Barnes, Presbyterian minister in Philadelphia, in 1845 publicly confessed the churches' dereliction to moral duty.

> Were all the ministers and members of the churches to do so simple a thing as the Society of Friends, after much toil and effort, have done, to remove from themselves the sin of slavery, and to stand before the world in the sublime and noble attitude of

---

[9]Theodore R. Hovet, "The Church Diseased: Harriet Beecher Stowe's Attack on the Presbyterian Church," *Journal of Presbyterian History,* 52 (1974): 172; William Lloyd Garrison, *The "Infidelity" of Abolitionism* (New York, 1860) 6, in Pease and Pease, *The Antislavery Argument,* 129.

[10]Baron Stow to W. H. Murch, 11 January 1839, printed in Arthur T. Foss and Edward Mathews, comps. *Facts for Baptist Churches* (Utica, 1850) 41. The letter was obtained by the Georgia *Christian Index,* which printed it on 12 February 1841; the exposure hardly improved attitudes toward the Boston Board among Baptists in the South.

having no connection whatever with the system, how soon would
the system come to an end! Could it be proclaimed throughout
the length and breadth of this land, as it can be of that society, that
no minister or member of any church is the owner of a slave, is
there a man who believes that the system could live? Would it not,
must it not, die?

The world could not uphold such a system, Barnes declared, "in the
face of a frowning church." This being the case, "on whom, then,
rests the responsibility of propagating this system from age to age?"
He reiterated the charge against the churches in a widely circulated
book first published in 1856, writing that "slavery could not be sustained in this land if it were not for the countenance, direct and in-
direct, of the churches." If the major denominations would emulate
the Quakers "and simply *detach* themselves from it, it is probable
that there is not power enough out of the church to sustain the system."[11]

But by the 1850s, it was too late. The Quakers had started firm-
ing up their opposition to slavery before the rise of the Cotton
Kingdom and were the only widely dispersed Christian body that
consistently exercised institutional discipline against all involvement with slavery.[12] The popular denominations, on the other
hand, had engaged in some early experiments in antislavery—
mainly verbal condemnation—but results were minimal. Presbyterians found the issue too divisive to handle above their regional
judicatories; Baptists had no authoritative denominational organizations to exercise control over the local churches; and Methodists quickly relaxed their early rules against slavery in response to
Southern objections. It followed that wherever a church would not
expel the evil from its own ranks, it could have little impact on slavery as a social institution.

The real problem was the perception on the part of the evangelicals that an antislavery church would necessarily remain a very

---

[11]*The Christian Reflector* (Boston), 24 April 1845; Albert Barnes, *The Church and
Slavery*, 2d ed. (Philadelphia, 1857) 28, 169.

[12]Cf. Lester B. Scherer, *Slavery and the Churches in Early America, 1619-1818*
(Grand Rapids, 1975) 69, 130. Albert Barnes had noted a few Scotch and German
churches that enforced antislavery regulations. Freewill Baptists, located mainly
in New England, also maintained a fairly consistent antislavery stance.

small church. Slaveholders made it known that they would more readily "part with their church privileges rather than with their slaves."[13] The churches persuaded themselves that their main mission was to "Christianize the nation" by multiplying converts, and their phenomenal success on this score seemed to justify the priority that placed "winning souls" above freeing slaves. But the soul-winning campaigns maintained their emotional momentum only by studious avoidance of all controversial issues. The churches' growth strategy depended on their not requiring converts to face the hard moral discipline demanded by Christian sensitivity to the evil of human bondage. So long as God seemed to smile on their zeal to bring in the unchurched, it was difficult to entertain any charge of fundamental wrongdoing. If slavery troubled a few sensitive spirits, its solution could still be delayed until a more convenient season.

Through their deliberate choice of expansion by evasion, the churches fatefully undermined whatever antislavery witness they might have had by consistently applying church discipline against slaveholding members. Every passing year found them entangled more inextricably with slavery, thus adding to the difficulty of dealing with the approaching conflict. When *Uncle Tom's Cabin* became as popular on stage as in book form, abolitionists noted wryly that "the theater became antislavery before many churches did."[14] Meanwhile, "the bondman's 250 years of unrequited toil" mounted inexorably into a debt that all the churches, along with the nation they were converting, would eventually have to pay. The moral anomaly was becoming so malignant as to threaten the very life of the body that sustained it.

It has been claimed that "revivalism and social reform" came to grips with slavery as a fundamental moral issue in American society, but this is far from clear. In Timothy L. Smith's well-known work there is a wistful passage arguing that leaders of the revival of 1858 "sought no escape from social responsibility" because they

[13]Rev. Benjamin Mills (a Kentucky Presbyterian) to the American Home Missionary Society, 1 June 1845, quoted in Walter Brownlow Posey, *Frontier Mission: A History of Religion West of the Southern Appalachians to 1861* (Lexington, 1966) 373.
[14]Ronald G. Walters, *American Reformers, 1815-1860* (New York, 1978) 96.

were "heirs of a tradition which judged sin even as it bore its cross."
Yet one must note that all controversial subjects were deliberately
excluded from the prayer meetings—the means by which revivals
spread—and that whatever "judgment" existed brought few slaveholders to the mourners' bench. By 1858 Southerners had long
since abandoned their earlier concessions that slavery was an evil
(though an inherited one in which Yankee traders shared complicity with Southern buyers) and were defending the slave system by
means of arguments derived from the same evangelical heritage as
the revival. Smith admitted that when the revivalists openly opposed slavery they were "heaping faggots on the fire of division,"
hardening Northern regionalism while wounding Southern pride.
And his further assertion that "the Awakening of 1858 appeared
to contemporaries to deepen the national soul-searching and so
pave the way to the election of Lincoln and the coming of the war"
seems tantamount to confessing that the revival was simply help-
less before the forces driving the nation to violence.[15] The social
import of the revival of 1858 in relation to the sectional conflict
needs much more probing by historians before plausible explanations can be advanced. On the face of things, one might think that
a fratricidal war in which Americans killed six hundred thousand
of their brothers marked a revival of the heritage of Cain rather than
of the religion of the Prince of Peace.

   The impotence of moral suasion is quite understandable in the
context of a "revival" that deliberately suppressed all discussion of
controversial issues. But there were many fervent soldiers in "the
evangelical warfare against slavery." Why did they persuade so few
of their coreligionists when, as it seems now, they were on the side
of the angels? One clue is in what George M. Marsden called "a
mentality attuned to finding moral absolutes." Whether the Northern evangelicals were confronting drunkards, Sabbath-breakers, or
slaveholders, for them each issue was a clear question of right or
wrong. In the absence of perceived ambiguities, no moderation was
necessary. "They lived in a world divided between Christ and Anti-
christ, the kingdom of God and the kingdom of Satan, the saved

---

[15]Timothy L. Smith, *Revivalism and Social Reform in Mid-Nineteenth-Century
America* (Nashville, 1957) 215-16, 223.

and the lost, and where conversions were sudden and radical. There was no middle ground."

Such an observation is confirmed by a passage in Daniel Webster's Seventh of March (1850) Speech, when he was decrying the schism in the Methodist Episcopal Church. After remarking that "religious disputes are apt to become warm in proportion to the strength of the convictions which men entertain of the magnitude of the questions at issue," Webster went on to declare:

> In all such disputes, there will sometimes be found men with whom every thing is absolute; absolutely wrong, or absolutely right. They see the right clearly; they think others ought so to see it, and they are disposed to establish a broad line of distinction between what is right and what is wrong. . . . [They] are ready to mark and guard [that line] by placing along it a series of dogmas, as lines of boundary on the earth's surface are marked by posts and stones.

Such an uncompromising dedication to purging all the sins of an entire nation led in inexorable steps to an all-out crusade. If public preachments against national sins failed to produce widespread repentance in the pattern made familiar by the evangelical revivals, the next step was legal coercion. If that failed, there remained only the wrath of God against sin—which easily translated into a holy war. Especially among the abolitionists, "immediatists sensed themselves involved in a cosmic drama, a righteous war to redeem a fallen nation. They now felt ready to make supreme sacrifices to prove their fitness in their new religion of antislavery."[16]

The mood of moral certainty among evangelicals masked a dearth of critical thinking, particularly about social systems, which in turn reflected the romantic mood of the whole period. John Higham pointed out that "the best thought of the period ran toward the aphoristic and prophetic. The age was uncongenial to analytical or systematic thinking." Revivalism, powerful as it was for producing a world of common experience, had created more a

---

[16]George M. Marsden, *The Evangelical Mind and the New School Presbyterian Experience: A Case Study of Thought and Theology in Nineteenth-Century America* (New Haven, 1970) 26; *The Works of Daniel Webster*, 16th ed., 6 vols. (Boston, 1872) 5:331-32; James Brewer Stewart, *Holy Warriors: The Abolitionists and American Slavery* (New York, 1976) 44.

union of hearts than of minds. It gave people sentimental visions but not realistic social strategies. Charles Francis Adams noted that the Boston Female Anti-Slavery Society, organized in 1832, held a single proposition: because slavery was "in direct violation of the laws of God," it ought to be abolished. But the well-meaning organizers had not the slightest idea of how to secure such an end other than condemning slaveholders as sinful. Rarely did they grapple even with the physical reality of the slave who was presumably their first concern.[17]

What rendered the churches vulnerable to sectionalism and dissolution, leaving them no more able than their unchurched contemporaries to eliminate slavery while saving both the Union and the peace, is that none of them had developed a comprehensive social ethic. Evangelical abolitionists may have been driven by an ethical vision, but they were poorly informed about the nature of social institutions and were therefore naive in devising strategies for dealing with systemic evil entrenched in social structures. Southern thinkers, on the other hand, were strongly committed to social order and strove mightily to convince themselves and others that slavery was ethically defensible. To oversimplify only slightly, Northern churches lacked a *social* ethic, Southern churches lacked a social *ethic*.

Sociology as a formal discipline, of course, was barely nascent. Indeed, the earliest attempt to formulate an American sociology was a labored apologia for the South's social system in the face of abolitionist attacks. The writings of Virginia's George Fitzhugh may be taken as typical of social thought in the antebellum South, although his work was more polemical than systematic. In *Sociology for the South*, published in Richmond in 1854, Fitzhugh apologized for using Auguste Comte's "newly-coined word," but explained that the "hundred open manifestations" of disease "lurking in the system of free society" now required doctors of society "to treat of its

---

[17]John Higham, *From Boundlessness to Consolidation: The Transformation of American Culture, 1848-1860* (Ann Arbor, 1969) 14-15; Pease and Pease, *The Antislavery Argument*, xxxvii-xxxviii.

complaints [and] propose remedies for their cure."[18] Fitzhugh's somewhat better known *Cannibals All! or, Slaves without Masters* (Richmond, 1857), whose subtitle refers to "wage slaves" in Northern industries, attacked the idea of a free economy based on notions of social contract and natural rights. Social order, he thought, must be grounded in Aristotle's theory of hierarchical classes. Thus Southern slavery was a positive good precisely because it provided a stable base for social hierarchy and thereby for social order. A modern scholar has observed that Fitzhugh's writings really "belong to the literature of slavery apologetics, for the 'sociology' is but incidental, being largely an attempt to erect an intellectual façade for the ante-bellum planter's regime."[19] Joseph LeConte, another pioneer Southern sociologist with similar purposes, adapted theories of natural science to a "growth-stage" theory of society that rejected reform (abolition) as interfering with the healthy development of the social "organism."[20]

Southern ministers had been thinking along these lines at least since 1822, when discovery of Denmark Vesey's plans for insurrection frightened whites into tightening their control over the slaves. In that year Richard Furman, pastor of Charleston's First Baptist Church, publicly addressed the governor of the state on behalf of South Carolina Baptists, expounding a biblical defense of slavery as a positive social good. Following Furman's lead, editors of Baptist periodicals in the South—ministers all—filled the columns of their papers with scriptural justifications of slavery.[21] By 1850 Ive-

---

[18]Harvey Wish, ed., *Antebellum: Writings of George Fitzhugh and Hinton Rowan Helper on Slavery* (New York, 1960) 45. Published the same year as Fitzhugh's *Sociology for the South* was Henry Hughes, *A Treatise on Sociology: Theoretical and Practical* (Philadelphia, 1854); cf. L. L. Bernard, "Henry Hughes, First American Sociologist," *Social Forces*, 15 (1936): 154-74.

[19]Harvey Wish, "George Frederick Holmes and the Genesis of American Sociology," *American Journal of Sociology*, 46 (1941): 698-707. Drew Gilpin Faust demonstrated that a "conservative organic view of social order" was implicit in the proslavery argument from the beginning; see *The Ideology of Slavery: Proslavery Thought in the Antebellum South, 1830-1860* (Baton Rouge, 1981) 9.

[20]See Theodore Dwight Bozeman, "Joseph LeConte: Organic Society and a 'Sociology for the South,' " *Journal of Southern History*, 39 (1973): 565-82.

[21]Richard Furman, *An Exposition of the Views of the Baptists Relative to the Col-*

son L. Brookes, another South Carolina Baptist minister, could combine arguments from scripture, sociology, and political theory to write *A Defence of the South Against the Reproaches and Encroachments of the North: in Which Slavery Is Shown to Be an Institution of God Intended to Form the Basis of the Best Social State and the Only Safeguard to the Permanency of a Republican Government*. Old School Presbyterians bolstered the Brookes-Furman-LeConte-Fitzhugh thesis by invoking the doctrine of predestination, whereby "God assigns to every man, by a wise and holy decree, the precise place he is to occupy in the great moral school of humanity."[22] Slaves were necessary not only as a system of labor but, in the expressive term of Senator James H. Hammond of South Carolina, as the indispensable "mud-sill of society and of political government."[23]

Examples like these could be multiplied indefinitely from a large body of literature produced in the Old South. One might even construct a "sociology of social theory" by noting the extent to which all of Southern society—its economy, political institutions, hierarchical stratification, and even its religious organizations—depended on the system of slavery for its structure and style.[24] The social theory articulated by such writers as those cited above was highly acceptable even to Southerners who owned no slaves because it furnished purportedly scientific justification for the values around which all Southern life was organized.

---

oured *Population of the United States, in a Communication to the Governor of South Carolina* (Charleston, 1823); Roger H. Crook, "The Ethical Example of the Editors of Baptist Journals Published in the Southeastern Region of the United States up to 1865" (Th.D. dissertation, Southern Baptist Theological Seminary, 1947); Stephen Paul Carleton, "Southern Church Leadership in the Emergence of Sectionalism and Schism, 1800-1850" (Ph.D. dissertation, University of Chicago, 1975).

[22][James Henley Thornwell?], "Address of the Presbyterian Church in the Confederate States of America" (1861), printed in *The Presbyterian Enterprise: Sources of American Presbyterian History,* ed. Maurice Whitman Armstrong et al. (Philadelphia, 1956) 216. Cf. also Theodore Dwight Bozeman, "Inductive and Deductive Politics: Science and Sociology in Antebellum Presbyterian Thought," *Journal of American History,* 64 (1977): 704-22.

[23]James H. Hammond, "Speech on the Admission of Kansas, under the Lecompton Constitution," U. S. Senate, 4 March 1858, in *Selections from the Letters and Speeches of the Hon. James H. Hammond of South Carolina* (New York, 1866) 318.

[24]Cf. Edmund S. Morgan, *American Slavery, American Freedom: The Ordeal of Colonial Virginia* (New York, 1975) ch. 18.

Antislavery evangelicals in the North rejected the "southern so-ciology," of course, but had little to offer in its place. Structural change as an approach to social reform was beyond their purview. Although Albert Barnes vigorously indicted the churches for not "detaching" themselves from slavery, he was unable to get much beyond individual action. "By prayer," he insisted, "by patience, by exhortation, by testimony, by the exercise of charity and forbear-ance mingled with Christian fidelity, by a growing conviction of the evil, by free discussion, by a deeper spirit of piety, the work [of emancipation] may be done,—done by each denomination for it-self; done by each family for itself; done by each individual for himself." The order of the admonitions is important. Barnes built his climax to the point of individual action, thus betraying the fact that he had scarcely escaped the romantic libertarianism of the post-Revolutionary generation that simply rejected any type of social or-ganicism as a violation of the autonomous individual.

A self-reliant individualism (Tocqueville invented the term and Emerson popularized it in the Age of Jackson) saw both the evils of slavery and their cure only in terms of individual actions. This atomistic view of society as an aggregate of individuals was a prod-uct of an Enlightenment that had given way to Romanticism and then fused with the evangelical revivals. Jefferson had needed no church at all, while Emerson and his anti-institutional followers were happy with "churches of two, churches of one." Methodists, the most vigorous church organizers in antebellum America, rarely ob-jected to large congregations but nonetheless sought social im-provement chiefly by means of individual piety. As Lois Banner put it, "the duty of the early Methodist was to perfect himself and to help others attain sanctification, not to engage in benevolence as a means of social improvement." Society would become Christian in proportion to the number of individuals pursuing Christian piety.[25]

It was Charles G. Finney who, more than anyone else, set the pattern of evangelical reformism, and his career affords some basic clues to the "impotence of moral suasion." Finney exalted individ-

---

[25]Barnes, *The Church and Slavery*, 166-67; Lois W. Banner, "Religious Benev-olence as Social Control: A Critique of an Interpretation," *Journal of American His-tory*, 60 (1973): 30.

ual piety over the organization and discipline of the Christian community. Insisting that the surest way to improve the social order was to secure the moral reform of individuals through the revivals, he taught converts to *"aim at being useful in the highest degree possible,"* to *"have moral courage,* and not to be afraid of going forward in duty." Whereas he wanted to "see what [converts] are willing to do for the education of ministers, for missions, for moral reform [such as temperance], for the slaves," he directed the overwhelming preponderance of Christian effort to "agonizing prayer for sinners . . . [and to] going about and pulling dying men out of the fire." Finney exemplified the "tendency among pietistic evangelicals to limit their horizon entirely to the regeneration of individuals and to deny or ignore the complexities of custom, prejudice, and sectional or class conflict that lie at the root of so much social injustice."[26]

To be sure, Finney attempted in the 1830s to exclude slaveholders from his Chatham Street Chapel in New York City, attended several meetings of the American Anti-slavery Society, and, as chairman of the 1839 anniversary of the Ohio Anti-slavery Society, introduced resolutions affirming the supremacy of God's law over human law. But by 1846 he began to think that it might be necessary to seek legislation to put away the "abominations" of "intemperance, licentiousness, slavery, etc." This was simply a change of strategy, not of fundamental social perception. As McLoughlin commented, "disappointed perfectionists often have a tendency to enact by force what they formerly thought could come about by spiritual means."[27] One might add that the tendency to resort to legislation also occurs in conjunction with the upward social mobility of successful denominations, particularly those with sectarian origins, as they begin to achieve social acceptance and the quasi-establishment status that goes with cultural dominance. Such groups

---

[26]Charles G. Finney, *Lectures on Revivals of Religion* (1835), ed. William G. McLoughlin (Cambridge MA, 1960) 404-405, 426, xliv.

[27]Ibid., li, n. 63. Charles C. Cole, *The Social Ideas of the Northern Evangelists* (New York, 1954) 204-11, offers a more favorable assessment of Finney's social strategy, arguing that Finney was committed to the "higher law" doctrine, that he wanted civil laws to be congruent with the higher law (for him, the Bible), and that in cases where they were not (for example, slavery sanctions) a Christian would be justified in disobeying them.

easily revert to a form of the state-church mentality that seeks to impose by legislation a morality that persuasion has failed to evoke.

But whether they resorted to legal coercion or not, antislavery evangelicals had great difficulty in coming to terms with the necessity of structural change as essential to social reform. For the most part, they were content to emphasize individual conversion as the most direct way to reach their goal of Christianizing the social order. But while this approach generated numerous reforming activities, it rarely disturbed basic social arrangements. How many people would have to be converted, or how long would it be before desirable social changes could become effective by such means? How would converts be instructed in the strategies for social change, and what were the mechanisms of structural reform? Nobody ever said. Before the Civil War (and long afterwards) evangelicals clung to the romantic vision that "when society is imbued with the spirit of Christianity, *it will come to order*—wrong and oppression of every kind, with all arbitrary and unnatural distinctions will be annihilated."[28]

Examples of such sociological innocence abound. Phoebe Palmer was not only a prominent revivalist in the holiness tradition; she was also one of the most vigorous pioneers in the evangelical attack on social evil. But as a recent biographer has concluded, she devoted her energies mainly to tract distribution and poverty relief, remaining "neutral on one great issue of her day, slavery. The other-worldly aspects of her consecration permitted compassion for the poor but not overt agitation for social change." The most aggressive abolitionists, though far from "neutral" on slavery, were equally unacquainted with the social mechanisms necessary to secure justice. James G. Birney instructed agents of the American Anti-slavery Society to "insist principally on the *sin of slavery*, because our main hope is in the consciences of men, and it requires little logic to prove that it is always safe to do right." William Adams, pastor of the Central Presbyterian Church in New York City, likewise urged would-be reformers to "begin, as God does, with

---

[28]*Christian Advocate and Journal* (New York), 5 July 1849, 106, quoted in James H. Moorhead, *American Apocalypse: Yankee Protestants and the Civil War, 1860-1869* (New Haven, 1978) 12.

the heart of the individual man; acquaint him with his destiny, and qualify him for it; and you may leave all other questions to an easy, natural, and inevitable solution." What social theory the antislavery evangelicals espoused never got beyond the notion that social evils were simply a compound of individual sins. The improvement of society, therefore, depended only on the conversion of a sufficient number of individual sinners.[29]

Lacking sociological comprehension, Northern evangelicals were trapped in an apparently insoluble conflict of values. Freeing the slaves, preserving the Union, and avoiding war became mutually exclusive goals. This defined a trilemma that impaled not only the ecclesiocrats but even the most astute politicians as well. Those who set a high value on freedom recognized the anomaly of slavery in a free republic and thus wanted to see Afro-Americans emancipated—even though few such people had any desire to see liberated blacks enter American society on equal terms with whites.[30] At the same time, devotion to the Union was so strong as to evoke a response sometimes designated, accurately enough, as religious. Those who regarded the Union as the chief bulwark of freedom, even the "last, best hope of earth," were thus caught in a tragic quandary. To call for emancipation was to provoke a reaction in the South that imperiled the Union, and to endanger the Union was clearly to risk civil war. More than a few Northerners declared that a Union that continued to tolerate slavery was not worth saving, while aroused Southerners volunteered their last ounce of blood and treasure to maintain the slavocracy—in the Union if possible, out of it if necessary. What made the conflict seem irrepressible was

---

[29]Henry W. Bowden, *Dictionary of American Religious Biography* (Westport CT, 1977) 350; Dwight L. Dumond, *Antislavery Origins of the Civil War* (Ann Arbor, 1959) 35; William Adams, *Christianity and Civil Government* (New York, 1851) 28. Cf. John L. Thomas, "Romantic Reform in America," *American Quarterly,* 17 (1965): 658-59.

[30]On racism among antislavery advocates, see George M. Frederickson, *The Black Image in the White Mind: The Debate on Afro-American Character and Destiny, 1817-1914* (New York, 1971); Leon F. Litwack, *North of Slavery: The Negro in the Free States, 1790-1860* (Chicago, 1961); Eugene H. Berwanger, *The Frontier Against Slavery: Western Anti-Negro Prejudice and the Slavery Extension Controversy* (Urbana, 1967); and V. Jacques Voegli, *Free but Not Equal: The Midwest and the Negro During the Civil War* (Chicago, 1967).

that no one seemed to know precisely how to free the slaves and at the same time preserve the Union without war. It was this cloud of unknowing that came between Northern and Southern churches in the 1840s, darkened their counsel, divided their ranks, and finally engulfed the whole nation in 1861.

Thus, in the period when American society was breaking apart, the churches found themselves unable to exercise effective leadership for the sake of social health and wholeness. Confronted with the glowering problem of slavery, revivalists were interested primarily in individual conversions, reformers naively urged pietistic solutions, independent Southerners set up a cry of *laissez nous faire,* and ecclesiocrats purchased a tenuous tranquillity by refusing to deal with the issue at all. The ethically sensitive urged at most a form of *charity,* but few called for systemic *justice.* That would have required fundamental changes in the institutional structure of American society, and no one could envision precisely what such changes might entail. The main churchly opposition to slavery came from Northern evangelicals, whose only strategies were to renounce personal complicity with the evil, resist its expansion into the territories and new states, and refuse to obey the Fugitive Slave Law. If such measures failed, the only recourse was to await Armageddon—or hurry it on.

Blanket indictments of this sort invariably invite a search for exceptions, and properly so. In the present instance, to be sure, there were a few, though their impact on nationwide, or even churchwide, thought seems to have been negligible. Horace Bushnell, who based his opposition to revivalism on convictions about the solidarity of the family, had little difficulty conceiving of the nation as a "family," a transcendent reality above the individuals who composed it. But Bushnell never constructed a truly *social* ethic on the basis of this concept. Ronald G. Walters turned up a handful of New England communitarians who announced their determination to "stay amid the great community [of the world], destitute of [church] communion, as it is, and go for *communitizing* the whole [nation]" by breaking down slavery and other destroyers of human community. There was also the case of Orange Scott, a Methodist evangelist in New England whom Donald G. Mathews called a "revolutionary" because Scott opposed both the romantic individualism of other evangelicals and the anarchical theories of the radical Garrisonians, seeking instead structural change through established social processes. For a brief period, Scott sought to bring justice to the slaves through a repentant electorate; if voters would "repent and do right," they could install a government instructed to overturn the legislative sanctions of slavery. But Scott soon became disillusioned with governmental institutions and called instead for the North to purge itself of the slaveholding states, in effect joining the radicals who regarded the Union as not worth saving.[31]

Another tentative effort to reach beyond romantic notions of immediacy and individualism was made by George Cole, a moderate Baptist, in the editorial columns of the *Cross and Journal* (Cincinnati) during the winter of 1846-1847. The sin and guilt of slavery, Cole argued, rested on the whole nation, since the North had been involved in the slave trade and continued to profit from the slave-dependent plantation economy of the South. But even though the system was morally wrong—and the South should be willing to admit it—no solution to the problem could come simply by denouncing the South. Cole suggested that a group of prominent Southerners who could admit the immorality of slavery should meet with a similar group from the North who could accept slaveholders as Christians; together they should draft a plan for gradual emancipation that would include some compensation for slaveholders and also distribute the costs so that all citizens might share in the sacrifices that would have to be made. Cole's proposal obviously had its own share of naive assumptions, particularly in minimizing the racial feelings involved, to say nothing of the difficulty of evoking a widespread willingness to sacrifice for a noble cause. But there was truth in his warning that "if slavery is ever abolished short of revolutions and bloodshed we believe that those who are willing to make some sacrifice will have the honor of the deed."[32]

---

[31]Walters, *American Reformers*, 77; Donald G. Mathews, "Orange Scott: The Methodist Evangelist as Revolutionary," in *The Antislavery Vanguard: New Essays on the Abolitionists*, ed. Martin Duberman (Princeton, 1965) 71-101.

[32]Cole's series of editorials appeared in the *Cross and Journal* from 27 November 1846 to 12 March 1847; they are summarized in Wesley Norton, *Religious Newspapers of the Old Northwest to 1861: A History, Bibliography, and Record of Opinion* (Athens OH, 1977) 120.

A hint of organicist thinking came belatedly from the editor of *Harper's Magazine* just as Lincoln was being inaugurated. Southern secessionists and Northern abolitionists, the editor wrote, were both doctrinaire groups who "persist in treating us as if we were got up by some chemical formula, and could be made and unmade at pleasure, instead of being a living body, with living antecedents and consequents." The division of the churches, he went on, had made many think that "the body of Christ is a nonentity, and Christianity is only a personal opinion." The same fuzzy thinking is now dividing the nation, as if "our nationality is little more than a bundle of ideas" and which of these is right must be settled by a contest of force. "[You might] as well say that a man's family is a bundle of opinions," the writer concluded, "and instead of cherishing the welfare of the household as a solid, vital fact, the great thing were to agitate it with discussions on the rights of parents and children, and let love starve itself out in the eternal war of words."[33] But his admonition came too late to do much good; the war of words was about to give way to a contest of cannon and muskets.

Probably the outstanding exemplar of organicism in the period was Edward Beecher, son of Lyman and president (1830-1844) of Illinois College. In the aftermath of the Alton riots in which editor Elijah P. Lovejoy was murdered, he denounced as fatuous the notion that "this age of the world needs nothing but the preaching of the gospel." Beecher was practically alone in antebellum America in speaking of "organic sin," an idea he expounded in a series of twelve articles in the Boston *Recorder* in 1845. Rebuking abolitionists who condemned individual slaveholders as sinners and who demanded emancipation without regard for the legal and social system in which slavery was enmeshed, Beecher argued that organic sin was not the wrongdoing of individuals but of the whole society; the "body politic" was the "great, omnipresent slaveholder." By this he meant even more than his father's catchword, "national sin," could convey. "If the organization of THE BODY POLITIC creates false and sinful *Permanent relations* between the individuals who compose the body politic, that . . . is an organic sin."

---

[33]"The End and the Beginning," *Harper's Magazine*, 22 (March 1861): 554.

In another context Beecher flew his evangelical colors by preaching that "SUPREME DEVOTEDNESS TO GOD" was the indispensable state of mind "which if first produced will secure all else." He proceeded to insist that the task of Christians was

> not merely to fill the earth with the knowledge of the Lord, not merely to preach the gospel to every creature, but to reorganize human society in accordance with the law of God. To abolish all corruptions in religion, and all abuses in the social system, and, so far as it has been erected on false principles, to take it down and erect it anew.[34]

There was more than a little romanticism in this position, of course, for Beecher made few concrete suggestions as to strategy. But not many evangelicals were listening anyway, and few of those understood even the tentative clues to social alternatives that he provided. The popular churches were simply unprepared to deal with slavery as a social institution; they had not developed an ethical stance that could help them perceive what would be necessary to uproot it from American society. Antislavery evangelicals were undoubtedly sincere in their wish to better the lot of the slaves, but their naiveté about social reality left them poorly equipped to come to grips with the complexity of slavery as a system deeply embedded in American history and life.[35]

That antebellum reformism—especially abolitionism—was overwhelmingly individualistic and atomistic is now an axiom of historical writing about the subject. Eric Foner observed that "historians as diverse in their ideological preconceptions as Stanley Elkins and William Appleman Williams severely chide the abolitionists for viewing slavery not as a functioning institution, embedded in a distinct society, but as a personal sin of the individual master

---

[34]Edward Beecher, *Narrative of the Riots at Alton, in Connection with the Death of the Rev. Elijah P. Lovejoy* (Alton IL, 1838) 156; Robert Meredith, *The Politics of the Universe: Edward Beecher, Abolitionism, and Orthodoxy* (Nashville, 1963) 113; Edward Beecher, "The Nature, Importance, and Means of Eminent Holiness Throughout the Church," in *The American National Preacher*, 10 (1835): 194.

[35]Cf. Moorhead, *American Apocalypse,* 125. Failure to deal adequately with the romantic individualism of the abolitionists is a serious flaw in John R. McKivigan's otherwise impressive work, *The War Against Proslavery Religion: Abolitionism and the Northern Churches, 1830-1865* (Ithaca, 1984).

against the individual slave." Both Elkins and Williams noted that the faith of the evangelical churches was captive to the prevailing romanticism of the time. Pointing as it did to the perfectibility of individual men and women, such faith was essentially anti-institutional and to that extent it nullified the *social* thrust of reform. As Williams put it, the revivalists "took the evangelical fervor of Hopkins and Edwards but abandoned their corporate ethic in favor of individualized religion." Elkins added that "religious vitality everywhere was overwhelming, but that vitality lay primarily in demands for individual satisfaction which took inevitable and repeated priority over institutional needs." Even the definition of sin, which is crucial to a people's sense of social responsibility, has historically been remanded in America to the individual, or worse, to itinerant preachers whose popularity rested on condemning immoralities that their hearers rarely committed.[36]

In a similar vein, David Potter viewed much of the abolitionist rhetoric as "unrewarding" simply because it regularly connected slavery with sin and emancipation with virtue but had no recommendation as to what the United States ought to do about slavery as a social system. The most enlightened discussion of the problem, Potter suggested, came not from any ecclesiastical figure but from Abraham Lincoln, who in debating with Stephen A. Douglas in 1858 "provided part of the American public with an overarching discussion of the real problems of slavery in American society—a discussion such as all the moralists in the abolition crusade and all the constitutional lawyers had not supplied." David Brion Davis also discerned "a wide gap between the abstract proposition that slavery was wrong, or even criminal, and the cautious formulation of antislavery policy." He as much as Potter decried the anti-institutional nature of evangelical abolitionism because it was an "essentially romantic" outlook that trusted "the innate moral capacities of the individual" and paid little attention to social structures and controls.

---

[36]Eric Foner, "The Causes of the American Civil War: Recent Interpretations and New Directions," *Civil War History,* 20 (1974): 205; William A. Williams, *The Contours of American History* (Cleveland, 1961) 251-52; Stanley M. Elkins, *Slavery: A Problem in American Institutional and Intellectual Life,* 2d ed. (Chicago, 1968) 28, 162 (see also the wider discussion on 140-206).

Thus abolitionist advocacy was largely ineffective, except to inspire the zeal that transformed a sectional conflict into a cosmic drama and escalated a fratricidal war into a holy crusade to redeem a fallen nation.[37]

Anyone who doubts the predominantly romantic character of white evangelicalism in the antebellum years should compare it with black religion of the same period. The latter was also fervently evangelical but was almost totally free from naive assumptions about the goodness and perfectibility of human nature. To the common condemnation of individual immorality, blacks added God's retributive justice against exploitation and oppression. Slavery was "the work of Satan," destined to be overcome as decisively and dramatically as God had delivered the Hebrews from Egyptian bondage. In the community of faith, moreover, God's purpose was to reunify a humanity fragmented by sin. A favorite text for the slaves was 1 Corinthians 12:13: "For by one Spirit we were all baptized into one body—Jews or Greeks, slaves or free—and all were made to drink of one Spirit." On the basis of such convictions, Christian slaves could sing:

> Am I not a man and a brother?
> Ought I not then to be free?
> Sell me not one to another.
> Take not thus my liberty.
> Christ, our Savior,
> Died for me as well as thee.[38]

Though they possessed no more sophisticated understanding of institutional realities than their would-be liberators, slaves fashioned from the experience of oppression a universalistic concept of liberation, justice, and community that escaped most white Christians of the period.

The Southern white churches, despite their efforts to construct a social theory in defense of slavocracy, operated with an understanding of social improvement much like that of their Northern

---

[37]David M. Potter, *The Impending Crisis, 1848-1861* (New York, 1976) 331-32, 355; David Brion Davis, "The Emergence of Immediatism in British and American Antislavery Thought," *Mississippi Valley Historical Review,* 49 (1962): 214, 229.

[38]*The Anti-Slavery Harp* (Boston, 1848) 10.

counterparts. They assumed that converted people became genuinely good, and this goodness was defined in terms of individual virtue rather than of abstractions like "equity" and "justice." A sufficient number of converts, it was assumed, would progressively rid society of all its evils, while masters could discharge their responsibility to slaves by providing religious instruction and treating them with kindness—which remained at best paternalistic and patronizing.

A typical example of this approach is John Holt Rice, founder of Richmond's First Presbyterian Church in 1812 and a leading voice of Southern Presbyterianism until his death in 1831. From his professorship in the newly established Union Theological Seminary, he wrote in 1827: "I am most fully convinced that slavery is the greatest evil in our country, except whiskey; and it is my ardent prayer that we may be delivered from it." Yet the church and its ministers must not interfere with slavery, for "there is nothing in the New Testament which obliges them to take hold of this subject directly." Rather, Rice advised, the church should confine itself to making good Christians.

> While we go on minding our own business, and endeavouring to make as many good christians as possible among masters and servants, let the subject of slavery be discussed in the political papers . . . as a question of political economy. Keep it entirely free from all ecclesiastical connexions . . . and treat it as a matter of state concernment. . . . Considerations of this sort, combined with the benevolent feelings growing out of a gradual, uninterrupted progress of religion, will, I believe, set the people of their own accord to seek deliverance. They will foresee the necessity of a change; soon begin to prepare for it; and it will come about without violence or convulsion.

Further, Rice feared that any ecclesiastical opposition to slavery would be counterproductive; people would "determine that the clergy shall not interfere in their secular interests, and their rights of property," and they would turn their backs on the church. To avoid such rejection, the church should address itself only to "spiritual" concerns.[39]

---

[39]John H. Rice to William Maxwell, 24 February 1827, in William Maxwell, *A Memoir of the Rev. John H. Rice* (Philadelphia, 1835) 306-308, 312-13.

With few exceptions, all Southern evangelicals agreed with this position. The only way a Christian could affect the world, they felt, was to renounce it. The first priority was to believe in Christ, the second to show one's love for God in a life of prayer and self-discipline; then one should persuade others to do the same. Churches composed of such people convinced themselves that their chief—nay, only—business was to save souls. They simply had no way, either in their theological framework or social perception, to address a deeply rooted social institution such as slavery.

More than one scholar has concluded that it was precisely the inability of the churches to do anything about eradicating slavery, no matter how uneasy their consciences may have been about the immorality of it, that confirmed their feeling of helplessness toward all social reforms demanding any kind of structural change. As Donald G. Mathews put it, "The bold, often quixotic confrontation with slavery [which occurred briefly in the Southern churches before the rise of the Cotton Kingdom] settled once and for all the problem of whether or not the moral struggle of the Christian would be carried on in the world of power and traditional relationships or within the mind and psychology of the individual believer." They concluded that the fight with evil was always an individual battle against individual sins. Converts were taught to strive for mastery of their own lives; beyond that, they received no guidance on how their religious commitments could affect social roles that were defined by race, sex, or power. By casting morality in purely individualistic terms, therefore, Southern evangelicals placed the institution of slavery beyond the reach of Christian social concern and their society beyond the pale of Christian action. Slavery was, in their insistent refrain, "purely a civil matter," and their refusal to confront it as a moral issue prevented them from ever learning the full extent of their moral responsibility in and for the whole society.[40]

This assertion suggests a further dimension of the social ethical failure of the antebellum churches. Their individualistic perspective, North and South, was consonant with prevalent notions about

---

[40]Donald G. Mathews, *Religion in the Old South* (Chicago, 1977) 77-78.

what has come to be called "the spirituality of the church." The phrase was especially popular with Old School Presbyterians and became a "distinctive" of the Southern wing of that denomination.[41] The concept, as they formulated it in 1845, runs as follows: "The church of Christ is a spiritual body, whose jurisdiction extends only to the religious faith and moral conduct of her members." The "moral conduct" with which the church should concern itself is limited to private behavior. Since slavery is exclusively a civil institution, the removal of which is within the power and competency of secular legislatures alone, it would be "peculiarly improper and inexpedient for this General Assembly to attempt, or propose measures on the work of emancipation."[42]

James Henley Thornwell, the most formidable voice of Southern Presbyterianism, elaborated further in 1861: Whether slavery exists or not "is a question which exclusively belongs to the State." The church has no right, duty, or competence to deal with it in any respect whatsoever.

> We have no right, as a Church, to enjoin it as a duty, or to condemn it as a sin. . . . The social, civil, political problems connected with this great subject transcend our sphere, as God has not entrusted to his Church the organization of society, the construction of Government, nor the allotment of individuals to their various stations.[43]

---

[41]See Ernest T. Thompson, *The Spirituality of the Church: A Distinctive Doctrine of the Presbyterian Church in the U. S.* (Richmond, 1961).

[42]General Assembly of the Old School Presbyterian Church, 1845, in *A Collection of the Acts, Deliverances, and Testimonies of the Supreme Judicatory of the Presbyterian Church,* ed. Samuel J. Baird (Philadelphia, 1855) 823-25.

[43]Address of the General Assembly of the Presbyterian Church in the Confederate States of America, 1861 (probably composed by James Henley Thornwell), in Armstrong, *Presbyterian Enterprise,* 214-15. See similar statements by Thornwell in Thompson, *Spirituality of the Church,* 24-25. Jack P. Maddex, "From Theocracy to Spirituality: The Southern Presbyterian Reversal on Church and State," *Journal of Presbyterian History,* 54 (1976): 438-57, has contested the "generally accepted premise" that Southern Presbyterians espoused the spirituality doctrine before the Civil War and that Thornwell was one of its major architects. His argument is based on highly selective evidence and ignores the fundamental philosophical presuppositions of Thornwell's social conservatism, which are ably expounded in Theodore Dwight Bozeman, "Science, Nature, and Society: A New Approach to James Henley Thornwell," *Journal of Presbyterian History,* 50 (1972): 307-25.

It is easy to see how this idea was inherently attractive to all evangelicals. Disestablishment in the Revolutionary period put all churches in the category of voluntary bodies of private individuals who join them because of personal needs and desires. A large portion of members came into the evangelical churches through revivalistic conversion in which they received salvation as a "spiritual" experience not necessarily related to the "material" world. Such people would naturally have very limited views of the church's role in society, and certainly few joiners would anticipate or intend a church-led assault on existing social arrangements. Before emancipation, such expectations made it easy for ecclesiastics of varying opinions about slavery, as part of their defensive reaction to abolitionism, to keep insisting that freeing the slaves was a question for the legislatures of the slaveholding states and not for the churches.

The Baptist General Committee of Virginia, for example, had acknowledged in 1785 that hereditary slavery was "contrary to the word of God" and resolved in 1790 to recommend the use of "every legal measure, to extirpate this horrid evil from the land." But local churches and regional associations bridled at such strong language and warned the General Committee not to interfere. In 1793 the committee consented lamely to relegate the slavery question entirely to the civil authorities.[44] When antislavery sentiment surfaced among Baptists in Kentucky, the Elkhorn Association resolved in 1805: "This Association Judges it improper for ministers Churches or Associations to meddle with emacipation [sic] from Slavery or any other political Subject and as such we advise ministers & Churches to have nothing to do therewith in their religious Capcities [sic]."[45]

The Baptists continued to reject social action as partisan politics. Typical of their attitude is an 1841 circular of the Executive

---

[44]See Reuben E. Alley, *A History of Baptists in Virginia* (Richmond, 1974) 124-27; and Smith, *In His Image, but,* 47-48. Only one congregation in the whole state (Black Rock Church) agreed with the General Committee that slavery was "unrighteous"; see James David Essig, "A Very Wintry Season: Virginia Baptists and Slavery, 1785-1797," *Virginia Magazine of History and Biography,* 88 (1980): 181.

[45]Document in William Warren Sweet, *Religion on the American Frontier: The Baptists, 1783-1830* (New York, 1931) 508.

Committee of the American Baptist Home Mission Society, based in New York City:

> The church has wisely and uniformly refused to furnish an armory for the secular conflicts of the times. When political opponents have struggled to proselyte or to subsidize the church, we believe it has been her policy, we are sure it has been her duty, to decline all knowledge of either party. Her prayers have gone up for the nation and its councils, its rulers, its union and its prosperity. But her members have been left individually to act upon the free impulse of their consciences, while the church as such, has turned to her own appropriate task, and, in the language of Nehemiah [6:3], replied to every appeal, "I am doing a great work, and I cannot come down."[46]

The statement was patently designed to disarm Southern suspicions about the intentions of the Home Mission Society in regard to slavery.

The strategy failed. When the Southern Baptist Convention was formed in 1845, its president, William B. Johnson, drafted an apologia for the organization. After rejoicing that the new denomination was now free "to promote slavery," Johnson declared that Southern Baptists were not organizing to promote "any form of human policy, or civil rights; but God's glory, and Messiah's increasing reign. . . . We will never interfere with *what is Caesar's*."[47] It is curious that Johnson should think that opposing slavery would be interfering in civil affairs, whereas promoting it would not be. His declaration that the Convention could now "promote slavery," moreover, seems an almost Freudian variant of the resolution of the 1844 General Missionary Convention that Baptists should be free to promote—outside the convention—their differing *views* about slavery.

---

[46]In Arthur T. Foss and Edward Mathews, comps., *Facts for Baptist Churches: Collected, Arranged, and Reviewed* (Utica, 1850) 70.

[47]Southern Baptist Convention, *Annual* (1845), 19. Johnson's celebration of Southern Baptists' new freedom "to promote slavery" was parallel to a speech of Alexander H. Stephens, who, shortly after being inaugurated vice-president of the Confederate States of America, dropped the standard Southern rhetoric about preserving strict constitutionalism and admitted that slavery and race domination constituted the cornerstone of the new Southern nation. See Frank Moore, ed., *Rebellion Record: A Diary of American Events* (New York, 1864) Supplement, 1:43.

Methodist preachers in their earliest conferences had adopted strict rules against slaveholding but soon had to qualify those rules with the proviso that they should apply "no farther than is consistent with the laws of the states in which [members] reside." It is striking that no one objected to this on the ground that it subordinated the demands of Christian conscience to civil jurisdiction. As the nineteenth century dawned, the official Methodist stand on slavery had relaxed to the point that Southerners were comfortable until the abolitionist attack began in the 1830s. The Methodist Episcopal Church, South, affirmed at its organizational meeting in 1845 that slavery was "a strictly civil institution exclusively in the custody of the civil power"; hence, the church should leave it completely aside.[48] Even Peter Cartwright, though believing that slavery was morally indefensible, admonished Methodists not to "meddle personally" with it.[49]

And so said they all. The American Tract Society poured out a veritable flood of evangelical literature condemning every conceivable sin—except that of slaveholding. The Protestant Episcopal Church refused to express itself on so "political" a matter. The Roman Catholic Church held to the same course; its hierarchy in America was still largely foreign-born, and prelates fearful of nativist reaction showed little interest in reform movements. John England, archbishop of Charleston, marshaled as many biblical proof texts in defense of the peculiar institution as his Protestant neighbors and concluded that "when it can and ought to be abolished is a question for the legislature and not for me."[50] Summing

---

[48]Henry B. Bascom, *Report of the Committee on Organization, Presented to the Convention of Delegates from the Annual Conferences of the Methodist Episcopal Church in the Southern and South-Western States, May 14, 1845* (Louisville, 1845) 5-7. Bascom was chairman of the committee.

[49]Peter Cartwright, *Autobiography of Peter Cartwright* (1856), ed. Charles L. Wallis (Nashville, 1956) 275.

[50]In 1840-1841 England published in the *United States Catholic Miscellany* eighteen "letters" defending the Roman Catholic Church's support of slavery as an institution. His biblical apologetic is most explicit in Letter 4, dated 21 October 1840, reprinted in *Letters of the Late Bishop England . . . on the Subject of Domestic Slavery* (Baltimore, 1844). The quotation is from Letter 18, dated 25 February 1841; see Joseph L. O'Brien, *John England—Bishop of Charleston: The Apostle to Democracy* (New York, 1934) 150-52.

up the unison chorus of Southern churchmen advocating "spirituality," Donald G. Mathews composed a whimsical litany:

> Slaveholding is a civil institution;
>    *and we will not interfere.*
> The character of civil institutions is governed by politics;
>    *and we will not interfere.*
> Politics are beyond the scope of the church;
>    *and we will not interfere.*[51]

There was a gross inconsistency between the Southern churches'
argument that slavery was a divine institution sanctioned in Scripture and their strident insistence that it was strictly a civil institution
beyond their concern. But the pathology of racism was rarely at-
tendant to logical consistency, and it is difficult to avoid the judgment that the churches were, to say it plainly, dismally derelict to
ethical duty. There was no other moral issue on which they de-
ferred so cravenly to civil authority. The political process was, to be
sure, often able to compromise contending interests, but it was
poorly equipped to deal with a fundamental moral question, especially one that ramified as widely throughout American society
as slavery. In their mounting agony over what was inescapably a
moral crisis, Americans were left without decisive guidance from
their moral mentors, and the nation descended inexorably into what
William Seward called, plausibly enough in 1858, an irrepressible
conflict.

An overemphasis on individualism, an inadequate social theory, a world-rejecting ecclesiology—these are clues to the inability
of the churches to achieve liberty and justice for enslaved Afro-
Americans and at the same time preserve the other fundamental
values that slavery threatened. Churches that maintained their internal tranquillity by refusing to confront the evil of human bondage simply immobilized themselves for any redeeming moral stance.
Those that divided to avoid further controversy between their contending factors wittingly pointed the nation toward rupture and
war. As sectional differences in the nation became irreconcilable,

---

[51]Mathews, *Religion in the Old South,* 157. I have transposed the lines from run-
in prose to the form of a litany.

antislavery evangelicals were unable to sort out the conflicting goals of abolishing slavery, avoiding war, and maintaining the Union— and so identified themselves uncritically with cries for a crusade against the slavocracy.

As agitation for secession increased in the South, churches of that region helped sustain an atmosphere of excitement that approached hysteria, so that "clergymen from the pulpit were almost as vocal as politicians from the stump in warning of the danger to the South, exhorting the people to declare their independence, and keeping emotions at high pitch."[52] The social ethical failure of American Christianity was here laid bare, and this dereliction has cast long shadows across all its subsequent history. In the judgment of Dwight Lowell Dumond, "the failure of the churches at this point in our history forced the country to turn to political action against slavery, and political action destroyed slavery as a system but left the hearts of the slaveholders [and, it must be added, of other white Americans] unregenerate and left oppression of the free Negro little less of an evil than slavery had been."[53]

Careful analysis of the political situation in 1860 has demonstrated that in neither North nor South was there a popular majority favoring extreme solutions. As James G. Randall put it, "It was small minorities that caused the war; then the regions and sections got into it."[54] In the words of the Charlottesville (Virginia) *Review,* South Carolina's headlong course toward secession in late 1860 stirred "the most bitter resentment." The Wilmington (North Carolina) *Daily Herald* asked scornfully whether North Carolina would "*submit,* to be dragged into revolution and anarchy, and all to please the State of South Carolina, who, by her insufferable arrogance, and conceited self-importance, has been a constant source of annoy-

---

[52]Potter, *The Impending Crisis,* 501.

[53]Dwight L. Dumond, *Antislavery: The Crusade for Freedom in America* (New York, 1961) 344. This work has been criticized as a moralistic tract whose historical rigor is compromised by the author's uncontrolled subjectivity; see C. Vann Woodward, "The Antislavery Myth," *The American Scholar,* 31 (1962): 312-28. As I argued in the introduction, no responsible historian should blink moral judgments on moral issues in history.

[54]James G. Randall, "The Blundering Generation," *Mississippi Valley Historical Review,* 27 (1940): 13. See also Pieter Geyl, "The American Civil War and the Problem of Inevitability," *New England Quarterly,* 24 (1951): 151.

ance and disquietude to the whole country, North and South, for the last thirty years?" Scattered voices from the churches, especially in the upper South, concurred. The *North Carolina Christian Advocate* accused South Carolina of "immoderate haste in seceding" and denounced Methodists of that state for approving the action. Virginia Presbyterian Robert Lewis Dabney condemned the Palmetto State as an "impudent little vixen [who] has gone beyond all patience. She is as great a pest as the Abolitionists."[55] Such vehement protests have led many historians to conclude that secession, on its face, was wantonly premature. But protests were ineffective, and other states soon followed South Carolina into schism, led "by a decisive minority, at a time when the majority was confused and indecisive."[56]

Many of the South's leading ministers were among the "decisive minority" that brought about secession and the formation of the Confederacy. Several outspoken critics of the time asserted unconditionally that without the active and energetic support of the clergy, already in defiant separation from their Northern ecclesiastical counterparts, secession would have had far less chance of adoption. William G. Brownlow, a pro-Union Methodist minister who edited the *Knoxville Whig* 1849-1861, testified that "the clergy of the South,—without distinction of sects,—men of talents, learning, and influence,—have raised the howl of Secession, and it falls like an Indian war-cry upon our citizens from their prostituted pulpits every Sabbath."[57] George Junkin, a Northern leader of Old

---

[55]*The Review* (Charlottesville VA), 4 January 1861, in *Southern Editorials on Secession*, ed. Dwight L. Dumond (New York, 1931) 389; *The Daily Herald* (Wilmington NC), 19 November 1860, ibid., 227-28; *North Carolina Christian Advocate*, 8 January 1861, quoted in W. Harrison Daniel, "A Brief Account of the Methodist Episcopal Church, South, in the Confederacy," *Methodist History*, 6 (1968): 28; Robert L. Dabney to his mother, 28 December 1860, in Thomas C. Johnson, *The Life and Letters of Robert Lewis Dabney* (Richmond, 1903) 215. South Carolina formally seceded on 20 December 1860.

[56]Don E. Fehrenbacher, "Disunion and Reunion," in *The Reconstruction of American History*, ed. John Higham (New York, 1962) 102. Cf. also Potter, *The Impending Crisis*, 502 n.

[57]*The Knoxville Whig*, 18 May 1861, reprinted in William G. Brownlow, *Sketches of the Rise, Progress, and Decline of Secession* (Philadelphia, 1862) 111-12. Brownlow expressed equal contempt for Northern clergy who had "kept [their] pulpits open to the abuse of Southern slavery and of the Southern people."

School Presbyterianism, laid special blame on his own denomination. Southern Presbyterians, he lamented, held the controlling power in their hands.

> I could name a half a dozen of Presbyterian ministers who could have arrested the secession, if they had seen fit. Notoriously, the Presbyterian ministers of the South were the leading supporters of the rebellion. It could not have been started without them.[58]

Thomas Smyth was undoubtedly one of those to whom Junkin referred. He preached secession as a divine right and a sacred duty, and on one occasion "composed a prayer explaining to God that His blessing on slavery committed Him to vindicate the Confederacy."[59]

Two weeks after the election of Lincoln, James Henley Thornwell upheld the essential rightness of the South's position, at the same time warning that "our path to victory may be through a baptism of blood." The Philadelphia *Presbyterian* noted that "many were led to the war . . . by his eloquent pleas." Thornwell's own South Carolina presbytery approved secession before the state convention did, and Virginia Presbyterians anticipated their state's secession with "trust in God . . . saying in the face of the world, and of honor itself—'IT IS RIGHT.' " Similarly, the Alabama Baptist Convention in 1860 unanimously adopted a resolution prepared by Basil Manly, Sr., affirming that since the federal Union had failed to answer the purpose for which it was created, Alabama Baptists felt constrained to declare themselves "subject to the call of proper authority in defense of the sovereignty and independence of the state of Alabama, and of her sacred right as a sovereignty to withdraw from this union." It was commonly believed that this declaration "did more to precipitate the secession of Alabama from the

---

[58]George Junkin, *Political Fallacies: An Examination of the False Assumptions, and Refutation of the Sophisticated Reasonings, Which Have Brought on This Civil War* (New York, 1863) 189.

[59]J. William Flinn, ed., *Complete Works of Thomas Smyth*, 10 vols. (Columbia SC, 1908-1912) 7:724-25; Robert L. Stanton, *The Church and the Rebellion: A Consideration of the Rebellion Against the Government of the United States; and the Agency of the Church, North and South, in Relation Thereto* (New York, 1864) 171; Maddex, "From Theocracy to Spirituality," 444.

Union than any other one cause." Methodist preachers at the 1860 Georgia Annual Conference favored secession by a vote of eighty-seven to nine. Criticism was stifled, loyalty to the South was equated with loyalty to God, and ministers suspected of disloyalty were dismissed from their posts. In May 1861 the Southern Baptist Convention, representing "a constituency of six or seven hundred thousand Christians," suddenly forgot its "spirituality" and enthusiastically voted approval of the Confederacy, "recognizing the necessity that the whole moral influence of the people, in whatever capacity or organizations, should be enlisted in aid of the rulers."[60]

After eleven states had seceded and formed the Confederacy, *The Richmond Christian Advocate* announced that the secession movement had been led by intelligent Christian men who were determined to protect their rights and make it possible for the South to live in peace. When the war began, the newly organized Presbyterian Church in the Confederate States of America urged its members to "put your treasures in the lap of your Country; throw your stout arms about her . . . if need be let your blood flow like water." As if in response, Georgia Baptists unanimously resolved "not to be behind any class of our fellow citizens in maintaining the independence of the South by any sacrifice of treasure or of blood." In Richmond, *The Central Presbyterian* announced proudly that "Virginia's gallant sons . . . have sprung forward to the defense of their insulted Mother; assured that they are contending for the most sacred rights, and for the dearest interests for which patriot soldiers ever drew the sword."

---

[60]James Henley Thornwell, "Our National Sins" (21 November 1860), in *Fast Day Sermons, or, The Pulpit on the State of the Country* (New York, 1861) 56; *The Presbyterian*, 23 August 1862, quoted in Lewis G. Vander Velde, *The Presbyterian Churches and the Federal Union, 1861-1869* (Cambridge MA, 1932) 30; "The Dreadful Sound," *The Central Presbyterian* (Richmond), 20 April 1861. Benjamin F. Riley, *History of the Baptists of Alabama* (Birmingham, 1895) 279-80; Walter Brownlow Posey, *Frontier Mission: A History of Religion West of the Southern Appalachians to 1861* (Lexington, 1966) 395-96; James W. Silver, *Confederate Morale and Church Propaganda* (New York, 1967) 18; Willard E. Wight, "The Churches and the Confederate Cause," *Civil War History*, 6 (1960): 368 (Wight gives several examples of Southern ministers dismissed for suspected disloyalty); Southern Baptist Convention, *Annual* (1861) 62-64.

Such expressions gratified Governor Francis W. Pickens of South Carolina, who praised the clergy and laity of all the Southern churches for their "fervor and religious zeal in our cause. . . . They have made it a holy war." In like vein, Thomas R. R. Cobb, a Presbyterian elder from Georgia and a general in the Confederate army, acknowledged gratefully that the Southern "revolution" had been accomplished "MAINLY BY THE CHURCHES." Cobb continued:

> I do not undervalue the name, and position, and ability of politicians; still I am sure that our success is *chiefly* attributable to the support which they derived from the co-operation of the *moral sentiment of the country*. Without that . . . *the enterprise would have been* A FAILURE.

Cobb referred glowingly to the Confederacy as the "GRAND CREATION" of the church, "the creature of her prayers and labors."[61]

Augustus B. Longstreet, a Georgia Methodist minister presiding over South Carolina College, hailed the beginning of the war as a crusade, the cause of God himself: "Gallant sons of a gallant State, away to the battle field, with the Bible in your arms and its precepts in your hearts. If you fall, the shot which sends you from earth, translates you to heaven." Reminiscent of the plenary indulgence offered to medieval crusaders, such promises were common. William G. Brownlow noted in 1862 that one often heard "secession chaplains, and other clergymen, teach soldiers from the pulpit, and assure the relations of soldiers in the event of their death, that the *cause* in which they fell, battling for the independence of the South in opposition to the Vandal hordes of the North, constitutes a passport sufficient to introduce them to all that exceeding weight of joy at God's right hand!" William Porcher Miles, chairman of the Military Commission in the Confederate House of Representatives, testified near the end of the war that "the clergy have

---

[61]*Richmond Christian Advocate*, 13 June 1861; Posey, *Frontier Mission*, 398; Georgia Baptist Convention, Minutes (1861) 5-6; *The Central Presbyterian* (Richmond), 18 May 1861, 78; Governor's Message to the South Carolina legislature, November 1862, quoted in Silver, *Confederate Morale and Church Propaganda*, 96; Thomas R. R. Cobb (presumed author), "The Church and the Confederate States of America," *Southern Presbyterian*, 20 April 1861, printed in Stanton, *The Church and the Rebellion*, 197-98.

done more for our cause, than any other class. . . . Not even the bay-onets have done more."[62] One modern historian, surveying testimonies like these, agreed that "in the period of warfare, as in that of the secession crisis, clergymen were second to no other professional class in buttressing the struggle for southern independence." Another concluded that "among the institutions within the Confederate States of America, none did more than the churches to further the Southern cause."[63]

Northern clergy seemed just as anxious as the Southerners for a Final Solution, even if that meant trampling out the grapes of wrath with the God of battles. A few, to be sure, were glad to see the South go, and good riddance. The Reverend Lester Williams, Jr., of Holden, Massachusetts, rejected President Buchanan's proclamation designating 4 January 1861 as a day of prayer for the preservation of the Union. "What is the Union worth today?" he asked.

> Every good thing pertaining to it is sacrificed to *one* thing in one half of the country. Trade, Friendship, Comity, Religion, Honor, Civilization, all yield to the clamors of slavery, and are brushed away before it. It is the Dagon god of the South to which everything else must fall down. The wrathful cry is, "Slavery shall have new and stronger guarantees, or the Union shall be dissolved." The Union, if it exists, must be made to bear slavery on its shoulders, and so become a bond of iniquity. Shall we be called upon to pray for *such* a Union? . . . I could as soon pray that Satan might be prospered and his kingdom come.[64]

---

[62]Augustus B. Longstreet, *Fast-Day Sermon, Delivered in the Washington Street Methodist Episcopal Church, Columbia, South Carolina, June 13, 1861* (Columbia, 1861) 10, quoted in Smith, *In His Image, but,* 191; Brownlow, *Sketches of the Rise, Progress, and Decline of Secession,* 177-78; *The Christian Observer,* 23 February 1865, quoted in Silver, *Confederate Morale and Church Propaganda,* 96.

[63]Smith, *In His Image, but,* 188; Wight, "The Churches and the Confederate Cause," 373.

[64]Lester Williams, Jr., *Freedom of Speech and the Union; A Discourse Delivered December 30, 1860, at Holden, Massachusetts,* quoted in Moorhead, *American Apocalypse,* 27-28. The Episcopal bishop of Florida, Francis H. Rutledge, likewise refused to attend prayers for the Union in one of his own churches on 4 January 1861; see Smith, *In His Image, but,* 175-76.

But most of the other ministers in the North were ready to fight, either to save the Union, or to punish the South, or both.

The General Conference of the Methodist Episcopal Church, meeting in May 1860, loudly applauded Missions Secretary John P. Durbin's call for military action to prevent secession: "As a citizen I have my opinion of the duty of maintaining the authority of the government, and if I were President of the United States, and any attempts were to be made, either North or South, to dissolve the Union, if there were ships enough, and men, and cannon, and powder, and ball enough, I would whip them in."[65] New School Presbyterians, meeting at the same time the Old School Assembly was dividing over the question of political loyalty, found no obstacle to declaring its "undiminished attachment" to the federal Union: "There is no blood or treasure too precious to be devoted to the defense and perpetuity of the Government in all its constituted authority."[66] The American Baptist Missionary Union (Northern successor to the General Missionary Convention after the division in 1845) met in Brooklyn on 29 May 1861 and resolved with some asperity that "what was bought at Bunker Hill, Valley Forge, and Yorktown, was not, with our consent, sold at Montgomery; that we dispute the legality of the bargain, and, on the strength of the Lord God of our fathers, shall hope to contest, through this generation, if need be, the feasibility of the transfer."[67]

The Northern clergy were no less ready than their Southern counterparts to transform the conflict into a crusade. As early as 1850, Aaron Chatterton, a Disciples of Christ preacher in Iowa, had declared: "I am for war, open war—a war of conquest and exter-

[65]*Daily Christian Advocate*, 25 May 1860, quoted in Robert D. Clark, "Methodist Debates and Union Sentiment on the Border, 1860-1861," in *Antislavery and Disunion, 1858-1861: Studies in the Rhetoric of Compromise and Conflict*, ed. J. Jeffery Auer (New York, 1963) 160.

[66]New School Assembly Minutes (1861) 12:447-48, quoted in Vander Velde, *The Presbyterian Churches and the Federal Union*, 344-45. The following year, with the war in full swing, the New School Assembly equated the Southerners with fallen angels and the disobedient Adam (ibid., 347).

[67]American Baptist Missionary Union, Minutes, 29 May 1861, American Baptist Historical Society. Cf. also Edward McPherson, *The Political History of the United States of America During the Great Rebellion*, 2d ed. (Washington, D.C., 1865) 475.

mination, to be prosecuted in the spirit of Him who 'goes forth conquering and to conquer,' and with weapons 'mighty through God to the pulling down of strongholds.' " Zachary Eddy of Northampton, Massachusetts, had been advocating peaceable disunion as late as 4 April 1861, but after receiving news of the fall of Fort Sumter three weeks later, he was ready for a crusade. "If the [medieval] crusaders, seized by a common enthusiasm, exclaimed, 'IT IS THE WILL OF GOD! IT IS THE WILL OF GOD!'—much more may we make this our rallying cry and inscribe it on our banners." Even the (Baptist) *Christian Review*, which had previously eschewed political controversy for the sake of national amity, now "pictured a fiendish South greedy for every inch of Northern territory, and called for the military obliteration of the Confederacy." Granville Moody of the Methodist Book Concern in Cincinnati wrote to Lincoln's secretary of the treasury, Salmon P. Chase, with instructions to "read this to the President and the Cabinet," that merely defensive measures would not do. The aims of war must be to destroy "the foes of law, order, and mutual rights." Cost should be no object, Moody declared; volunteers from Ohio are ready to rush to the place of greatest danger and fight to the last man. "The route through Maryland must be kept open [even] if we make it a graveyard. . . . Let them know that *our flag is still there.*' "[68]

This kind of vindictiveness, coming as it did from recognized religious figures and supported by their invocations of divine providence, readily conditioned public opinion in the North to baptize the war as a holy cause. To the extent that it is legitimate to call the Confederacy the "grand creation" of the Southern churches, one must also regard the war for the Union as the "grand crusade" of the Northern churches—an Armageddon which for them augured the Day of the Lord. Pastors who did not clearly identify themselves as loyal supporters of the federal government by preaching patriotic sermons and praying for the success of the Union armies

---

[68]*Western Evangelist*, August 1860, quoted in Winfred E. Garrison and Alfred T. DeGroot, *The Disciples of Christ: A History* (St. Louis, 1948) 333; Moorhead, *American Apocalypse*, 37, 41; Granville Moody to Salmon P. Chase, 30 April 1861, Chase Papers, Library of Congress.

met with severe displeasure if not outright rejection. If moral suasion had been impotent, patriotic gore was not.

By the time the war was fully under way, most members of the popular churches, North and South, were ready to believe that the Lord God Almighty was resolving their trilemma by taking the slavery issue into his own hands. Northerners believed the crusade would purge the land of its sin and set the nation back on course to its providential destiny. Southerners were convinced that the holy mission of a Christian America would simply be transferred from the perfidious North to the faithful Confederacy. Neither side questioned the sacredness of its cause, and each interpreted the conflict in all the richness of biblical imagery. When a Baltimore mob attacked Massachusetts troops marching to Washington in response to Lincoln's mobilization call (19 April 1861), the New Orleans *True Witness* hailed the skirmish as Marylanders' "sacrifice" of the aggressors on the altar of God's righteous purpose.

> Baltimore has stood at the font of *baptismal blood, in solemn covenant* for the Confederate States; and Providence ordered that this thrilling deed, *this sealing ordinance,* should be on the anniversary of the battle of Lexington, Mass., the memorable 19th of April. Thus the same day beheld the first blood of '76 and of '61—fortunate omen of the result.[69]

What James H. Moorhead wrote of "Yankee Protestants" could apply with equal truth to the mood of both North and South: "The almost joyous abandon with which the churches had thrown themselves into the business of war was in part an escape from ambiguities that had become too burdensome to sustain, and the apocalyptic trumpet sounded the glad promise that these uncertainties would be forever eliminated when God shortly made perfect his model republic."[70] There seem to have been few voices raised within the churches recognizing the possibility that God, as President Lincoln was to put it in the cadences of the Second Inaugural, had given "to both North and South this terrible war as the woe due to those by whom the offence [of slavery] came."

---

[69]*The True Witness* (New Orleans), 27 April 1861, in Stanton, *The Church and the Rebellion,* 185. The Battle of Lexington, of course, occurred in 1775, not 1776.

[70]Moorhead, *American Apocalypse,* 82.

Shortly after Southern guns opened fire on Sumter, the *Syracuse* (New York) *Daily Courier and Union* linked all the churches with the whole process of national breakdown:

> The churches North and South, in their conflicting lessons to the people of the different sections, are equally with the politicians responsible for present disasters. Perhaps as they speak with more power and greater influence, they are more responsible! And if war and bloodshed become inevitable, they will certainly be more responsible, for no one can fail to see that the enthusiasm of religion superadded to the mere opinion of patriotic duty,—and the holy sanction of the Church,—inspirit politicians of either section and tend [to] make them more dogmatic and resolute, and to render the war, in either section, a holy as well as a patriotic war![71]

The Reverend Granville Moody happily accepted the charge. "I believe it is true that we did bring it about," he exclaimed, "and I glory in it, for it is a wreath of glory around our brow!"[72] His fellow Methodist, Pennell Coombe of the Philadelphia Conference, agreed, though with less lightness of heart: "The chief responsibilities of our national calamities" do lie with the churches, for "the sundering of the Churches has prepared the way for the sundering of the States."[73]

It would be problematic, if not downright fatuous, to claim that if the popular denominations had held fast to their early condemnations of slavery and had nurtured an unswerving commitment to oppose it consistently within their own ranks, they could have maintained a united moral witness and saved the nation from its long and bloody tragedy. History never discloses its alternatives. But one can legitimately decry what Allan Nevins, an astute historian

---

[71]*Syracuse Daily Courier and Union,* 1 June 1861, in *Northern Editorials on Secession,* ed. Howard C. Perkins (New York, 1942) 1092.

[72]Reported in *The Crisis* (Columbus OH), 15 August 1861, 1. Moody was pastor at Morris Chapel (Methodist) in Cincinnati and agent of the Methodist Book Concern. In 1861 he accepted a commission as colonel in the U. S. Army, commanding the 74th Regiment of the Ohio Voluntary Infantry. Concerning Moody's pro-war sentiments, the editor of *The Crisis* commented that "the pulpits of such savages resemble a good deal more a butcher's shambles than the altars of that divine religion whose founder was the Prince of Peace."

[73]*Western Christian Advocate* (Cincinnati) 28:30:1-2, quoted in Chester F. Dunham, *Attitude of the Northern Clergy Toward the South, 1860-1865* (Toledo, 1942) 128.

with profound human insight, called "wretched leadership" in a
time of deepening crisis.

> To hold that the Civil War could not have been averted by
> wise, firm, and timely action is to concede too much to determin-
> ism in history. . . . Passionate unreason among large sections of
> the population was one ingredient in the broth of conflict. Acci-
> dent, fortuity, fate, or sheer bad luck (these terms are inter-
> changeable) was another. . . . But beyond these ingredients lies
> the further element of *wretched leadership*. Had the United States
> possessed three farseeing, imaginative, and resolute Presidents
> instead of Fillmore, Pierce, and Buchanan, the war might have
> been postponed until time and economic forces killed its roots.[74]

That is a counterfactual argument, of course, but even so, it has a
poignant persuasiveness. Applied to the behavior of the churches,
it may make an even stronger case, for if political leadership was
wretched, so was religious. Ernest T. Thompson, magisterial historian of Southern Presbyterianism, deplored the lack of decisive
leadership in both church and state: "The fact that this bloody and
unnecessary war took place is a mark of the failure not only of the
political but also of religious leaders, both North and South."[75]

The fatal flaw in antebellum church leadership was that ecclesiastics were less distressed by the evils of human bondage than
concerned with the tasks of institutional maintenance. In the critical decades of the 1830s and 1840s, their efforts were directed more
to muting the moral issue of slavery than to confronting it forthrightly. Even "church-oriented abolitionism," as John R. Mc-
Kivigan termed it, though resolute enough in its own circles, had
minimal impact on denominational leaders because for them, ecclesiastical peace was always more important than antislavery activity. By the time they were forced to take a position, it was too late
to prevent schism or even to shore up their stand against slavery.
Even after the schisms, Northern religious bodies continued to reject abolitionism in order to court supporters in the upper South
and border states.[76]

---

[74]Allan Nevins, "The Needless Conflict," *American Heritage, The Magazine of
History,* 7 (August 1956): 6; emphasis mine.

[75]Thompson, *The Spirituality of the Church,* 23.

[76]McKivigan, *The War Against Proslavery Religion,* 16, 74-92.

This so outraged Harriet Martineau that she wrote scornfully of "the acquiescing clergy, who, if they do not understand [Christianity's] principles, are unfit to be clergymen; and if they do, are unfit to be called Christians." She neatly caught the paradox of those who "uphold a faith which shall remove mountains, who teach that men are not to fear 'them that kill the body, and afterwards have no more that they can do,' [and yet] are the most timid class of society; the most backward in all great conflicts of principles." Observing in 1836 that "the clergy have not yet begun to stir upon the Anti-Slave question," she wondered what kind of apostle Paul would have been "if he had preached on everything but idolatry at Ephesus, and licentiousness at Corinth." Her sarcastic answer: "Very much like the American Christian clergy of the nineteenth century," who preach against every sin but slavery.[77]

In the same vein John Quincy Adams confided to his diary in May 1838:

> There is in the clergy of all the Christian denominations a time-serving, cringing, subservient morality, as wide from the spirit of the gospel as it is from the intrepid assertion and vindication of truth. The counterfeit character of a very large portion of the Christian ministry in this country is disclosed in the dissensus growing up in all the Protestant Churches in the South on slavery.[78]

That was a New England liberal speaking, of course. From another angle, one could say that Southern clerical leadership was all *too* effective, since it marshaled such massive support for the slavocracy and the Confederacy. To add that such leadership was also wretched is to pass deliberate moral judgment.

In the midst of the war an antislavery member of the Old School Presbyterian Church, Robert Livingston Stanton, attempted a major assessment of the churches' role in bringing on the national tragedy. His 562-page book, *The Church and the Rebellion* (the title

---

[77]Martineau, *Society in America*, 2:321, 350.
[78]Charles Francis Adams, ed., *Memoirs of John Quincy Adams*, 12 vols. (Philadelphia, 1874–1877) 9:544.

either betrays his presuppositions or announces his conclusions), written from the border state of Kentucky, placed a major portion of blame on the Southern clergy for fomenting the "rebellion" by supporting the breakaway states. But Stanton also passed critical judgment on the centrist ecclesiocrats of the North who throughout the antebellum years had discouraged all discussion of slavery in order to placate the South.

> The fact is undeniable, that a large and influential class among clergymen and editors in the Church of all branches at the North, exerted such an influence for a long course of years, whether so intended or not, as to foster that spirit and countenance those claims put forth by the South, which led Southern demagogues to believe that they could rule the country according to their own peculiar notions, and could count upon their Northern friends to sustain them; or, failing to rule it, could divide the country, and still look with confidence to their support. . . . *It tended to deceive the Southern Church.*

Northern ecclesiastics whose silence on slavery encouraged the South to think it could continue on its arrogant way with impunity, Stanton continued, had their counterparts in national politics. The Northern moderates had "ever been crying out about an infringement of Southern rights, making apologies for the South, courting the smiles of the Southern people, and yielding, step by step, to their extreme demands." Leaders of the Southern churches were thus "stimulated to become active promoters of the rebellion, by virtue of the hold which they believed they still had upon their special friends at the North; supposing at first that their secession might be effected peaceably, or, if it came at last to an open clash of arms, that their faithful allies would still stand by them."

How many "special friends at the North" the Southern churches still had in 1860 is questionable, but there was much truth in Stanton's charge that Northern attempts to suppress antislavery activity during the thirty years prior to the war encouraged the South in its fateful course. Thus what Northern ecclesiastics intended as a strategy to maintain unity became itself a contributing cause of division—and further evidence of irresolute leadership. Stanton's main accusation, however, was against the Southern clergy. Its support of slavery and secession, he charged repeatedly, was the keystone of Southern morale and a leading provocation of the war.[79]

Similar accusations came from the prolific pen of William G. Brownlow, "the fighting parson." As a Methodist minister and editor of *The Knoxville Whig* (he was also governor of Tennessee, 1865-1869), he blamed the Southern ministry, and especially the Methodists, for leading the South out of the Union.

> I have no hesitancy in saying, as I now do, that the worst class of men who make tracks upon Southern soil are Methodist, Presbyterian, Baptist, and Episcopal clergymen, and at the head of these for mischief are the Southern Methodists. I mean to say that there are honorable exceptions in all these churches; but the moral mania of Secession has been almost universally prevalent among the members of the sacred profession.

As far away as the Wisconsin frontier, Alfred Brunson reiterated Brownlow's charges: "No well-informed person doubts that if those Southern Methodist preachers had not fomented the rebellion, it would not have occurred. The statesmen who led in it could not have carried the mass of people with them, if those preachers had been against them, nor if they had been neutral."[80]

What passed for leadership in the antebellum churches was not only wretched; it was also racist. That accusation presumably needs no further documentation with respect to the Southern clergy—witness their repetitions *ad nauseam* that slavery was a biblical institution and a positive social good, their interest in Christianizing the slaves primarily as a means of social control, and their refusal to accord equal privileges to black members of their own churches.[81] (An

---

[79]Stanton, *The Church and the Rebellion*, 93, 87, 95, 393. Stanton—Presbyterian minister, seminary professor, confidant of Lincoln, and brother-in-law to Elizabeth Cady Stanton—seems under-studied. See the tantalizing essay by Timothy F. Reilly, "Robert L. Stanton, Abolitionist of the Old South," *Journal of Presbyterian History*, 53 (1975): 33-49.

[80]Brownlow, *Sketches of the Rise, Progress, and Decline of Secession*, 189-90; Alfred Brunson, *A Western Pioneer*, 2 vols. (New York, 1872) 1:395.

[81]Smith, *In His Image, but,* furnishes massive and irrefutable documentation. There is, of course, a poignancy about a minister like Charles Colcock Jones, who apparently tried conscientiously to mitigate the harshness of the system he inherited by an accident of birth. But as the acquiescent beneficiary of an oppressive, racist society which the churches were helping to maintain, he falls under judgment along with his fellow ministers who made a career out of supporting the slavocracy. See Robert Manson Myers, *The Children of Pride: A True Story of Georgia in the Civil War* (New Haven, 1972).

old ex-slave testified that he never joined a church because the white preachers talked less about the Lord God Almighty than about the Master and Mistress.)

But what of the Northern traditionalists who tried during the crucial years of the 1830s to placate slaveholders while turning a hostile hand against abolitionists—indeed, against all discussion of slavery in the churches? Few Northern ecclesiastics regarded the system of human bondage as grievously wrong and held that the church should strive consistently to subject it to moral judgment. Few spurned the bugbear of "miscegenation" and believed that blacks could be incorporated into American society on equal terms with whites.[82] Indeed, Northern church folk seemed no more anxious than their Southern counterparts to grant equal status to black members, even among themselves. The editor of *The Colored American*, for example, became a member of the Presbytery of New York in 1821. Sixteen years later he was complaining that in spite of an agreement that the privilege of serving as a delegate to the General Assembly would be rotated among the members, he had always been passed over, sometimes in favor of inexperienced younger ministers, some of whom were "unnaturalized foreigners" whose "foreign brogue" enthralled native Presbyterians. Alas, the black editor exclaimed, "like the Declaration of Independence, the good brethren did not mean by *every brother, a colored brother! not at all—not at all!*" Because of intransigent racism, he concluded, the "grave divisions" of 1837 were making "a shameless wreck" of the Presbyterian church.[83]

As for the abolitionists and their "war against proslavery religion," it is a common conclusion among historians that they probably did less to clarify moral insight in the North than to harden proslavery sentiment in the South. Their chief accomplishment in the North seems to have been to consolidate the self-righteousness that turned a war for the Union into a holy crusade. Charles C. Cole, although allowing somewhat more room than Nevins for the "ir-

---

[83]Cf. Frederickson, *The Black Image in the White Mind;* Litwack, *North of Slavery: The Negro in the Free States;* Berwanger, *The Frontier Against Slavery;* and Voegli, *Free but Not Equal.*

[83]Reported in the *Alton* (IL) *Observer,* 27 July 1837.

repressible conflict" thesis, condemned "the Finneys, Bushnells, Leavitts, and Waylands" for allowing themselves to be swept into fratricidal violence as a means of achieving their antislavery objectives. The coming of the war "indicated a failure in leadership on the part of the [Northern] clergy just as much as on the part of statesmen and politicians."[84] In his more recent and detailed study of the Christian abolitionists, John R. McKivigan provided convincing documentation of the failure of Northern religious leaders to advocate vigorous antislavery measures, even after Southerners withdrew from the national denominations.[85] Both Northern and Southern church leaders, therefore, must be charged with serious dereliction to moral duty in shaping public opinion on the monumental immorality of slavery and in directing popular sentiment away from disruption and war.

Several members of the antebellum clergy, even in the South, betrayed their feelings of guilt on this point. Robert Lewis Dabney, Presbyterian theologian of the Old Dominion, thought that the four million church members in America should have been able to exert enough Christian love to stem the angry tides of conflict. In a prescient piece of 1856 he envisioned the approaching "national convulsion" and asked sorrowfully:

> What, was there not enough of the oil of love in all these four millions of the servants of the God of love to soothe the surging billows of party strife? Was there not enough of the majority of moral weight in these four millions of Christians to say to the angry waters, "Peace, be still"? Were not all these strong enough to throw the arms of love around their fellow-citizens, keep down the hands that sought each others' throats, and constrain them by a sweet compulsion to be brethren?

Perhaps this was simply more romanticism. Dabney's wistful questions did not reckon with the racism that has undermined the credibility of Christian charity throughout American history. But in suggesting that the churches could have done more than "stand idly

---

[84]Cole, *Social Ideas of the Northern Evangelists*, 219-20. Joshua Leavitt (1794-1873) has not been mentioned previously in this work; a Congregational minister and an abolitionist, he edited *The Independent* in New York City, 1848-1873.

[85]McKivigan, *The War Against Proslavery Religion*, 82.

by and see phrenzy immolate so many of the dearest hopes of man and so much of the glory of God on her hellish altar," Dabney put his finger squarely on a major precipitant of national disruption: "the fiend had borrowed the torch of discord from the altar of Christianity." His reference was unmistakably to the denominational schisms that preceded the war by sixteen years.[86]

Racism aside—or better, under judgment—it is not unreasonable to suppose that there were several actions the churches could have taken to fulfill their responsibility as moral guides of a society that professed to respect the Christian message. They might, for example, have opposed the statutes that denied to slaves basic civil rights and educational privileges, pressed for legal recognition of slave marriages, sought repeal of laws against manumission, encouraged feasible procedures for slaves to gain their freedom, tried to mitigate prejudice against free blacks, provided equal treatment for blacks within the fellowship of their own congregations, and heeded the chorus of warnings about the apocalyptic results of schism. Even if the churches were unable or unwilling to exercise their influence to bring about structural changes in American society, they nonetheless had the option of making slaveowning by church members morally questionable and therefore subject to church discipline—but they refused to act before it was too late to avoid disruption. Quakers, to point to one notable example, were sufficiently resolute on this point to show what could be done, and their behavior demonstrates that the popular denominations did have, for a while at least, other alternatives.[87]

A sociologically astute reader might protest that Quakers were a small "sect" able to enforce moral discipline, while mainline denominations were inclusive "churches" with inevitably greater lax-

---

[86]Robert Lewis Dabney, "Christians, Pray for Your Country," *The Central Presbyterian* (Richmond), 29 March 1856; also in Dabney, *Discussions: Evangelical and Theological,* 2 vols. (1891; rpt. London, 1967) 2:398. See his 1860 sermon on "The Christian's Best Motive for Patriotism," in which he shamed "the boasted Christianity of America, and of the nineteenth century," in *Fast-Day Sermons; Or, The Pulpit on the State of the Country,* 81-97.

[87]Cf. T. Scott Miyakawa, *Protestants and Pioneers: Individualism and Conformity on the American Frontier* (Chicago, 1964) 195-96. McKivigan, *The War Against Proslavery Religion,* makes the case for the Freewill Baptists as "second only to the Friends in terms of early religious antislavery prominence" (28; see also 43-44, 162).

ity. But the familiar "church/sect" typology, originally constructed for a European setting, must be invoked with great caution in American religious history. For the antebellum groups under consideration here, it has little relevance. At the beginning of the nineteenth century, Quakers were as much a denomination as Methodists, more numerous than Presbyterians, and almost as widely dispersed as Baptists. Their antislavery stance had less to do with their sociological typology than with a determination to make their behavior consistent with their moral convictions. Table 5 helps to demonstrate this by comparing Quakers' growth to that of the popular denominations in the first four decades of the century.[88]

|  |  | | | | TABLE FIVE |
|---|---|---|---|---|---|
| Popular Denominations Compared to Quakers:<br>Membership Growth 1800–1840 (in thousands) | | | | | |
|  | 1800 | 1810 | 1820 | 1830 | 1840 |
| Baptists | 170 | 200 | 265 | 320 | 560 |
| Methodists | 70 | 160 | 250 | 500 | 820 |
| Presbyterians | 20 | 40 | 80 | 200 | 275 |
| Quakers | 60 | 72 | 86 | 100 | 109 |

The explosive growth of the popular denominations was due, in significant part, to an early decision by the leadership that nothing so controversial as antislavery should be allowed to hinder the enlisting of new members. Leaders of all groups realized correctly that an antislavery church would remain a small church, and few were willing to accept the limitations that a consistent stand against human bondage would impose on church growth. In starkest terms, most churchmen chose institutional concerns over human liberation, and that choice has to be judged a moral failure of enormous proportions.

History, of course, is irreversible. It may seem pointless to conjecture alternative scenarios or to suggest that if church leaders had chosen to value racial equality and human liberation above enlarg-

---

[88]My figures are extrapolated from graphs in Edwin S. Gaustad, *Historical Atlas of Religion in America* (New York, 1962) 52, 96. Presbyterians did not surpass Congregationalists until 1823, but that is not an important fact here because the latter was a regional body clustered primarily in the Northeast.

ing their membership, results might have been different. But if any "lessons" remain for those who have ears to hear, perhaps a clue to the failure of ecclesiastical leadership lies in Alexis de Tocqueville's discovery that in the America of the 1830s "you meet a politician where you expected to find a priest."[89] Tocqueville was a liberal Roman Catholic with a strong sense of the church as a basic value-creating and value-sustaining institution in society, and one would not stretch his meaning overmuch to interpret him as saying that everywhere he expected to find a minister of God working faithfully at the care and cure of souls—with the comprehensive moral discipline that such ministry necessarily requires—he found instead an "operator" who knew how to "work the system." His statement was as true of the parish clergy as of top-ranking ecclesiocrats, and it simply underscored the fact that leaders of the popular churches derived both their position and their power from staying closely tuned to the thoughts and feelings of their people. From such a base of support, effective moral leadership on any controversial issue was extremely difficult.

It is a commonplace of social psychology that what elites can communicate is constrained by popular notions, current folkways, and what the masses will accept. A generation ago, Methodist historian William Warren Sweet observed that "the church does not lead public opinion on such matters as the slavery issue, but rather, tends to follow public opinion."[90] More recently George M. Marsden concluded that American Protestant denominations were (and are) "too democratic for effective social action." A deeply ingrained individualism always militates against success in reform movements that require effective group discipline.

> The republican ideology demands that the denominations follow, rather than lead, their constituencies. If the constituency is significantly divided, as is nearly bound to be the case on crucial social issues, effective denominational reform is impossible. Dissenters from the majority opinion, viewing the church as a free

[89]Alexis de Tocqueville, *Democracy in America* (1835), trans. George Lawrence, ed. J. P. Mayer (New York, 1969) 293.

[90]William Warren Sweet, *Methodism in American History*, rev. ed. (Nashville, 1953) 233.

agency, which they have every right to leave, in the face of institutional pressure will simply leave.[91]

"Republican ideology," moreover, was reinforced by revivalistic appeals, which had swelled the ranks of the popular churches
while reducing the demands of moral discipline. The result was to
move those churches far away from the classical Puritan sense of
corporate responsibility for the total society. Thus in the face of
threats by disaffected church members to defect, Tocqueville's ecclesiastical politicians simply decided that institutional maintenance had to take precedence over prophetic moral leadership.
Intoxicated by their success among unchurched masses in post-
Revolutionary America, the clergy found the cost of defying popular feeling toward blacks and their enslavement too high a price
to pay.

It has been one of the lesser noticed tragedies of America's tragic
era that the nation's moral and spiritual mentors were either unwilling or unable to exercise decisive leadership toward a more just
and humane society. Committed to church growth, swayed by sectional interest, and silent about racial prejudice, they could neither
swim against the stream nor redirect its flow and so chose to protect
their position by staying close to the main currents. But at too many
crucial points in the fateful onrush of events, they sounded all too
dismally like the tragicomic character in some legendary revolution
who is reported to have cried at a moment of crisis, "The mob is in
the street! I must find out which way they are going, for I am their
leader."

How prescient, we can see now, were the warnings of so many
within the churches and outside them who predicted, as did Thomas
Crowder of Virginia in 1844, that if the national church bodies
should divide, "a civil division of this great confederacy may follow
that, and then hearts will be torn apart, master and slave arrayed
against each other, brother in the Church against brother, and the
north against the south—and when thus arrayed, with the fiercest

---

[91]George M. Marsden, *The Evangelical Mind and the New School Presbyterian Experience*, 89; cf. also 236. Jeffrey Hadden, *The Gathering Storm in the Churches* (New
York, 1969), described the same tensions arising from congregations' displeasure
with the clergy's participation in the civil rights movements of the 1960s.

passions and energies of our nature brought into action against each other, civil war and far-reaching desolation must be the final results."[92] But such warnings went unheeded, and even after six hundred thousand American men had died by their brothers' hands, in the stillness at Appomattox there was little contrition in the broken churches that had prefigured the broken nation.

---

[92]Robert A. West, ed., *Report of Debates in the General Conference of the Methodist Episcopal Church* (New York, 1855) 95.

# INDEX